Brödermann/Etgen

CIETAC Arbitration Rules 2024

Institutional Arbitration

Schütze (ed.)

CIETAC Arbitration Rules 2024

Article-by-Article Commentary

by

Eckart Brödermann
Björn Etgen

2024

BECK • HART • NOMOS

Published by
Verlag C.H.Beck oHG, Wilhelmstraße 9, 80801 München, Germany,
email: bestellung@beck.de

Co-published by
Hart Publishing, Kemp House, Chawley Park, Cumnor Hill, Oxford, OX2 9PH, United Kingdom,
online at: www.hartpub.co.uk

and

Nomos Verlagsgesellschaft mbH & Co. KG, Waldseestraße 3–5, 76530 Baden-Baden, Germany,
email: nomos@nomos.de

Published in North America by Hart Publishing
An Imprint of Bloomsbury Publishing 1385 Broadway, New York, NY 10018, USA
email: mail@hartpub.co.uk

beck.de

ISBN 978 3 406 81228 6 (C.H.BECK)
ISBN 978 1 5099 8437 4 (HART)
ISBN 978 3 7560 1813 0 (NOMOS)

Printed in Germany by
Beltz Grafische Betriebe GmbH
Am Fliegerhorst 8, 99947 Bad Langensalza

Typeset by
Reemers Publishing Services GmbH, Krefeld
Cover: Druckerei C.H.Beck Nördlingen

myclimate
shape our future

chbeck.de/nachhaltig

Foreword

It has been over a decade since the first edition of Institutional Arbitration was published in 2013 and the time for a second edition is more than ripe. However, legal commentaries of any kind are faced with the challenge of publication before legislative reforms or case law render a commentary out of date from the outset. With 14 different sets of rules from across the globe, the second edition of Institutional Arbitration was continuously delayed by a cycle of reform projects and the need to update the texts to ensure that they correspond to the state of the law at the time of publication – it is of course essential that users of a commentary can rely on the information given therein! To end the cycle and avoid further delays, the editor and the publishers decided to move away from a single volume and focus on separate publications containing more detailed commentaries on the most important international arbitration institutions. In this long term, this allows not only for a quicker response to future legislative changes but also greater detail.

The first separate commentary (Wiegand/Altenkirch, HKIAC Administered Arbitration Rules 2021) was published in 2021 and has been well received in arbitration practice. Further commentaries are expected in due course, continuing at this time with expert explanations of Chinese arbitration rules and procedure pursuant to the recently reformed CIETAC Arbitration Rules. Arbitration in China is particularly significant as court proceedings in Chinese on international disputes can prove to be especially challenging for foreign parties. With two highly experienced practitioners, Eckart Brödermann and Björn Etgen, taking over from Michael J. Moser and Sabine Stricker-Kellerer, as authors, users of this commentary will be able to navigate arbitration in China under the CIETAC Arbitration Rules.

The editor and the publisher kindly thank the authors of this, and subsequent editions, for their understanding and patience in the drafting process.

Stuttgart
January 2024

Rolf A. Schütze

Preface

In a world which is facing global challenges and disruptions, arbitration is an important tool to cope with their economic consequences for business relationships. No matter how strong the impact of such challenges and disruptions may be, it is timely and important to remember the powerful Chinese principle of "Peace shall have Priority" (*yi he wei gui:* 以和为贵) which calls for the universal renunciation of violence. Domestic and international arbitration provides an important tool to realize that principle by solving economic disputes and contributing thereby to peace. In this spirit we ourselves hope to contribute with this book to the understanding of arbitration in China and especially under the arbitration rules of the China International Economic and Trade Arbitration Commission (CIETAC), further developed yet again with their 2024 version that has come into force on **January 1, 2024**.

Among the over 1,000 options for institutional arbitration offered by various arbitral institutions around the globe, **CIETAC ranks at the top**, both through the numbers for arbitrations as a whole and for international arbitrations. In many situations, foreigners doing business in China are bound to consider or to work with them. When negotiating contracts with a Chinese party, the combination of an arbitration clause with a choice of the general principles and rules as developed by the International Institute for the Unification of Private Law (UNIDROIT), i.e., the UNIDROIT Principles of International Commercial Contracts, has been described as **"Simplified Global Contracting"** (→ Art. 52 mn. 8).

According to a European saying, the devil lies in the details. This is also true for the interpretation of the CIETAC Arbitration Rules. While there exist excellent books on Chinese arbitration law, even in English (*Kun Fan*, *Jingzhou Tao*), and also on the CIETAC Arbitration Rules (*Jianlong Lu/Lijun Cao*, 2020), this article-by-article commentary provides an **international perspective** with a focus on the challenges which an arbitration in China provides for a foreign entity or the foreign shareholders of a Chinese subsidiary. Moreover, the 2024 CIETAC Arbitration Rules include several **noteworthy changes**, e.g., with regard to the digitalisation of CIETAC arbitration, third party funding, interim awards, early dismissal, the approach to *ad hoc* arbitration and the adaptation of the choice of law regime in Art. 52 which now includes explicitly the possibility to choose or apply general principles of law in the area of international contracting, namely the UNIDROIT Principles of International Commercial Contracts. In contrast, the changes to Chinese arbitration law as discussed since a few years under the **Draft Revised PRC Arbitration Law (2021)** have not seen the daylight and the law is likely to undergo further changes. It has been discussed in this book where relevant and appropriate.

This book covers all changes of the 2024 edition by comments. It thereby continues a tradition of observing the CIETAC Rules from an international, multi-jurisdictional perspective with article-by-article comments which was started in 2006 by *Sabine Stricker-Kellerer* (Germany) and *Michael Moser* (Hong Kong) under the editorship of *Rolf Schütze*.[1]

---

[1] The comments were initially published in German by Sabine Stricker-Kellerer/Michael J. Moser, 'Schiedsordnung der China International Economic and Trade Arbitration Commission (CIETAC)' in

Preface

Both authors – connected with each other through the **Inter-Pacific Bar Association (IPBA)** – are international arbitration practitioners with a long-standing focus on China and Chinese arbitration law. **Eckart Brödermann** (born 1958) encountered Chinese arbitration law first during the research for his LL.M. thesis on Chinese admiralty law at the East Asian Legal Studies Program of Harvard Law School in 1982/83, when China started to open both to international business and towards re-admitting the profession of lawyering. He has observed Chinese arbitration law for many years, acting *inter alia* from 2012 to 2020 as managing director of the Chinese European Arbitration Centre (now, since 2023, the Asian European Arbitration Centre) in Hamburg, Germany, which he cofounded jointly with the Hamburg Bar in friendly cooperation with CIETAC and CCPIT in 2008. In his teaching of international arbitration as professor at the University of Hamburg, the CIETAC Arbitration Rules are never missing. Considering the options offered by international arbitration with an open mind, there is never only one solution. Students and practitioners need to know options; and in several situations the choice of the CIETAC Arbitration Rules may be the best solution under the specific circumstances of the case. In Shanghai, he has experienced the CIETAC Arbitration Rules also as a chairman in an international arbitration. **Björn Etgen** (born 1962), a fluent mandarin speaker, spent over 20 years as a lawyer in Beijing, Hong Kong and Taiwan. He has been a pioneer in legal advice to German companies in Asia, particularly in China. He is admitted as an arbitrator at various Asian and international arbitration institutions and has been serving as arbitrator in a substantial number of CIETAC arbitrations over the last 20 years and has been closely following the developments of arbitration in China. In 2023 alone, he has been involved in CIETAC arbitration cases with a total amount of the disputes exceeding 150 million EUR.

With these article-by-article comments, the authors strive to provide the legal community with **a tool** which may be helpful when diving into the adventure of foreign-Chinese business.

The authors wish to thank CIETAC for valuable comments and insights offered during the preparation of this revision, especially with regard to recent developments in 2022/2023 on the digital organization of arbitration under the CIETAC Arbitration Rules.

The authors further wish to thank their law firms and their colleagues for their support of this book project: Attorney-at-law HE Mingjie (何铭杰) (Graf von Westphalen) who assisted with research and was responsible for the comparison of the new and old CIETAC Arbitration Rules and Ms. WANG Rumeng (王如梦) (Graf von Westphalen – Shanghai office) who assisted with extensive research of the latest developments in arbitration in Mainland China. The team of students at the University of Hamburg, Verena Ernst, Kai Kunad, Jakob Schüssler and Paul Vogel (all Brödermann Jahn) provided substantial background research.

Hamburg and Munich
May 2024

Eckart Brödermann
Björn Etgen

Schütze (ed.), Institutionelle Schiedsgerichtsbarkeit, 1st edn, Munich 2006 and 2nd edn, Munich 2011 (in German) and 1st edn, Munich 2013 (in English); published with revisions by Eckart Brödermann/Björn Etgen, ibid., in 3rd edn, 2018 (in German). Over time, with multiple adaptations of the CIETAC Rules on their way towards internationalization, few roots have remained from the initial comments, but the authors would like to acknowledge their alignment to the tradition established by the initial commentators to whom the authors are connected in multiple ways, e.g., in one case by joint studying of Chinese law over 40 years ago when China started to open up towards the international world.

Authors

Professor Dr. Eckart Brödermann is a lawyer, arbitrator – who is listed with CIETAC – and a professor of law with a focus on private international law, international contracting and international arbitration at the University of Hamburg, Germany. He holds an LL.M. title from Harvard University (East Asian European Legal Studies '83) and titles of *License en droit* and *Maître en droit* from the University of Paris V (*René Descartes*, Malakoff). He is admitted to practice in New York (since 1984) and in Germany (since 1990). He is a fellow of the chartered institute of arbitrators (FCIArb, London) and a German bar approved specialist (*Fachanwalt*) for cross-border business law. Professor Brödermann has written and co-authored multiple books and articles, including an article-by-article commentary on the general principles and rules of international contract law as compiled and developed by the International Institute for the Unification of Private Law (Unidroit), namely The Unidroit Principles of International Commercial Contracts (2nd edn 2023; Chinese translation: Wang, 国际统一私法协会国际商事合同通则 – –逐条评述, Beijing 2021). *[Chapter 1; Chapter 2; Art. 1–22; Art. 24–47, 51–52; Chapter 4 and Art. 49–50 co-written with Björn Etgen]*

Dr. Björn Etgen is a lawyer and arbitration practitioner with a focus on China. He has been listed as CIETAC arbitrator for more than 20 years and is also an appointed arbitrator with various other arbitration institutions in China and Asia. He has acted in numerous arbitration cases with CIETAC as counsel and arbitrator and is one of the few European arbitrators who also arbitrates in Chinese (Mandarin). He studied law and Chinese in Tübingen, Münster and Taipei and is admitted to the bar in Germany since 1995. He holds a Dr. iur. title from the University of Münster (1995). He lived and worked in Beijing (1996–2005) and Hong Kong (2005–2013) as partner and Head of China Practice of an international law firm. Dr. Etgen has written and co-authored multiple books and articles on business law and arbitration in China and is a frequent speaker on topics related to China arbitration. He is listed in "Best lawyers in Germany" for Dispute Resolution (2024). *[Chapter 3; Art. 23, 48, 53–88; Chapter 4 and Art. 49–50 co-written with Eckart Brödermann]*

Table of contents

Abbreviations

AAA	American Arbitration Association
ADR	Alternative Dispute Resolution
AIAC	Asian International Arbitration Centre
Am. U. Int'l L Rev.	American University International Law Review
approx.	approximately
Arb. Int'l	Arbitration International (Journal)
Art.	article(s)
ASEAC	Asian European Arbitration Centre
BAC/BIAC	Beijing Arbitration Commission/Beijing International Arbitration Center
BGB	Bürgerliches Gesetzbuch (German Civil Code)
BGBl.	Bundesgesetzblatt (German Federal Law Gazette)
CCOIC	China Chamber of International Commerce
CCPIT	China Council for the Promotion of International Trade
CEAC	Chinese European Arbitration Centre
cf.	confer (refer to)
CIETAC	China International Economic and Trade Arbitration Commission
CISG	United Nation Convention on Contracts for the International Sale of Goods
Cornell Int'l L. J.	Cornell International Law Journal
DIS	Deutsche Institution für Schiedsgerichtsbarkeit (German Arbitration Institute)
Draft Revised PRC Arbitration Law (2021)	Draft Revised Arbitration Law of the People's Republic of China, published by the Ministry of Justice of the PRC on July 30, 2021
ed.(s)	editor(s)
edn	edition
e.g.	exempli gratia (for example)
et seq.	et sequentia
fn.	footnote
FS	Festschrift (*Liber Amicorum*)
GDPR	Regulation (EU) 2016/679 of the European Parliament and of the Council of 27 April 2016 on the protection of natural persons with regard to the processing of personal data and on the free movement of such data (General Data Protection Regulation)
HKD	Hong Kong Dollar
HKIAC	Hong Kong International Arbitration Centre
IBA	International Bar Association
ICC	International Chamber of Commerce
ICDR	International Centre for Dispute Resolution
i.e.	id est (that is)
IPBA	Inter-Pacific Bar Association
J. Int. Arb.	Journal of International Arbitration
MedArb/ArbMed	A combination of arbitration and conciliation/meditation
mn.	margin number(s)
NJW	Neue Juristische Wochenschrift
no.	number(s)
NYC	New York Convention on the Recognition and Enforcement of Foreign Arbitral Awards
p(p).	page(s)
para.	paragraph(s)/clause(s)
PRC	People's Republic of China

Abbreviations

RabelsZ	Rabels Zeitschrift für ausländisches und internationales Privatrecht (The Rabel Journal of Comparative and International Private Law)
RIW	Recht der internationalen Wirtschaft (Law of the International Economy)
RMB	Renminbi Yuan
Rome I Regulation	Regulation (EC) No 593/2008 of the European Parliament and of the Council of 17 June 2008
SAR	Special Administrative Region
SchiedsVZ	Zeitschrift für Schiedsverfahren (German Arbitration Journal)
sent.	sentence
SIAC	Singapore International Arbitration Centre
SIDRC	Seoul International Dispute Resolution Centre
suppl.	supplement
SPC	Supreme People's Court of the People's Republic of China
THAC	Thailand Arbitration Centre
UIA	Union International des Advocats
UNCITRAL	United Nations Commission on International Trade Law
vol.	volume
ZPO	Zivilprozessordnung (German Code of Civil Procedure)

Glossary of Latin legal terms

English has become a global language. In the civil law parts of the world, the law goes back to Roman roots and the former global language "Latin". This brings along that a civil trained lawyer (as well as some of the sources cited in this commentary) tend to sometimes tie in the Latin language. For those lawyers who come from jurisdictions where Latin expressions are not taught as part of the legal training, this glossary may be helpful.

ad hoc	non-institutional
argumentum	argument, argument based on
de facto	in fact
ex aequo et bono	according to what is fair and good
ex officio	resulting from a function
forum	court, place of the court
lex fori	law of the forum
favor arbitri	arbitration favor (preference to the solution that preserves the effectiveness of the arbitration agreement rather than its destruction)
verbatim	in a way that uses exactly the same words as were originally used
res iudicata	a matter already adjudicated upon
prima facie	at first sight/as it seems first

Bibliography and sources*

A. Literature on CIETAC/CIETAC publications

Budke, 'Party Autonomy and its Limitations in International Commercial Arbitration in Mainland China under the CIETAC Arbitration Rules' in Glöckner et al (eds), Rechtliche Funktionsbedingungen von Märkten und Formen der Konfliktbeilegung in China und Europa, Lausanne 2017, pp. 191–218

CCPIT, Annual Working Report 2023 on CIETAC, available under https://www.cietac.org

CIETAC, Annual Yearbook of CIETAC 2022 [贸仲委 2022 年工作报告], at http://www.cietac.org

CIETAC, CIETAC Guidelines on Proceeding with Arbitration Actively and Properly during the COVID-19 Pandemic, issued on 28 April 2020 [中国国际经济贸易仲裁委员会关于新冠肺炎疫情期间积极稳妥推进仲裁程序指引（试行）], available under http://www.cietac.org

Kniprath, Die Schiedsgerichtsbarkeit der Chinese International Economic and Trade Arbitration Commission (CIETAC), Cologne 2004

Laprès, 'The Role of Foreign Lawyers in CIETAC Arbitration Proceedings' China Business Review (May-June 2009), 46–49

Meng, 'CIETAC's latest emergency arbitration: an inside look', China Business Law Journal 2022, at https://law.asia/cietacs-latest-emergency-arbitration/

Neelmeier, 'CIETAC: Chinese Supreme People's Court klärt Zuständigkeitsfragen', SchiedsVZ 2015, 251–253

Öhlberger, 'China-Related Contracts: What to Consider When Agreeing on CIETAC Arbitration' in Klausegger et al (eds), Austrian Arbitration Yearbook 2009, Munich 2009, pp. 113–145

Stricker-Kellerer/Moser, 'Schiedsordnung der China International Economic and Trade Arbitration Commission (CIETAC)' in Schütze (ed.), Institutionelle Schiedsgerichtsbarkeit, 2nd edn, Munich 2011

Yu/Cao, A Guide to the CIETAC Arbitration Rules and Practice, Oxford 2020

B. Further literature on arbitration in China

Bell/Chong/Sharp, 'The "Golden Landmark Case" – A new dawn for enforcement of foreign arbitral awards in China?' (May 2016) available under: https://www.lexology.com

Beneyto/Brödermann/Meyer/Zhao, 'Neue Wege in der Schiedsgerichtsbarkeit: Das Chinese European Arbitration Centre (CEAC) für China-Verträge', RIW 2011, 12–21

* The original titles of publications available only in Chinese are provided in brackets. For ease of reading, the English translation is used in the references made in the footnotes. Unless stated otherwise, all websites cited in this book were last visited on May 22, 2024. To avoid citation of long and complicated web addresses, only the homepage is cited.

Bibliography and sources

Brödermann
- 'The Chinese European Arbitration Centre – An Introduction to the CEAC Hamburg Arbitration Rules' J. Int. Arb. 2013, 303–328
- 'Chinesische und chinabezogene Schiedsverfahren – Beobachtungen aus Wissenschaft und Praxis' in Ebke/Olzen/Sandrock (eds), Festschrift für Siegfried H. Elsing zum 65. Geburtstag, Frankfurt a.M. 2015, pp. 53–71
- 'Chinese European Arbitration Centre (CEAC)' in World Arbitration Report (2018)

Brödermann/Etgen/Zong, 'Länderbericht China (Volksrepublik)' in Geimer/Schütze (eds), Internationaler Rechtsverkehr in Zivil- und Handelssachen, 58th suppl., October 2019

Brödermann/Heeg-Weimann, 'The Chinese European Arbitration Centre – Hamburg' in Respondek (ed.), Asia Arbitration Guide, 8th edn, Berlin 2023, pp. 61–69

Burkardt/Zapletal/Guo, 'China' in Respondek (ed.), Asia Arbitration Guide, 8th edn, Singapore 2023, pp. 43–60

China Academy of Arbitration Law, 'Annual Report on International Commercial Arbitration in China' (2014)

Choong, 'First reported case of China ICC award being enforced in China' in Practical Law, October 2009, available under: https://uk.practicallaw.thomsonreuters.com
- 'China', The Asia-Pacific Arbitration Review 2014, 40–45

Dong/Brödermann, 'Chinese European Arbitration Centre (CEAC) in Hamburg and CEAC Arbitration Rules in International Comparison, Arbitration and Law' Journal of CIETAC (仲裁与法律) 2010, 104–130

Dong/Meng, 'Does Supreme People's Court's Decision open the Door for Foreign Arbitration Institutions to Explore the Chinese Market?' Kluwer Arbitration Blog, July 15, 2014, available under: http://kluwerarbitrationblog.com

Fan, 'Arbitration in China. A Legal and Cultural Analysis (2013)' discussed by Brödermann/Eckart, Global Arbitration Review, March 19, 2014

Fourth Senate for Civil Proceedings of the Supreme People's Court
- 'Annual Report of the Supreme People's Court about the Judicial Examination of Commercial Arbitrations 2019', Beijing 2021
- 'Annual Report of the Supreme People's Court about the Judicial Examination of Commercial Arbitrations 2020', Beijing 2021

Huang (ed.), International Private Law and International Commercial Arbitration [国际私法与国际商事仲裁], Wuhan 1994

Jiang/Xiao (eds), Arbitration Law [仲裁法], 3rd edn, Beijing 2016

Johnston, 'Bridging the Gap Between Western and Chinese Arbitration Systems – A Practical Introduction for Businesses', Journal of International Arbitration 2007, 565–580

Moser, 'Commentary on Arbitration and Conciliation Concerning China' in van den Berg (ed.), New Horizons in International Commercial Arbitration and Beyond, Alphen aan den Rijn 2005, pp. 89–98

Moser/Yuen, 'Chinese Supreme People's Court Provides Clarification – and Confusion – on Arbitration Issues' in van den Berg (ed.), New Horizons in International Commercial Arbitration and Beyond, Alphen aan den Rijn 2005, pp. 99–111

Rogers/Townsend
- '"Hybrid" clauses in China Ningbo court upholds validity of hybrid clause', International Arbitration Report 2014, 18–20
- 'The Longlide decision', April 2015, available from: https://www.nortonrosefulbright.com

Song (ed.), Arbitration Law, Beijing 2016

Song/Yang/Chen, 'Annual Review on Commercial Arbitration in China' in Commercial Dispute Resolution in China: An Annual Review and Preview, Hong Kong 2015, pp. 9–44

Tang/Sun (eds), The new Interpretation of Arbitration Law [仲裁法及配套规定新释新解], Beijing 2002

Tao, 'Salient Issues in Arbitration in China', Am. U. Int'l L Rev. 2012, 807–832

Tevini, 'Besonderheiten des chinesischen Schiedsverfahrensrechts, SchiedsVZ 2010, 25–31

Trappe
- 'Conciliation in the Far East', Arb. Int'l 1989, 173–185
- 'Streiterledigung im Chinageschäft', RIW 1989, 107–112

Utterback/Blackwell, 'Enforcing foreign arbitral awards in China – a review of the past twenty years', September 15, 2016 available from: www.kwm.com

Wang, 'Investigation and Thinking on the Operation of Interim Award of Commercial Arbitration in China', Beijing Arbitration vol. 1 2017, 31–48

Weimann/Heeg/Hasenstab, 'CEAC Arbitration – Bridging the Gap between China and Europe – Arbitration Tailored for Sino-European Disputes Administered by the Chinese European Arbitration Centre' in Klausegger et al. (eds), Austrian Yearbook on International Arbitration 2013, Munich 2013, pp. 125–148

Wiegand/Ye, 'International Arbitration in China (People's Republic)' in Balthasar (ed.), International Commercial Arbitration – A Handbook, 2nd edn, Munich 2021, pp. 320–357

Xia, 'Implementation of the New York Convention in China', Arbitration Brief 2011, 20–24

Yang, The Effect of International Commercial Arbitral Award, Shanghai 2021

Zhang, 'Enforceability of Ad Hoc Arbitration Agreements in China: China's Incomplete Ad Hoc Arbitration System', Cornell Int'l L. J. 2013, 361–399

C. Further literature

BAC/BIAC, Annual Yearbook of BAC/BIAC 2019 [北京仲裁委员会/北京国际仲裁中心 2019 年度工作总结], at: https://www.bjac.org.cn

BAC/BAIC, Annual Yearbook of BAC/BIAC 2020 [北京仲裁委员会/北京国际仲裁中心 2020 年度工作总结], at https://www.bjac.org.cn

BAC/BIAC, Annual Yearbook of BAC/BIAC 2021 [北京仲裁委员会/北京国际仲裁中心 2021 年度工作总结], at https://www.bjac.org.cn

Bonell, 'The law governing international commercial contracts und the actual role of the UNIDROIT Principles', Uniform Law Review 2018, 15–41

Born, International Commercial Arbitration, 3rd edn, Alphen aan den Rijn 2021

Brödermann
- 'Die Bedeutung des (internationalen) Gesellschaftsrechts in internationalen zivil- und handelsrechtlichen Schiedsverfahren – Zugleich ein Beitrag zur Auslegung von Art. II, IV und V Abs. 1 (a) des New Yorker Übereinkommens' in Cascante/Spahlinger/Wilske (eds), Global Wisdom on Business Transactions, International Law and Dispute Resolution – Festschrift für Gerhard Wegen zum 65. Geburtstag, Munich 2015, pp. 591–604
- 'Choice of Law and Choice of UPICC Clauses in the Shadow of the Dispute Resolution Clause – Fundamental Aspects of Developing a Coherent Basis for Cross-Border Contracts', Hamburg Law Review 2016, 21–51
- '§ 6 Internationales Privatrecht' in Piltz (ed.), Münchener Anwaltshandbuch Internationales Wirtschaftsrecht, Munich 2017
- 'Bridge over Troubled Waters for International Commercial Contracts – The UNIDROIT Principles 2016, An Overview form a Long Time User', Tulane J Int Comp L 2020, 193–257
- Unidroit Principles of International Commercial Contracts, An Article-by-Article Commentary', 2nd edn, Baden-Baden, 2023; Chinese translation (1st edn): Wang, 国际统一私法协会国际商事合同通则——逐条评述, Beijing 2021

Bibliography and sources

Brödermann/Rosengarten, Internationales Privat- und Verfahrensrecht, 9th edn, Munich 2024

Brödermann/Wegen
- 'IPR-Anh 1' in: Prütting/Wegen/Weinreich (eds), BGB – Bürgerliches Gesetzbuch, 17th edn, Munich 2022 (cited as: PWW/Brödermann/Wegen)
- UNIDROIT Principles of International Commercial Contracts, An Article-by-Article Commentary, 1st edn, Alphen aan den Rijn 2018; Chinese translation: Wang, 国际统一私法协会国际商事合同通则——逐条评述, Beijing 2021
- UNIDROIT Principles of International Commercial Contracts, An Article-by-Article Commentary, 2nd edn, Alphen aan den Rijn 2023 (cited as: Brödermann, UNIDROIT Principles Commentary)

Deißner, Interregionales Privatrecht in China, Tübingen 2012

Hausmaniger, 'Civil Liability of Arbitrators – Comparative Analysis and Proposals for Reform', Journal of International Arbitration 1990, 7–48

Jiang (ed.), Understanding and application of the provisions of the new Civil Procedure Law, Beijing 2022

Klages/Leibküchler/Pißler, 'Allgemeiner Teil des Zivilrechts der Volksrepublik China', Zeitschrift für Chinesisches Recht 2017, 208–238

Laumen, '§ 286 ZPO' in Prütting/Gehrlein (eds), ZPO Kommentar, 14th edn, Munich 2022 (cited as Laumen/Prütting/Gehrlein)

Leading Small Group of the Supreme People's Court to work on the implementation and enforcement of the Civil Code [最高人民法院民法典贯彻实施工作领导小组], Encyclopedia of the application of the Civil Code of China [中国民法典适用大全], Volume I on Foreign-related Commerce and Maritime trade [涉外商事海事卷（一）], Beijing 2022

Leibküchler, 'Comments on the Supreme People's Court's Interpretation No. 1 on the Private International Law Act of the PRC', China-EU Law Journal 2013, 201–216

Ling, Contract Law in China, Hong Kong 2002

Office of Leading Small Group of the Supreme People's court to the work on the implementation and enforcement of the Civil Code [最高人民法院民法典贯彻实施工作领导小组办公], Understanding and application of the provisions of the new Interpretation of the Civil Procedure Law [最高人民法院新民事诉讼法解释理解与适用], Beijing 2022

Pißler, 'Das neue Internationale Privatrecht der Volksrepublik China: Nach den Steinen tastend den Fluss überqueren', RabelsZ 2012, 1–46

Samuel, Jurisdictional problems in international commercial arbitration: a study of Belgian, Dutch, English, French, Swedish, Swiss, U.S., and West German law, Zürich 1989

Schubert, 'Der Grundsatz von Treu und Glauben im chinesischen Zivilrecht – zur Bedeutung eines chinesischen Gesetzeskommentars', Zeitschrift für Chinesisches Recht 2019, 34–41

Trappe, 'Maritime Schiedsgerichtsbarkeit' in Plantey/Böckstiegel/Bredow (eds), Festschrift für Ottoarndt Glossner zum 70. Geburtstag, Frankfurt a. M. 1994, pp. 459–476

Vogenauer (ed.), Commentary on the UNIDROIT Principles of International Commercial Contracts, 2nd edn, Oxford 2015

Yu/Shore, 'Independence, Impartiality, and Immunity of Arbitrators: US and English Perspectives', International and Comparative Law Quarterly 2003, 935–967

Zhan, 'Commentary to the Liability of Arbitrators in Hong Kong and Mainland China', Research of Arbitration 2004 No. 1, 31–37

Zhang/Zhang, 'Annual Review on Commercial Mediation in China' in Commercial Dispute Resolution in China: An Annual Review and Preview, Hong Kong 2015, pp. 45–55

D. Chinese law

Arbitration Law of the People's Republic of China [中华人民共和国仲裁法] adopted at the 9th Session of the Standing Committee of the 8th National People's Congress on August 31, 1994, and promulgated by Order No. 31 of the President of the People's Republic of China on August 31, 1994. English version: https://www.chinajusticeobserver.com/law/x/arbitration-law-20170901 (last visited November 27, 2023)

Arrangement Concerning Mutual Assistance in Court-ordered Interim Measures in Aid of Arbitral Proceedings by the Courts of the Mainland and of the Hong Kong SAR [关于内地与香港特别行政区法院就仲裁程序相互协助保全的安排] signed on April 2, 2019, and in force as of October 1, 2019. English version: https://www.doj.gov.hk/en/mainland_and_macao/pdf/arbitration_interim_e.pdf (last visited December 31, 2023)

Arrangement Concerning Mutual Enforcement of Arbitral Awards between the Mainland and the Hong Kong Special Administrative Region [最高人民法院关于内地与香港特别行政区相互执行仲裁裁决的安排] in force since February 1, 2000. English version: https://www.doj.gov.hk/en/legal_dispute/pdf/mainlandmutual2e.pdf (last visited July 19, 2023)

Circular of the Supreme People's Court on Implementing Convention on the Recognition and Enforcement of Foreign Arbitral Awards Entered by China [最高人民法院关于执行我国加入的《承认及执行外国仲裁裁决公约》的通知] promulgated on April, 10 1987, and in force as of April, 10 1987. Chinese version https://flk.npc.gov.cn (last visited December 31, 2023)

Circular of the Supreme People's Court on Issuing the 36th Batch of Guiding Cases, Fa [2022] No.267 [最高人民法院关于发布第 36 批指导性案例的通知) 法〔2022〕267号], issued on December 27, 2022

Civil Code of the People's Republic of China [中华人民共和国民法典] adopted at the 3rd Session of the 13th National People's Congress on May 28, 2020. English version: http://www.npc.gov.cn (last visited July 19, 2023)

Civil Procedure Law of the People's Republic of China [中华人民共和国民事诉讼法] adopted at the 4th Session of the 7th National People's Congress on April 9, 1991, amended for the fifth time in accordance with the Decision of the Standing Committee of the National People's Congress on Revising the Civil Procedure Law of the People's Republic of China at the 5th session of the Standing Committee of the 14th National People's Congress of the People's Republic of China on September 1, 2023. English version: https://www.lawinfochina.com (last visited November 27, 2023)

Foreign Investment Law of the People's Republic of China [中华人民共和国外商投资法] adopted at the 2nd Session of the 13th National People's Congress and promulgated by Order No. 26 of the President of the People's Republic of China on March 15, 2019, in force as of on January 1, 2020. English version: https://shlx.pkulaw.com (last visited December 31, 2023)

Interpretation of the Supreme People's Court concerning the "Civil Procedure Law of the People's Republic of China" [最高人民法院关于适用《中华人民共和国民事诉讼法》的解释] adopted at the 1,866th Meeting of the Judicial Committee of the Supreme People's Court on March 22, 2022, in force since April 10, 2022. Chinese version: http://lawinfochina.com (last visited November 27, 2023)

Interpretation of the Supreme People's Court concerning Some Issues on the Application of the "Arbitration Law of the People's Republic of China" [最高人民法院关于适用《中华人民共和国仲裁法》若干问题的解释：（最高人民法院关于适用《中华人民共和国仲裁法》若干问题的解释）adopted at the 1,375th Meeting of the Judicial Committee of the Supreme People's Court on December 26, 2005, in force since September 8, 2006. English version: https://cicc.court.gov.cn (last visited May 15, 2024). Cited as 2006 Interpretation of the Supreme People's Court.

Interpretation of the Supreme People's Court on Several Issues Concerning the Application of the "Law of the People's Republic of China on the Law Applicable to Foreign-Related Civil Relationships" (I) [最高人民法院关于适用《中华人民共和国涉外民事关系法律适用法》若

干问题的解释（一）] adopted at the 1,563rd Session of the Judicial Committee of the Supreme People's Court on December 10, 2012 and amended in accordance with the Decision at the 1823rd meeting of the Judicial Committee of the Supreme People's Court on December 23, 2020. English version: https://shlx.pkulaw.com (last visited November 27, 2023)

Law of the People's Republic of China on the Law Applicable to Foreign-Related Civil Relationships [中华人民共和国涉外民事关系法律适用法] adopted at the 17th session of the Standing Committee of the 11th National People's Congress on October 28, 2010 and promulgated by Order No. 36 of the President of the People's Republic of China on October 28, 2010. English version: https://cicc.court.gov.cn (last visited November 27, 2023)

Legislation Law of the People's Republic of China [中华人民共和国立法法] adopted at the 3rd Session of the 9th National People's Congress on March 15, 2000, and amended for the second time in accordance with the Decision at the 1st Session of the 14th National People's Congress on March 13, 2023. English version: https://shlx.pkulaw.com (last visited November 27, 2023)

Mediation Law of the People's Republic of China [中华人民共和国人民调解法] adopted at the 16th meeting of the Standing Committee of the 11th National People's Congress of the People's Republic of China on 28 August 2010, and promulgated by Order No. 34 of the President of the People's Republic of China on August 28, 2010. English version: https://www.lawinfochina.com/ (last visited November 27, 2023)

Opinions of the Supreme People's Court on Providing Judicial Guarantee for the Building of Pilot Free Trade Zones [最高人民法院关于为自由贸易试验区建设提供司法保障的意见] issued on December 30, 2016. English version: https://shlx.pkulaw.com (last visited December 31, 2023)

Provisions by the Supreme People's Court on Evidence in Civil Procedures [最高人民法院关于民事诉讼证据的若干规定], adopted at the 1,201st meeting of the Judicial Committee of the Supreme People's Court on December 6, 2001, and amended for second time in accordance with the Decision at the 1777th meeting of the Judicial Committee of the Supreme People's Court on October 14, 2019. Chinese version available at: http://gongbao.court.gov.cn (last visited November 27, 2023)

Provisions of the Supreme People's Court on Several Issues concerning Arbitration-related Judicial Review Cases [最高人民法院关于审理仲裁司法审查案件若干问题的规定] adopted at the 1728th meeting of the Judicial Committee of the Supreme People's Court on December 4, 2017, and in force as of January 1, 2018. Chinese version available at: https://flk.npc.gov.cn (last visited December 31, 2023)

Provisions of the Supreme People's Court on Several Issues concerning the Enforcement Work of the People's Courts (for Trial Implementation) (Revised in 2020) [最高人民法院关于人民法院执行工作若干问题的规定(试行)] adopted on June 11, 1998, and effective as of July 8, 1998. English version: https://shlx.pkulaw.com (last visited December 31, 2023)

Provisions of the Supreme People's Court on Several Issues concerning the Handling of Cases by People's Courts to Enforce Arbitration Awards [最高人民法院关于人民法院办理仲裁裁决执行案件若干问题的规定], promulgated on February 22, 2018, and in force as of March 1, 2018 (cited as: SPC Enforcement Provisions 2018) English version available at: http://www.lawinfochina.com (last visited December 31, 2023)

Provisions of the Supreme People's Court on the Application of Law in the Trial of Taiwan-Related Civil and Commercial Cases (Revised in 2020) [最高人民法院关于审理涉台民商事案件法律适用问题的规定] adopted on April 26, 2010, and effective as of January 1, 2011. Chinese version: https://flk.npc.gov.cn (last visited December 31, 2023)

Relevant Provisions of the Supreme People's Court on the Reporting and Verification of Arbitration Judicial Review Cases (Revised in 2021) [最高人民法院关于仲裁司法审查案件报核问题的有关规定] adopted on December 24, 2021, and effective as of January 1, 2022. Chinese version: https://flk.npc.gov.cn (last visited August 11, 2023)

Supplemental Arrangement Concerning Mutual Enforcement of Arbitral Awards between the Mainland and the Hong Kong Special Administrative Region [高人民法院关于内地与港特别政区相互执仲裁裁决的补充安排] signed on November 27, 2020, in force since May 19, 2021. English version: https://www.doj.gov.hk (last visited January 4, 2024)

E. Chinese court decisions*

Civil Judgment of the SPC, (2021) Supreme Court Intellectual Civil Final No.924 [(2021)最高法知民终 924]

Civil Judgment of the No. 4 Intermediate People's Court of Beijing, (2021) Beijing 04 Civil Special No.715 [（2021）京 04 民特 715 号]

Civil Judgment of Shenzhen Intermediate People's Court, (2019) Yue Enforcement Review No.912 [(2019) 粤执复 912 号]

Civil Judgment of Intermediate People's Court of Nanjing, (2018) Su 01 Assist Foreign Recognition No.8 [(2018)苏 01 协外认 8 号]

Civil Judgment of Intermediate People's Court of Shenzhen, (2018) Yue 03 Civil First No.2267 [(2018)粤 03 民初 2267 号]

Civil Judgment of Wuhan Maritime Court, (2014) Wu Maritime Court Other No.00038[(2014)武海法他字第 00038 号]

F. International and foreign sources of law

German Code of Civil Procedure [*Zivilprozessordnung*], promulgated on December 5, 2005 (BGBl. I p. 3202; 2006 I p. 431; 2007 I p. 1781), last amended by Art. 1 of the Act dated October 10, 2013 (BGBl. I p. 3786) and Book 10 last amended by Art. 1 of the Act of October 5, 2021 (BGBl. I, p. 4607)). English version: https://www.gesetze-im-internet.de/englisch_zpo

Hague Judgments Convention: Convention of 2 July 2019 on the Recognition and Enforcement of Foreign Judgments in Civil or Commercial Matters, to enter into force on September 1, 2023. Text available at: https://www.hcch.net

NYC: New York Convention on the Recognition and Enforcement of Foreign Arbitral Awards from June 10, 1958. Text available at: www.newyorkconvention.org/text

Rome I Regulation: Regulation (EC) No 593/2008 of the European Parliament and of the Council of 17 June, 2008 on the law applicable to contractual obligations (Rome I)

UNCITRAL, HCCH and Unidroit, Legal Guide to Uniform Instruments in the Area of International Commercial Contracts, with a Focus on Sales (United Nations, February 2021) (cited as: UNCITRAL et al., Tripartite Legal Guide)

UNCITRAL Model Law on International Commercial Arbitration, accepted by the UN Commission on International Trade Law on June 21, 1985, adopted by the General Assembly on December 11, 1985, with amendments as adopted on December 4, 2006; text available at: https://uncitral.un.org

UNIDROIT Principles of International Commercial Contracts 2016, text available at: https://www.unidroit.org

G. Relevant websites

http://www.cietac.org/

https://cicc.court.gov.cn/

https://www.unidroit.org/

https://newyorkconvention1958.org/

---

* All decisions cited here are available under https//wenschu.court.gov.cn.

PART I
CIETAC AND ARBITRATION IN CHINA

Chapter 1
Introduction – Importance of CIETAC Arbitration

A. The need for arbitration in Foreign-Chinese legal relations

This Commentary on CIETAC arbitration is written from a continental European and in particular German perspective, bearing also a US and a global perspective in mind. It is based on studies of Chinese law and experiences with Chinese parties over several decades, both in Europe (under different arbitration rules) and in China, including experience as chair in a CIETAC arbitration. Against this background, it is observed that legal relations between foreign and Chinese companies often end in arbitration. This is unavoidable for economic, procedural and, most importantly, legal-cultural and sociological reasons. 1

I. Economic reasons

From an economic perspective, the intensity of foreign-Chinese relations leads to the conclusion of numerous contracts. This entails the risk of legal dispute. 2

II. Legal-cultural and sociological reasons

From a legal-cultural and sociological perspective, the **different understanding of the concept of "contract"** in large parts of the world like Europe (Germany) or, e.g., the United States, and in the People's Republic of China (PRC) induces the **risk of legal dispute**.[1] Western business partners tend to focus on the details of duties and rights as regulated in the contract. In contrast, Chinese contract partners are inclined to go beyond the specific wording and to rather concentrate on the concept of **fairness and equality** (in case of a dispute this may sometimes lead to an overreaction). The goal to act "in accordance with the principle of universal harmony" (*he wei gui:* 和为贵)[2] is more important than the formal language of the contract. A Chinese expert has expressed this observation as follows: "The Germans are '*frantic to apply any detailed clause*' and tend to an '*over-engineering*', while 'the Chinese'[3] are masters of improvisations. As long as the parties have an agreement on their joint goal, it is not so important which way they 3

[1] Brödermann in FS Elsing, p. 57.

[2] Fan, Arbitration in China (2013), p. 185. According to The Commentary of the Conversations [論語論疏] of XING Bing [刑昺], (932–1010 AD), this phrase originated in Chapter I "*Xueer*"[学而] of the "Conversations of Confucius"[论语]. In the original context, it says "In enforcing the rites, emphasis is placed on harmony." [礼之用，和为贵。] Harmony in this context means "the rites must be appropriate to nature". The meaning "Peace shall have priority" used in the preface was only derived later.

[3] For the Greater China area one must distinguish between 23 provinces, 4 municipalities (Beijing, Tianjin, Shanghai, Chongqing), 5 autonomous regions (Guangxi, Inner Mongolia, Tibet, Ningxia, Xinjiang) and 2 special administrative regions (Hong Kong, Macau); therefore, there is not one "China" but several.

take."[4] This can lead to an **expectation** of the Chinese business partner to implement contractual clauses not too strictly and to perceive rules as negotiable with regard to changing circumstances.

4 To emphasize, while western international businesspersons, e.g., from Europe or the United States, wish to negotiate all details of a contract with an interest to focus, as of the contract conclusion, on a good execution of the agreement, Chinese businesspersons tend to perceive the contract conclusion as an initiation of a real relationship which provides a frame for the negotiations. From the perspective of Chinese businesspersons, the admissibility of contract adaptation because of (fundamental) change of circumstances is quasi integrated into a contract.[5] Therefore, in the process of transaction, specifically with a local partner in a developing region in China, a Western investor generally struggles against persuading the local partner to sign a detailed contract. The Chinese reluctance to sign a detailed contract is due to the Chinese style of substance over form. This understanding follows from the perception of the "law" (which is transposed to "contracts"), which reminds an educated Chinese by its mere term of the negative (punishing) side of law (while for a German businessperson, thinking in the spirit of enlightenment ("*Aufklärung*") or the German constitution (*Grundgesetz*), the word "law" might make it think of the (positive) freedom of contract when thinking about law): The old and complex sign 灋 (for ***Fa*** **= law**), usually represented today by a more simple, shortened form (法), has two sides:[6] One side stands for a "one horned imaginary animal" ("*zhi*"), which can **distinguish good and evil** from each other. It removes those who are not upright. The left side of the sign for *Fa* stands for water and may awake the association of a criminal, who is drifted away by the stream of the river.[7] These two sides of the sign are united by a verb, which stands for "to get rid of". To avoid being pushed into the water, a Chinese businessperson – associating with *Fa*[8] only the punishing side of the law – may feel "obliged" to renegotiate core points of a contract after contract conclusion with the goal to develop a "Chinese" and not a Teutonic solution.[9] It will do so (i) in the interest of its company and with regard to the goal of living according to the "**principle of universal harmony" (*he wei gui:* 和为贵)**[10] and (ii) also in its own interest. As a result, Chinese and foreign business partners may operate on the basis of **two fundamentally different understandings** of contract.[11] These aspects can shape a European-Chinese or other foreign-Chinese arbitration.[12] Sometimes, they *may* also explain the approach of Chinese arbitrators.

5 The observations above are pertinent in many situations (they have been confirmed by many Chinese colleagues during several intensive discussions), but they are **certainly not always** correct, specifically in the case of a transaction in a big city with international exposure. Many Chinese are internationally educated, understand the importance of

---

[4] Sen Gao in a presentation on June 15, 2016 on the "Munich Summit on China Arbitration" organized by CIETAC and CEAC (now ASEAC).

[5] Brödermann in FS Elsing, p. 56.

[6] Summary according to Fan, Arbitration in China, p. 184, fn. 13 with a quote by Shen Xu: "Fa *is also* zhi, *in that it strikes those who are not upright and removes them*", German summary by Brödermann in FS Elsing, pp. 55–56 (with reference to further sources).

[7] Fan, Arbitration in China, p. 184.

[8] Brödermann in FS Elsing, p. 56.

[9] Brödermann in FS Elsing, p. 57 (with an example).

[10] → mn. 3.

[11] Brödermann in FS Elsing, pp. 54–55, 57.

[12] A German-Chinese arbitration case serves as an example: Brödermann in FS Elsing, p. 58 (after a deliberate overselling of its products by a Chinese producer, it argued as a *force majeure* event that the construction of a second production facility to create the necessary production capacities was not approved by the competent authorities).

compliance with a contract and may insist under certain circumstances on the execution of the concrete wording of a contract, possibly by pointing at Art. 509 PRC Civil Code. Also, many Chinese prestigious companies pay full attention to western contractual culture. However, the different basic understanding of contracts in China and in Germany and other Western countries creates a necessity to insist on agreeing upon a good dispute resolution clause including an arbitration agreement. It is worth investing **market strength** into the negotiation of an arbitration clause (→ Ch. 2 mn. 6 et seq.).[13]

III. Procedural reasons

From a procedural perspective, even though there are no bilateral or multilateral treaties which govern or facilitate the execution of German state court judgments in the PRC and vice versa, the **recognition and enforcement of German state court judgments** in the PRC has in recent years become more predictable. Both countries have recognized judgments of the other country[14] and therefore reciprocity does exist.[15] There may be even more clarity if China decides to join the Hague Judgments Convention. Currently, however, there exist no signs in this regard.[16] **6**

Many foreign parties are reluctant to agree on the **competence of Chinese state courts** for various reasons, partly (i) due to risk management considerations (Chinese law experienced practitioners generally feel that based on their practical experience the level of legal proficiency among judges, differs from region to region and person to person; there is also a risk of local protection), and (ii) due to emotions. For example, some international companies feel that the communist party – acting in accordance with its leadership role as set forth in the preamble of the Chinese constitution – might take some influence on the appointment of judges via its committees "*on politics and law*". This feeling has gained even more momentum in recent years, where the role of the party has been emphasized by the political leadership. It might thereby develop influence into the Chinese system of state court justice, thereby contravening the independence of judges as guaranteed by Art. 126 of the Chinese Constitution.[17] **7**

The safest possibility to combine a procedure outside China with execution and enforcement, if necessary, of a foreign title in the PRC, i.e., in the state of the business partner, is the agreement on an arbitration clause. It opens the door to an **arbitration** and the recognition and execution of an arbitral award as protected by the **New York Convention** (NYC) and by the provisions in **Art. 291 of the Civil Procedure Law of the People's Republic of China** (PRC Civil Procedure Law) which, from a Chinese **8**

---

[13] See in this context already the pleading of the author in Piltz, Münchener Anwaltshandbuch Internationales Wirtschaftsrecht, § 6 mn. 165.

[14] Brödermann, J. Int. Arb. 2013, 303, 305, and in FS Elsing, p. 60 with reference in fn. 30 to a decision by the High Regional Court of Berlin dated May 18, 2006, whereas in a reversed case the reciprocity of § 328 ZPO was acknowledged (KG Berlin, 18.5.2006 – 20 SCH 13/04, SchiedsVZ 2007, 100); Weimann/Heeg/Hasenstab, Austrian Yearbook on International Arbitration 2013, pp. 125 et seq. See also the court decision of the Intermediate People's Court of Wuhan, (2012) E Wuhan Zhong Min Shung Wae Chu Zi. No. 00016.

[15] Brödermann/Etgen/Zong, Internationaler Rechtsverkehr, 58th suppl., p. 1057.

[16] For an overview on the Contracting Parties of the Hague Judgments Convention see https://www.hcch.net/en/instruments/conventions/status-table/?cid=137.

[17] See also Brödermann in FS Elsing, pp. 59–60.

perspective, takes priority over the New York Convention because these rules are in conformity with the NYC.[18]

9 The arbitration solution is particularly helpful in negotiations on Chinese-foreign **Joint Venture** companies. According to Art. 279 No. 3 PRC Civil Procedure Law, foreign state courts may decide about such disputes from a Chinese perspective; on the other hand, the quoted provision does not refer to whether or not such disputes may be settled by arbitration.

B. Arbitration and Chinese legal culture

I. Dispute resolution as last resort

10 In the PRC, resolving a dispute by arbitration is usually the "last resort" (in fact, it applies not only in the PRC but also in the vast majority of Asian countries). In view of the search for harmony (*he wei gui:* 和为贵),[19] as noted above, mutual **negotiations** and mediation provide the essential part of dispute resolution in the PRC (→ Art. 47 mn. 10).[20] Thus, contractual dispute resolution schemes often provide that arbitration requires failed negotiation as prerequisite. Even if this is not the case, such negotiations are often possible and meaningful. Also, it is often difficult to determine whether the parties fulfilled their duty of negotiation.

To avoid long consultation processes, parties are well advised to provide for time limits for the preceding negotiations in their arbitration clauses.

11 In practice, the consultation phase may be used to manage expectations and to fence the dispute into realistic dimensions.

Example: After 10 years of contract duration – and a change of the arbitration clause at the occasion of a contract prolongation –, a German company terminated the framework agreement of an exclusive agency agreement which served as a basis for 300 individual contracts. The Chinese party felt deeply hurt in its honor and initially requested a compensation of all marketing activities in the past 10 years. Conciliation efforts reduced the claims for damages to a reasonable amount which then became subject of an arbitration proceeding.[21]

12 In China, **mediation** has a long tradition. Thus, several arbitration organizations including CIETAC (as discussed → mn. 21 et seq.; → Art. 47 mn. 1–9), the Beijing Arbitration Commission (**BAC**), the Joint Mediation Center of the China Council for the Promotion of International Trade, **CCPIT**) and the China Chamber of International Commerce (**CCOIC**) or the **Beijing ADR Center** provide and organize mediation opportunities.[22] Further, for German-Chinese disputes it is a viable option to turn to the Beijing Hamburg Conciliation

[18] Circular of the Supreme People's Court on Implementing Convention on the Recognition and Enforcement of Foreign Arbitral Awards Entered by China; Art. 271 and Art. 304 PRC Civil Procedure Law; as well as: Fan, Arbitration in China (2013), pp. 101 et seq.; Brödermann/Rosengarten, Internationales Privat- und Verfahrensrecht, mn. 807; Brödermann in FS Elsing, p. 69.

[19] → mn. 3.

[20] See also Wiegand/Ye in Balthasar, International Arbitration in China, p. 324 (at mn. 2): "Distinct features of international commercial arbitration in China include […] an emphasis on conciliation".

[21] A CEAC (now ASEAC) case from 2016, see in general for the Asian European Arbitration Centre "ASEAC": www.aseac-arbitration.com (last visited July 19, 2023).

[22] See Zhang/Zhang, Commercial Dispute Resolution in China, p. 45.

Centre in Beijing[23] or to its sister institution in Hamburg[24]. According to Art. 31(1) of the Chinese Mediation Law, a settlement agreement concluded during a mediation proceeding is binding in China. In case of non-performance of the obligations undertaken in such a settlement agreement, the other party can file a claim.[25] Art. 33 of the Chinese Mediation Law further provides for options of execution by Chinese courts in case of non-performance of mediation-based settlement agreement.

II. Development of arbitration in the PRC

Arbitration in the PRC has undergone an impressive development in the past years. **13**
There are approximately 270 arbitration institutions in the PRC.[26] Many administer not only national but also international and foreign related arbitrations.

1. Top-down approach

As observed by *Kun Fan*, Chinese arbitration commissions administer Chinese **14**
arbitrations with a **"top-down" approach**. It is due to the powerful role of the arbitration commission, as opposed to the "bottom-up" approach of arbitration in a European-American spirit with a focus on party autonomy.[27] The arbitrator concludes not only an arbitrator contract with the parties but also, and possibly even more importantly, a **cooperation contract** with the arbitration commission;[28] for each transfer of arbitrator fees to a foreign arbitrator, CIETAC concludes an additional agreement on the payment of the arbitration fee with the foreign arbitrator. The **CIETAC Arbitration Rules** reflect this top-down approach on three levels:

1. The rules on the **tasks of CIETAC** itself demonstrate its **powerful function**, e.g.
   i) Art. 6(1) and (7) on the power of CIETAC to determine the validity of an arbitration agreement and its own jurisdiction over an arbitration case (as opposed to the "competence-competence" approach in Europe which places that authority with the Arbitral Tribunal);[29]
   ii) in the provisions on the acceptance of arbitration claims (Art. 13(1));
   iii) the rules on the admission of a Request for Joinder (Art. 18(1) sent. 2);
   iv) the rules on the nomination of an arbitrator (Art. 26);
   v) the rules on the replacement of arbitrators (Art. 33);
   vi) in the rules on scrutiny of the arbitral award (Art. 51);
   vii) in the rules on a decision about the prolongation of the time period available for rendering an award (Art. 51(2)).
2. In the **role of the Arbitral Tribunal** to decide whether to accept a joint intention of the parties (e.g., Art. 38(1) on the decision to admit an open hearing).
3. In the **role of the presiding arbitrator** who decides alone if the Arbitral Tribunal cannot reach a majority opinion (Art. 49(6) sent. 1).

---

[23] For information (in German) see www.hk24.de/produktmarken/beratung-service/recht_und_steuern/schlichtung/beijing-hamburg-conciliation-centre/beijing-hamburg-conciliation-centre_index/1168144.

[24] Founded in 1987, to be found at www.hk24.de in the category of "*Recht und Steuern*", there under "*Schlichtung*/Conciliation"; see also Trappe, Arb. Int'l 1989, 173–185, and RIW 1989, 107–112, as well as Trappe in FS Glossner, pp. 461 et seq.

[25] Art. 32 PRC Mediation Law.

[26] See https://practiceguides.chambers.com/practice-guides/international-arbitration-2023/china at 1.4.

[27] Fan, Arbitration in China, pp. 179 et seq.; see also the summary by Brödermann in FS Elsing, pp. 65–66.

[28] Fan, Arbitration in China, pp. 176–177.

[29] The 2024 CIETAC Rules take a step towards international practice in the new Art. 6(1) which delegates the competence to the Arbitral Tribunal after its formation.

15 The currently discussed Draft Revised PRC Arbitration Law (2021)[30] is bound to attenuate the top-down approach over some aspects, especially by shifting the competence-competence to the Arbitral Tribunal (Art. 28, also → Art. 6 mn. 2) and by admitting *ad hoc* arbitration for commercial disputes involving foreign-related elements (Art. 91, 93, also → mn. 34). Culturally, however, the top-down approach remains the starting point for the assessment of arbitration in China.

2. Legal basis

16 The legal basis of arbitration in China is in particular the **PRC Arbitration Law**[31] which first came into force on September 1, 1995, and which correlates, in several points with the UNCITRAL Model Law on International Commercial Arbitration.[32] In this context it is important to consider the binding interpretation of the Supreme People's Court concerning some issues on the application of the PRC Arbitration Law which came into force on September 8, 2006 (hereinafter referred to as 2006 Interpretation of the Supreme People's Court.[33]

17 Art. 21 et seq. PRC Arbitration Law[34] regulate many core issues which the CIETAC Rules pick up and regulate in more detail. Art. 65 et seq. PRC Arbitration Law[35] provide the basis for foreign related CIETAC arbitrations, Art. 67 PRC Arbitration Law[36] provides the basis for the nomination of foreigners with special know-how (e.g., about a chosen contract law) as arbitrators. Further, the PRC Arbitration Law also provides **limits** to party autonomy (e.g., Art. 68 PRC Arbitration Law[37] on conservation of evidence). In line with the Chinese orientation on harmony which also influences the density of dispute, a "*good faith competition*" is a **goal** of Chinese (CIETAC) arbitration.[38]

18 When conducting arbitration in the PRC against a Chinese company, **multiple further sources of law** may become important, even if the parties have agreed as a matter of a compromise on German contract law for the substance and on a Chinese seat of the Arbitral Tribunal[39]. Such further sources of law include, for example:[40]

---

[30] The Ministry of Justice of the PRC published a revised draft for an updated PRC Arbitration Law on July 30, 2021. For the full text of this PRC Arbitration Law (Revised) (Draft for Public Comments) see Mao, FLIA Review 2021, 177–216.

[31] Further (binding) interpretation by the People's Court as reported by Wiegand/Ye in Balthasar, International Arbitration in China, p. 326 mn. 10.

[32] Accepted by the UN Commission on International Trade Law on June 21, 1985. Text and status at ww.uncitral.org (last visited July 19, 2023).

[33] Interpretation of the Supreme People's Court concerning Some Issues on the Application of the "Arbitration Law of the People's Republic of China", in force since September 8, 2006. English version available at https://cicc.court.gov.cn/html/1/219/199/201/672.html.

[34] Art. 35 et seq. Draft Revised PRC Arbitration Law (2021).

[35] Art. 88 et seq. Draft Revised PRC Arbitration Law (2021).

[36] Art. 89 Draft Revised PRC Arbitration Law (2021).

[37] According to Art. 43–49 Draft Revised PRC Arbitration Law (2021), the Arbitral Tribunal shall have the power to grant interim measures like the conservation of evidence.

[38] Li Hu, Ph.D., Deputy Secretary General of CIETAC in a presentation on June 15, 2016, on the "Munich Summit on China Arbitration" organized by CIETAC und CEAC (now ASEAC); see also Art. 2 (1) and 7 CIETAC Rules.

[39] See critical observations of Brödermann in Piltz, Münchener Anwaltshandbuch Internationales Wirtschaftsrecht (2017), § 6 mn. 95, 113–114 (implementation of the dispute resolution clause as the more important clause in comparison to the choice of applicable law); Brödermann, Hamburg Law Review 2016, 21 et seq. (concerning "Choice of Law and Choice of UPICC Clauses in the Shadow of the Dispute Resolution Clause").

[40] Enumeration according to Brödermann in FS Elsing, p. 67.

- the Civil Procedure Law of the PRC[41] with further (binding[42]) interpretation by the People's Court[43];
- the Chinese private international law is applicable at the Chinese seat of the Arbitral Tribunal, i.e., the Law of the Application of Law for Foreign-related Civil Relations of the PRC which was adopted on October 28, 2010,[44] with additional (binding) interpretations by the People's Court of December 28, 2012;[45]
- the Chinese company law to decide whether the Chinese Party is properly represented by the right organs as well as
- (binding) interpretations of the People's Court on the taking of evidence[46] as well as
- SPC Guiding Cases in the field of judicial review in arbitration cases.[47] Such 36th Batch of Guiding cases cover the scope of review in cases of confirmation of validity of arbitration agreement, independence of arbitration agreement, implied arbitration clause, expansion of validity of arbitration agreement, public interest and *ad hoc* arbitration.

On a case-by-case basis, further Chinese sources of law may become relevant, such as rules on intertemporal law.[48] To the extent that only foreign lawyers based in the PRC are active in an arbitration, the necessary **pleadings on Chinese law** can become difficult because foreign law firms may not give advice on Chinese law according to the prevailing – though debated – opinion in the PRC (→ Art. 22 mn. 2). **19**

An Arbitral Tribunal consisting solely of foreign arbitrators can organize – with due consent and/or upon the selection of the parties – an **expert on procedural questions** (without admitting such expert as an additional *de facto* arbitrator in the hearing).[49] In preparation of a hearing, such a procedural expert can help, for example with advice on several formal questions, for instance the admissibility of management directors of a party offered as witness during the arbitration. **20**

C. China International Economic and Trade Arbitration Commission (CIETAC)

The "Arbitration Institute of the China Chamber of International Commerce", known as the China International Economic and Trade Arbitration Commission ("CIETAC") was founded over 65 years ago in 1956 by the China Council for the Promotion of International Trade (**CCPIT**) as the "Foreign Trade Arbitration Commission" of the CCPIT.[50] **21**

---

[41] Passed on the 4th conference of the 7th National People's Congress on April 9, 1991, 3rd revision on June 27, 2017. English version available at http://cicc.court.gov.cn/html/1/219/199/200/644.html (last visited May 22, 2024).

[42] Cf. Burkardt/Zapletal/Guo, '4. China' in Respondek (ed.), Asia Arbitration Guide, p. 43.

[43] Opinions on Several Issues concerning the Application of the PRC Civil Procedure Law by the Supreme People's Court, passed on July 14, 1992, at the 528th conference of the committee on judicature of the Supreme People's Court, SPC's Official Journal 1992, No. 3, pp. 70 et seq.

[44] See Pißler, RabelsZ 2012, 1–46; Leibküchler, China-EU Law Journal 2013, 201–216.

[45] Interpretation of the Supreme People's Court on Several Issues Concerning the Application of the "Law of the People's Republic of China on the Law Applicable to Foreign-Related Civil Relations" (I).

[46] Provisions by the Supreme People's Court on Evidence in Civil Procedures.

[47] Circular of the Supreme People's Court on Issuing the 36th Batch of Guiding Cases, Fa [2022] No.267.

[48] Art. 104 PRC Legislation Law; and Art. 2 of the Interpretation of the Supreme People's Court on Several Issues Concerning the Application of the "Law of the People's Republic of China on the Law Applicable to Foreign-Related Civil Relations" (I), which foresees a limited retroactive effect of such conflict of laws rules that did not exist at the time of the contract conclusion.

[49] Brödermann in FS Elsing, p. 68.

[50] Art. 1(1) CIETAC Rules.

CIETAC is the largest and most important arbitration institution in the PRC.[51] The number of new cases received in 2023 by CIETAC was 5237, with a total amount in dispute of RMB 151 billion, a record high.[52] Among them were 645 foreign-related cases with a disputed amount of RMB 52.7 billion, and 4592 domestic cases with a disputed amount of RMB 98.2 billion. 209 cases had an amount in dispute over 100 million yuan, including 19 cases over 1 billion yuan. The internationalization factor of cases increased. The number of international cases in which both parties were foreign parties amounted to 62 cases. The cases involved 88 countries and regions. The top 10 sources of foreign-related cases included Hong Kong, the United States, Germany, South Korea, Singapore, the British Virgin Islands, and the United Kingdom.[53]

22 In 2022, the "Internal Guidelines on Case Management under the CIETAC Arbitration Rules" were issued to enhance the ability to apply international rules in resolving disputes; the Secretary's Guide to Handling Cases and the Procedural Provisions of the Advisory Committee of Experts were revised to improve the professionalism and standardization of case management.

23 As of 2023 there were 1,897 arbitrators from 144 countries and regions on the arbitration panel, among them were 591 foreign arbitrators. A total of 136 foreign arbitrators were involved in 125 cases. In 2023, 90 cases were handled exclusively by foreign arbitrators. In a total of 93 cases English and Chinese or only English applied as the language of arbitration.[54]

24 CIETAC has now created a new cloud-system which has significantly improved the efficiency of procedural management.[55] In 2023, 1,804 applications were filed online, accounting for nearly one third of the total number of cases filed; 1,906 online court sessions were held, accounting for nearly one-third of the total number of cases, involving parties from 35 countries and regions.[56]

25 CIETAC has made efforts to strengthen the information technology systems, to optimize the online flow of cases, and to improve efficiency. An external company has developed an electronic signature seal and a signature seal system for the secretary-general to improve the efficiency of signing and approving.[57] However, this system works currently primarily in Chinese and is not yet ready for international and foreign-related cases.

26 The **structure** used by CIETAC for its arbitration rules is logical and familiar mainly from a civil law perspective. **Chapter I** contains the "**General Provisions**": on organizational matters and competence, including the relation of CIETAC to its subsidiaries (sub-commissions, arbitration centers) and references to CIETAC under wrong nominations, e.g., "arbitration by the CCPIT" (Art. 2–4), arbitration agreement (Art. 5–6), seat (Art. 7), service of documents (Art. 8), principle based on good faith (Art. 9–10). **Chapter II** regulates the "arbitration proceedings": (i) in **Section 1** Request for Arbitration, Defense and Counterclaim (Arts 11–12), the acceptance of a case (Art. 13), procedures relating to multiple contracts (Art. 14), the core briefs to be submitted following the commencement of arbitration which determine the scope of the arbitration proceeding (Art. 15–17), joinder and consolidation (Art. 18–19), organization of the arbitration proceeding (Art. 20–21), conservatory and interim measures (Art. 23); (ii) in **Section 2** Arbitrators and the Arbitral Tribunal (Art. 24–34); (iii) in **Section 3** the Hearing (Art. 35–50 including the combination

---

[51] See Fan, Arbitration in China, p. 16 (at fn. 32); Budkein in Glöckner et al., Rechtliche Funktionsbedingungen, p. 192.
[52] CCPIT, Annual Working Report 2023 on CIETAC.
[53] CCPIT, Annual Working Report 2023 on CIETAC, p. 10.
[54] CCPIT, Annual Working Report 2023 on CIETAC, p. 10.
[55] CCPIT, Annual Working Report 2023 on CIETAC, p. 10.
[56] CCPIT, Annual Working Report 2023 on CIETAC, p. 10.
[57] CCPIT, Annual Working Report 2023 on CIETAC, p. 10.

with Conciliation in Art. 47) ("Med-Arb"/"Arb-Med"-options). **Chapter III** contains provisions on the "**Arbitral Award**": the award including issues of costs (Art. 51–57), performance and non-performance of the award, i.e., the application for enforcement of the award (Art. 58). **Chapter IV** regulates a summary proceeding applicable by party agreement or, absent a party agreement, to smaller amounts (Art. 59–67). **Chapter V** provides special provisions for domestic arbitration (Art. 68–75), and **Chapter VI** contains special provisions for CIETAC arbitration in Hong Kong (Art. 76–83). **Chapter VII** contains supplementary provisions including, e.g., a provision on language, on **interpretation** and the entry into force of the arbitral rules (Art. 84–88).

D. Distinguishing CIETAC-Proceedings in comparison to its international competitors

The PRC Arbitration Law distinguishes quite rigidly between foreign-related, interna- 27
tional, and domestic arbitrations.[58] With due regard to this distinction, the option of CIETAC Arbitration will have to be balanced against different alternatives from a foreigner's and in particular continental European perspective. The agreement on an *ad hoc* arbitration does not yet offer an alternative, although this is about to change.

I. "Domestic" contracts

From a Chinese perspective, disputes between **Chinese subsidiaries of foreign com-** 28
panies (or of Chinese joint venture companies with a foreign shareholding) with Chinese companies are classified as **"domestic" disputes**.[59] They cannot be administered by a foreign arbitral institution.[60] In case of a negotiation of a dispute resolution clause for such contracts, the CIETAC-arbitration rules (with its special provisions for domestic arbitrations in Chapter 5, Art. 65–72 since 2005) have to compete with (i) national Chinese state courts, and (ii) with other Chinese arbitration institutions of which there are approx. 270 (→ mn. 11). Well known examples include the **Beijing Arbitration Commission** ("BAC") or the **Shanghai International Arbitration Centre**[61] (a kind of spin-off of CIETAC which separated from CIETAC in 2013 invoking older rights, and by taking over the full panel of CIETAC arbitrators as admitted at that time)[62] or the **Shenzhen Arbitration Commission**. All big cities in China, such as **Jinan, Shanghai, Guangzhou, Shenzhen**, have an arbitration institution. CIETAC operates in 15 cities with its arbitration centers (→ Art. 2 mn. 1). What is decisive from a foreign perspective is the question whether the different rules permit to implement a neutral presiding arbitrator (chairperson) who is considered also as neutral from the foreign perspective.[63] In view of

[58] Wiegand/Ye in Balthasar, International Arbitration in China, p. 324 (at mn. 2), pp. 327 et seq. (at mn. 16–27); cf. Xia, Arbitration Brief 2011, 20 (21) (with a reference to various rules which apply for enforcement; here it is – because of an amendment of law after the publication of the article by Xia – Art. 248 PRC Civil Procedure Law for national arbitration proceedings; Art. 291 PRC Civil Procedure Law for foreign related arbitration proceedings and Art. 304 PRC Civil Procedure Law (which implements the New York Convention) for international arbitration proceedings.

[59] Tevini, SchiedsVZ 2010, 25 (26).

[60] Wiegand/Ye in Balthasar, International Arbitration in China, p. 324 (at mn. 3), pp. 327, 328 (at mn. 16–20), p. 333 (at mn. 41).

[61] Song/Yang/Chen, Annual Review on Commercial Arbitration in China, p. 41.

[62] Choong, The Asia-Pacific Arbitration Review 2014, 40.

[63] Cf. e.g. Art. 8 and 9(3) in conjunction with Art. 6 of the ASEAC Rules; see also Brödermann, World Arbitration Report, at I.A.1.

the longstanding experience of CIETAC with international arbitration, the CIETAC Rules have a good chance to win the competition in these cases and to be chosen as the governing arbitration rules.

29 If one wishes to obtain the same freedom as for international contracts (→ mn. 30 et seq.), it is possible to contemplate a **"Paramount-clause"** by which the dispute is drawn to the shareholder level: If the parties to the contract both have strong shareholders (e.g., in Taiwan or Hong Kong or in any offshore jurisdiction), it is possible to stipulate that all disputes between the operator subsidiaries shall be deemed to be disputes between their shareholders, the mother-companies.[64] This scheme is sometimes chosen in framework-contracts in which subsidiaries of the "mother-companies" do business with each other in different jurisdictions. In such cases, the parties undertake to delegate the dispute resolution from the Chinese parties to their international shareholders.

II. International and foreign-related contracts

30 For international or foreign-related[65] contracts (→ Art. 3 mn. 3), the CIETAC Rules are in competition with all known models of institutional arbitration. This includes in particular arbitration under the arbitration rules of the **ICC** (with a seat in Hong Kong)[66], the **ICDR**[67], the **HKIAC**[68] in Hong Kong, the **SIAC**[69] in Singapore, and the **AIAC**[70] in Kuala Lumpur. It is to be observed that parties often tend to overlook that the agreement on a seat in Hong Kong, Singapore or Kuala Lumpur includes an arbitral procedural switch to *common law* style arbitration.[71]

Example: The determination of the contents of German law becomes "a question of fact" as opposed to a "question of law" which the arbitrators are free to research and assess; a different basic understanding of taking of evidence and interpretation applies.[72] Those who wish to avoid this may think about alternatives on neutral ground: e.g., arbitration under the rules of the **THAC**[73] in Bangkok, the **SIDRC**[74] in Seoul or the **Asian European Arbitration Centre**[75]

---

[64] See Brödermann in Piltz, Münchener Anwaltshandbuch Internationales Wirtschaftsrecht, § 6 mn. 165–167 for arbitration clauses with paramount clauses.

[65] For a definition of the term "foreign-related" see the Interpretation of the Supreme People's Court on Several Issues Concerning the Application of the "Law of the People's Republic of China on the Law Applicable to Foreign-Related Civil Relations" as reported by Burkardt/Zapletal/Guo in Respondek, Asia Arbitration Guide, p. 44.

[66] International Court of Arbitration, https://iccwbo.org/dispute-resolution/dispute-resolution-services/arbitration/rules-procedure/.

[67] International Centre for Dispute Resolution (ICDR) of the American Arbitration Association (AAA), www.icdr.org.

[68] Hong Kong International Arbitration Centre, www.hkiac.org.

[69] Singapore International Arbitration Centre, www.siac.org.sg.

[70] Asian International Arbitration Centre, www.aiac.world.

[71] Art. 74 CIETAC Rules; see also Deißner, Interregionales Privatrecht in China, p. 373 (at mn. 1010) for the application of common law in Hong Kong; Brödermann in Piltz, Münchener Anwaltshandbuch Internationales Wirtschaftsrecht, § 6 mn. 297.

[72] Brödermann in Piltz, Münchener Anwaltshandbuch Internationales Wirtschaftsrecht, § 6 mn. 298–308. According to Art. 74 CIETAC Rules, the arbitration law of Hong Kong is applicable if the arbitration proceedings are administered by the CIETAC Hong Kong.

[73] Thailand Arbitration Centre, thac.or.th.

[74] Seoul International Dispute Resolution Centre, www.sidrc.org/idrc/en/main/main.do.

[75] https://www.aseac-arbitration.com/arbitration/model-choice-of-law-clause/. See also Brödermann/Heeg-Weimann in Respondek, Asia Arbitration Guide, pp. 61–69; Brödermann, J. Int. Arb. 2013, pp. 301–325; Weimann/Heeg/Hasenstab, Austrian Yearbook on International Arbitration 2013, pp. 125–148.

(ASEAC), formerly known as **Chinese European Arbitration Centre (CEAC)**, founded in 2008 in in Hamburg, Germany, especially for these kind of cases.

ASEAC has cooperated with CIETAC since its conception.[76] It integrates Chinese experts in its organs (including in particular the "Appointing Authority") in a spirit of "sensed neutrality".[77] Several details of the ASEAC rules are organized with a special regard to Chinese needs.[78] 31

From an international perspective, when negotiating a Chinese arbitration clause, it is important to focus on the **question of execution**. In case of an execution, in line with a standard practice in other jurisdictions, a Chinese arbitral award will be tested against the arbitration law in China. The provision in Art. 291 PRC Civil Procedure Law (which is a subject of discussions in smaller circles also in China) corresponds at large to Art. V NYC. The criterion that the procedure for arbitration needs to be "in conformity with the rules of arbitration" (Art. 291(1) no. 3 PRC Civil Procedure Law) – which implies a possible deviation from the arbitration agreement and therefore entails a risk of unenforceability – now tends to be interpreted not too rigidly. However, there is always a procedural risk that an arbitral award may be unenforceable because of a formal error.[79] If an arbitral award is not enforceable because of such a formal error, Art. 292 PRC Civil Procedure Law offers a repetition of the arbitration proceeding or to bring the action before a state court. 32

III. Not a realistic alternative (yet): *ad hoc* arbitration

Current Chinese law does not recognize *ad hoc* arbitration in China,[80] whereby the recent trend as captured in Art. 2(7) of the 2024 CIETAC Rules points in the opposite direction. Even though "*ad hoc*" arbitration may not be formally prohibited,[81] the separation of arbitration from any administrating (and thereby somehow supervising) institution is unknown to Chinese legal culture in the PRC. Art. 4(3) sent. 1 of the CIETAC Rules only grants the parties a right to submit the arbitration to "other arbitration rules" or to mutually amend the CIETAC rules as long as the agreed rules do not infringe mandatory arbitration law. In line with Art. 4(3) sent. 2, the Beijing Higher People's Court has accepted (and not qualified as an "*ad hoc*" arbitration) a clause where the parties have agreed on the UNCITRAL arbitration rules **in connection with an agreement of CIETAC as the arbitral commission** administrating the arbitration.[82] 33

---

[76] An example for an article on ASEAC is the publication of Dong/Brödermann, Arbitration and Law, Journal of CIETAC 2010, 104–130.

[77] Beneyto/Brödermann/Meyer/Zhao, RIW 2011, 12 (14); Brödermann/Heeg-Weimann in Respondek, Asia Arbitration Guide, pp. 64–65.

[78] See Brödermann, J. Int. Arb. 2013, 301 (307 et seq.) ("enhanced neutrality"); World Arbitration Report, at I.A.1; see also Brödermann/Heeg-Weimann in Respondek, Asia Arbitration Guide, pp. 61–62.

[79] See the critical observations by Brödermann in FS Elsing, pp. 66–67.

[80] Arg. Art. 16(3) PRC Arbitration Law as well as the Supreme People's Court in People's Insurance Company of China, *Guangzhou Branch v. Guandong Guanghe Power Co. Ltd.* (2003) Min Se Zhong Zi No. 29; see also Wiegand/Ye in Balthasar, International Arbitration in China, p. 330 (at mn. 29–30) as well as Yu/Cao, A Guide to the CIETAC Arbitration Rules and Practice, mn. 5.23–5.24. Art. 21 of the 2021 Draft Revised PRC Arbitration Law does not require the designation of an arbitration institution anymore.

[81] Cf. only Art. 16 and 18 PRC Arbitration Law concerning the necessity to choose an arbitration institution in the arbitration clause; see also Moser in van den Berg, New Horizons in International Commercial Arbitration and Beyond, p. 91.

[82] → Art. 4 mn. 4 (at fn. 11) as well as → Ch. 3 mn. 10, 11.

Even though the 2024 CIETAC Rules allow the technical support of *ad hoc* arbitration cases, given the current Arbitration Law of the PRC, such cases may only be validly conducted in case of foreign parties and foreign law applicable to the arbitration case. Nevertheless, given the current uncertainty it would not be advisable to proceed with *ad hoc* arbitration in Mainland China, as the losing party might still challenge such award, claiming a **formal violation of the PRC Arbitration Law**.

34 For quite a while, Chinese courts have already tended to recognize arbitration clauses providing for an *ad hoc* arbitration outside China as **foreign-related arbitrations**.[83] In recent years, several foreign *ad hoc* arbitration awards were recognized and enforced in China. In 2014, the Wuhan Maritime Court acknowledged and enforced an *ad hoc* arbitration award made in London.[84] In 2018 the Intermediate People's Court of Nanjing recognized and enforced an *ad hoc* award rendered in Sweden.[85] Also in 2018, the Intermediate People's Court of Shenzhen acknowledged and enforced an *ad hoc* arbitration award made in Hong Kong.[86] Despite these several recognitions and enforcements of foreign *ad hoc* arbitration awards in China a risk remains. It may work,[87] but who wants to take the risk? The draft provisions of the Supreme People's Court of December 31, 2003[88] relating to foreign-related and international arbitrations (which was not integrated into the published **2006-Interpretation of the People's Supreme Court**[89] on rules on foreign-related and foreign arbitrations) declared an arbitration clause providing for *ad hoc* arbitration as "invalid"[90] unless (i) the parties come from member states of the NYC and (ii) the applicable national laws permit *ad hoc* arbitration.[91] In other words, an arbitration award rendered in an *ad hoc* arbitration (e.g. from Switzerland on a "Paramount" clause[92] and the UNCITRAL-arbitration rules) between foreign shareholding companies would be recognized in China. Nonetheless, the enforcement of awards rendered in *ad hoc* arbitrations remains, combined with risks of time and cost which need to be taken into account. For example, in a remote part of China (beyond the "first class" cities – "*yi xian cheng shi*" in Chinese) there may be **practical difficulties** to convince the Chinese domestic court judge of the admissibility of *ad hoc* arbitration because of its 'strange' character from a Chinese perspective (the

---

[83] Zhang, Cornell Int'l L. J. 2013 361 (365, 368); see also Tao, Am. U. Int'l. Rev. 2012, 807 (812).

[84] Civil Judgment of Wuhan Maritime Court, (2014) Wu Maritime Court Other No.00038.

[85] Civil Judgment of Intermediate People's Court of Nanjing, (2018) Su 01 Assist Foreign Recognition No.8: "The Court concluded that, based on the facts found and determined, the arbitral award made by an *ad hoc* arbitral […] tribunal did not fall into the non-recognition and non-enforcement circumstances stipulated in Article V(1)(b), (c) and (d) of the Convention on the Recognition and Enforcement of Foreign Arbitral Awards, nor did it violate the terms of the reservation made by China when it acceded to the Convention, or the public policy of China or the fact that the matter in dispute could not be resolved by arbitration".

[86] Civil Judgment of Intermediate People's Court of Shenzhen, (2018) Yue 03 Civil First No.2267.

[87] Chinyen Wang (Professor at Providence University in Taiwan) has informed the author regarding the recognition of an arbitral award rendered in London in 1992; according to Wiegand/Ye in Balthasar, International Arbitration in China, p. 331 mn. 30, foreign *ad hoc*-arbitration awards will be enforced pursuant to Art. II and IV NYC.

[88] Supreme People's Court, Provisions on Handling Foreign-Related Arbitrations and Arbitrations Adjudicated Abroad by People's Courts, People's Court Daily, December 31, 2003, at 1–3 as reported by Chen, Arbitration Law Review 2018, 35 (43 et seq.).

[89] Interpretation of the Supreme People's Court concerning Some Issues on the Application of the "Arbitration Law of the People's Republic of China", in force since September 8, 2006. English version available at https://cicc.court.gov.cn/html/1/219/199/201/672.html.

[90] Budke in Glöckner et al., Rechtliche Funktionsbedingungen, p. 197.

[91] Commented by Stricker-Kellerer/Moser in Schütze, Institutionelle Schiedsgerichtsbarkeit, Introduction mn. 18.

[92] → mn. 29.

Chinese domestic court judge is likely not to have studied *ad hoc* arbitration in his legal education). In international practice, the recognition of foreign arbitral awards in *ad hoc* arbitration is taken for granted. The Supreme People's Court has confirmed the recognition of such "*ad hoc* arbitration awards" for Hong Kong *ad hoc* arbitration awards in the Supreme People's Court Notice of Relevant Issues on the Enforcement of Hong Kong Arbitral Awards in the Mainland of December 30, 2009.[93]

E. Method

The comments on the CIETAC Rules are made from the perspective of an international, and in particular a German-European, lawyer whereby one of the co-authors is also admitted in New York. The comments will place particular emphasis on streaming the differences between the CIETAC Rules and the arbitration rules of the German *Deutsche Institution für Schiedsgerichtsbarkeit* (German Arbitration Institute – DIS) as well as the UNCITRAL-Arbitration Rules and the correlating ASEAC-Arbitration Rules (the arbitration rules of the Hamburg-based ASEAC are based on the UNCITRAL Arbitration Rules). Special attention is given to the changes of the CIETAC Rules in recent years and the proposals in the Draft Revised PRC Arbitration Law (2021). In particular, CIETAC has added rules on the Emergency Arbitrator (Art. 23). The Draft Revised PRC Arbitration Law (2021) is further developing this subject at Art. 43 et seq. in a new section on interim measures. Other essential developments include the rules on consolidation and joinder (both as a consequence of multiple contracts, Art. 14, and of additional parties). Further, there are amendments throughout the CIETAC Rules in order to integrate the Arbitration Court. Finally, CIETAC has reacted by several small amendments to practical needs (e.g., Art. 40(3) which now explicitly permits court reporting). **35**

In addition to the CIETAC Rules, the comments include excerpts from the PRC Arbitration Law and the PRC Civil Procedure Law, which are important for the execution of CIETAC arbitral awards. **36**

---

[93] The Supreme People's Court Notice on Issues relating to the Enforcement of Hong Kong Arbitral Awards in the Mainland China, Fa [2009], effective from December 30, 2009, as reported by Yu/Cao, A Guide to the CIETAC Arbitration Rules and Practice, mn. 1.33 (fn. 36); see also Arrangement Concerning Mutual Enforcement of Arbitral Awards between the Mainland and Hong Kong Special Administrative Region, in force since February 1, 2010. English version available at www.doj.gov.hk/en/mainland_and_macao/pdf/mainlandmutual2e.pdf (last visited July 19, 2023). See also Tao, Am. U. Int'l. Rev. 2012, 807 (813) and there fn. 23; for further examples, see Zhang, Cornell Int'l L. J. 2013, 361 (365–366) with further references there in fn. 17.

Chapter 2
CIETAC-Standard Arbitration Clauses

A. Model arbitration clauses

1 On its official website, CIETAC offers **two Model Arbitration Clauses**:[1]

Model Arbitration Clause (1)

Any dispute arising from or in connection with this Contract shall be submitted to China International Economic and Trade Arbitration Commission (CIETAC) for arbitration which shall be conducted in accordance with the CIETAC's arbitration rules in effect at the time of applying for arbitration. The arbitral award is final and binding upon both parties.

Model Arbitration Clause (2)

Any dispute arising from or in connection with this Contract shall be submitted to China International Economic and Trade Arbitration Commission (CIETAC) ________Sub-Commission (arbitration centre) for arbitration which shall be conducted in accordance with the CIETAC's arbitration rules in effect at the time of applying for arbitration. The arbitral award is final and binding upon both parties.

2 On the official website of the CIETAC European Arbitration Centre, CIETAC offers another Model Arbitration Clause (which in its para. 1 is identical to the Model Arbitration Clause (1), merely adding language regarding the seat of arbitration, the place of the hearing as well as the language of arbitration):[2]

Model Arbitration Clause (3)

Any dispute arising from or in connection with this Contract shall be submitted to China International Economic and Trade Arbitration Commission (CIETAC) for arbitration which shall be conducted in accordance with the CIETAC's arbitration rules in effect at the time of applying for arbitration. The arbitral award is final and binding upon both parties.
The seat of arbitration shall be [...]
The hearing shall be held in [...]
The language to be used in the arbitration shall be [...]

B. Comments

3 The model clauses regulate the following as a minimum:

1. Qualification of the object of the arbitration ("dispute arising from or in connection with this Contract").
2. Determination of the competent authority to administer the arbitration, either the CIETAC **commission itself at its headquarter** in Beijing (Model Clause 1) **or** at any of its **subcommissions/arbitration centres** (Model Clause 2, Art. 2(3) sent. 1, to be read in connection with Appendix I).
3. Element of time; the Model Clause refers to the arbitration rules in effect **at the time of applying** for arbitration and not at the time of the conclusion of the arbitration

[1] See www.cietac.org under "guide".
[2] See https://www.cietac-eu.org/model-clause/.

agreement;[3] from a German perspective, this reflects a "procedural" approach known to German lawyers from state court proceedings.

4. A declaratory hint at the **principle of finality** of a CIETAC arbitration award, which reflects Art. 49(9) CIETAC Rules and which finds its ultimate foundation in Art. 9(1) PRC Arbitration Law.[4]

Absent a deviating party agreement (as recommended in Model Clause 3; Art. 7(1); Art. 36(1)), the parties' choice of the competent main or sub commission of CIETAC also implies **the choice of the place** where the arbitration proceeding will take place (Art. 7(2); Art. 36(2)). This includes the venue for each meeting of the Arbitral Tribunal with the parties. 4

In an international or foreign-related CIETAC Arbitration, it may also become necessary for the arbitrators or parties to travel to China even for merely a one day hearing. The decision on the place of the hearing is therefore very important. A change of venue to a foreign jurisdiction or to Hong Kong can imply a change of the applicable arbitration law (arg. Art. 74).

In arbitration practice, the change of the **place of the oral hearing** (Art. 36(2)) to a place outside China faces particular practical obstacles: (i) the payment of initial costs whereby non-payment implies a change of venue (Art. 82(3)) and, more importantly, (ii) practical questions of a visa for the CIETAC case administrator (Art. 13(4)),[5] who must or would like to attend the hearing. As an arbitrator, there is an interest to keep the relationship with CIETAC in a cooperative spirit. CIETAC is not only competent for the scrutiny of the award (Art. 51) for which there may be a need that it happens fast to meet deadlines; it is also in charge of each transfer of installments of the arbitrator fees due under the agreement with the arbitrators. 5

From a foreign perspective, if it is necessary to accept a Chinese venue, one may contemplate choosing a **remote place in China** to equalize the disadvantage of traveling so that the contract partner may also not fully feel "at home" at the arbitration venue. A more cost-efficient alternative may be to watch for good travel connection to the home jurisdiction.
From a continental European, German and from a **risk management perspective** it may be reasonable to **supplement** the CIETAC model clause by using the party autonomy provided by Art. 4(3) sent. 1 on a series of issues as set out in the following.

I. Contracts between two parties

For contracts between two parties, it may be reasonable to enlarge the scope of the possible **object of the arbitration**, e.g., on "any disputes arising from or in connection with the contract (including its conclusion, validity and termination)". 6

Further, depending on the circumstances and the results of the negotiations, additional **provisions** may be necessary on: 7

1. the **qualification** of the arbitrators or at least of the presiding arbitrator (however, very qualified requirements, like "a German lawyer with a Chinese background from a neutral jurisdiction" may render the implementation and application of the provisions impossible in practice);

---

[3] Cf. for the opposite e.g.the regulation in (f) of the ASEAC Arbitration Clause, which allows each party on the basis of party autonomy to insist on the application of the version in force at the time of contract conclusion.

[4] Art. 9(1) PRC Arbitration Law is expected to remain mainly unchanged in the new PRC Arbitration Law; for foreign-related cases see Art. 290 PRC Civil Procedure Law.

[5] In practice, this job is done by a Chinese lawyer.

2. an agreement that the parties may choose an arbitrator also from **outside the CIETAC list of arbitrators** pursuant to Art. 26(2) and subject to the confirmation by the chairman[6] of CIETAC;[7]
3. the **agreement on the presiding arbitrator** by agreement of the party appointed arbitrators (making use of the procedure set forth in Art. 27(3)), so as to increase the chances of indirect influence on the person of the presiding arbitrator);
4. the **background** of the presiding or sole arbitrator (e.g., from a neutral jurisdiction; ever since arbitrators need not necessarily be listed on the CIETAC arbitration list (Art. 26(2)), the parties have more freedom to shape their arbitration agreement in this respect (→ Art. 27 mn. 4);
5. the **number** of the arbitrators (however → Art. 25 mn. 1);
6. the **language** including, e.g., a provision on the language in which documents may be submitted, Art. 81(1) sent. 1 (as recommended in Model Clause 3); without such provisions the procedure will take place in Chinese (Art. 81(1) sent. 2); bilingual procedures are also possible, have been conducted on various occasions but are costly and time consuming. CIETAC lacks the ability to deal effectively with bilingual cases, other than English-Chinese, such as German-Chinese[8] or French-Chinese;
7. the **venue of the hearings** (as recommended in Model Clause 3; Art. 36(2)); if this venue shall be at a different place as compared to the seat of the arbitration commission;
8. the degree of confidentiality which shall apply to the **arbitration proceeding**;
9. the **timing** as of when the arbitration proceeding may start as compared to preceding conciliation efforts (e.g., "In the event that no settlement is reached within [30] days from the date of notification by either party to the other party that it intends to submit a dispute, controversy or claim to arbitration, then such dispute, controversy or claim shall be submitted to the China International Economic and Trade Arbitration Commission ("CIETAC") for arbitration …");
10. the **choice of law** for the arbitration agreement (this possibility is presupposed in Art. 5(3));
11. the non-applicability of the **CIETAC Guidelines on Evidence**[9] (which, in essence correlate with the IBA Rules on the Taking of Evidence[10], → Art. 41 mn. 5), if and to the extent one wishes to exclude the influence of common law elements, e.g., on discovery in an arbitration between parties stemming both from civil law jurisdictions.

8 Further, one might consider adding provisions on a **maximum period** for the arbitration proceeding; while such initiation is not necessary in view of Art. 51(1) of the CIETAC Rules, this may not harm but rather serve as a "reminder" to the parties in the light of the reports on multiple deadline prolongations and sometimes very long duration of arbitration proceedings. Such an explicit agreement may also help to reduce the number of prolongations of deadlines.

[6] A note on gender: The official translation of the CIETAC website describes the chairperson of CIETAC (and the chairperson of any CIETAC tribunal) as "chairman". Any use of the generic masculine in this commentary is purely made to be consistent with the official text, integrating all chairpersons.

[7] In this regard, also see Art. 50 Draft Revised PRC Arbitration Law (2021).

[8] The co-author has just recently experienced a German-Chinese CIETAC arbitration, where the translation of the CIETAC appointed translators, as well as the "bi-lingual" transcripts were not acceptable and by no means "international standard".

[9] At CIETAC's website www.cietac.org under "Rules".

[10] https://www.ibanet.org/resources.

Rules on the **conduct of the hearing** are accepted under Art. 35(2), (3) and (5) (and may be reasonable, e.g., if a shareholding company wants to ensure that its representative or organ may be present in the oral hearing). **9**

In practice, the agreement on such useful additions to the CIETAC model clause will be subject to the probable unwillingness of the parties (or clients) to concentrate on that level of details during the contract negotiation. Yet, it minimizes risks of dispute if these issues receive some attention during the contract negotiation. **10**

II. Contract with multiple parties

For a contract with multiple parties, depending on the circumstances, it may be sensible to add provisions on **11**

1. the applicability of the CIETAC arbitration clause also for **connected contracts** or to subsequent contracts (Art. 14);
2. possible **joinders** of parties[11] (with regard to Art. 18(2)), e.g., by determining the moment in time, like one month after receipt of the statement of defense in the knowledge that such an agreement may imply a new composition and constitution of the Arbitral Tribunal (if the arbitration agreement provides for the allocation and payment of (partial) costs payable to the arbitrator who is leading the Arbitral Tribunal, this is likely to enhance the consent of CIETAC pursuant to Art. 18(1), (3) and (7), because a joinder under such circumstances will not bring any detriment to CIETAC);
3. all issues mentioned above (→ mn. 6 et seq.) in the knowledge that the right to nominate an arbitrator is easily lost in case of multiple parties which may be detrimental if one party faces a multitude of parties for the mere reason of a different (or financially driven) organization of "the other party"; like in the context of many other arbitration rules,[12] to safeguard the right to nominate an arbitrator by the party standing alone requires particular and specific wording in the arbitration clause.

---

[11] In major and complex contracts, these rules can be helpful despite the costs which can possibly arise (in practice, complex arbitration clauses – which may exceed 20 pages – are sometimes used under particularly complex circumstances in confidential multi-party situations).

[12] Art. 12(8) ICC Arbitration Rules; Art. 12(3) ICDR Arbitration Rules; Art. 20.3 and 20.4 DIS Arbitration Rules.

Chapter 3
Recognition and enforcement of arbitral awards in the People's Republic of China

A. Introduction

1 As concerns the enforcement of arbitral awards in China, a distinction must be made between foreign arbitral awards and national arbitral awards (e.g. CIETAC awards). While foreign arbitral awards shall be recognized and enforced[1], national awards only require enforcement. The SPC has issued rules on matters relating to the judicial review of arbitration cases and their enforcement.[2]

2 Enforcement usually takes place in two or three stages: (i) First, the party who won the case has to find out about the **assets** of the Chinese party and where such assets are located (this assessment might have already been done at an earlier stage). In a second step, in case of a foreign award the foreign party must (ii) **file the application** for recognition before the competent national court and after the recognition or in the case of a national award (iii) **apply for enforcement** of the arbitral award before the competent court that is locally competent for assets of the Respondent or at the place where the party against whom enforcement is sought has its registered seat.[3]

3 The application for enforcement of an arbitral award in China is to be submitted within two years. The deadline starts when the deadline for the performance according to the arbitral award expires.[4] If a foreign defendant has no property in Mainland China, upon which the meaures of a compulsory enforcement can be undertaken, this period will only commence again, once such a property is founded in Mainland China.[5]

4 It is also possible that the Chinese party who lost the arbitration case has assets outside of China. China has been a member of the UN Convention on the Enforcement of Foreign Arbitral Awards (**New York Convention**) since 1987 and therefore, CIETAC awards have already been successfully enforced in many countries, also in Germany, France, Italy and in the USA. Of course, the procedure is then in turn dependent on the national laws of the country where enforcement shall take place. Even if at the time the arbitral award is rendered, a Chinese company does not yet have assets outside of China, for instance, non-performance of an arbitral award could still have implications on that company's ambitions to become active in international business.

---

[1] Art. 304 PRC Civil Procedure Law and Art. 544 of the Interpretations of the Supreme People's Court on the Application of the Civil Procedure Law of the People's Republic of China.

[2] Provisions of the Supreme People's Court on Several Issues Concerning the Judicial Review of Arbitration Cases; Provisions of the Supreme People's Court on Several Issues Concerning the Handling of Cases by People's Courts to Enforce Arbitration Awards and the Relevant Provisions of the Supreme People's Court on the Reporting and Verification of Arbitration Judicial Review Cases (Revised in 2021).

[3] Art. 2 Provisions of the Supreme People's Court on Several Issues Concerning the Handling of Cases by People's Courts to Enforce Arbitration Awards.

[4] Art. 250 PRC Civil Procedure Law.

[5] See: Guiding Case No. 37 of the Supreme People's Court: *Shanghai Jwell Machinery Co., Ltd. v. Retech Aktiengesellschaft.*

There were **some important court rulings on various issues of enforcement of arbitral awards** in China in the last few years: 5

I. *Duferco S.A. v. China-Base Ningbo Foreign Trade Company and Ningbo Arts & Crafts Import & Export Co., Ltd*

In important decisions in 2009,[6] the Intermediate People's Court Ningbo ordered enforcement of two arbitral awards where the place of arbitration was in China, but the procedure had been carried out by a foreign court of arbitration, i.e., the International Chamber of Commerce (ICC).[7] In the past, there was significant uncertainty as to whether arbitral awards that had been rendered by a foreign arbitration institution in China would be enforceable in China. In the concrete cases, a Swiss steel company (Duferco S.A.) enforced two ICC arbitral awards against two companies in Ningbo (*14005/MS/JB/JEM v. China-Base Ningbo Foreign Trade Company and 14006/MS/JB/JEM v. Ningbo Arts & Crafts Import & Export Co., Ltd*). 6

The disputes between the company in Ningbo and the Swiss companies were about sales contracts which were governed by the UN Convention on the International Sale of Goods (CISG) and which provided for arbitration proceedings in China according to the ICC Rules. 7

These were the first reported cases where a Chinese court granted the requests for enforcement of ICC judgments where the seat of the Arbitral Tribunal was in China. 8

II. *Anhui Longlide v. BP Aganati S.R.L.*

In March 2013, the Supreme Court of the People's Republic of China confirmed in a request of a court concerning a dispute between Anhui Longlide Packing and Printing Co., Ltd. ("Anhui Longlide") and BP Agnati S.R.L. ("BP Aganati")[8] with regard to an arbitration clause that the choice "ICC International Court of Arbitation" together with the choice "place of jurisdiction at Shanghai" would be valid.[9] With the explanation that such a clause, in this case of the ICC, would be valid, the Supreme Court eliminated a major obstacle for arbitration procedures of foreign institutions in China. 9

III. *Zhejiang Yisheng v. INVISTA*

The 2014 case of *Zhejiang Yisheng Petrochemical Co., Ltd.* ("Zhejiang Yisheng") *v. INVISTA Technologies S.à.r.l.* ("Invista") was a dispute on the validity of an arbitration clause that provided for CIETAC arbitration proceedings according to the UNCITRAL Rules. The Intermediate People's Court in Ningbo confirmed in its decision that such a "hybrid agreement" would be valid.[10] 10

---

[6] *Duferco S.A. v. China-Base Ningbo Foreign Trade Company* available under https://newyorkconvention1958.org/; *Ningbo Arts & Crafts Import & Export Co., Ltd* (2008) Yong Zhong Jian Zi No. 4 (2008).

[7] Available under https://newyorkconvention1958.org, see also Choong, First reported case of ICC award being enforced in China in: https://uk.practicallaw.thomsonreuters.com/9-500-3353.

[8] [2013] Min Si Ta Zi No. 13.

[9] Dong/Meng, Kluwer Arbitration Blog, July 2014; Rogers/Townsend, The Longlide decision.

[10] Rogers/Townsend, International Arbitration Report 2014, pp. 19–20; Annual report on International Commercial Arbitration in China (2014), pp. 68–69; Yu/Cao, A Guide to the CIETAC Arbitration Rules and Practice, mn. 3.12.

11 The dispute had arisen from two technology licensing agreements. The parties had agreed the following: "The arbitration shall take place at CIETAC, Beijing, P.R. China and shall be settled according to the UNICITRAL Arbitration Rules as at present in force". Invista commenced arbitration proceedings in July 2012 and Zhejiang Yisheng then challenged the validity of the arbitration clause, stating that those "*ad hoc*" arbitration proceedings would not be admissible for arbitration clauses in China. Pursuant to the internal reporting system of the courts already mentioned above, the Intermediate People's Court in Ningbo and the People's Court of the Zhejiang province reported the case to the Supreme Court. After a proceeding which lasted 18 months, the Ningbo court followed the instructions of the Supreme Court and rejected Yisheng's pleas from their submission of March 18, 2014. This is an important confirmation that hybrid clauses are valid under Chinese law.

IV. *Siemens International v. Golden Landmark*

12 In a judgment of November 27, 2015, the Intermediate People's Court, Shanghai No. 1, decided to accept and enforce an arbitral award from Singapore despite the fact that the parties were two Chinese parties (Siemens International Trading (Shanghai) Co. Ltd. ("Siemens International") and Shanghai Golden Landmark Co., Ltd ("Golden Landmark")).[11]

13 A sales contract was the subject matter of the dispute. Both parties were so-called Wholly Foreign Owned Enterprises (i.e., Chinese legal persons) with their registered seat in the Free Trade Zone in Shanghai. The parties had agreed that disputes would have to be settled in Singapore before the Singapore International Arbitration Center (SIAC). There was a dispute on the sales contract and the purchaser-initiated arbitration proceedings in Singapore in 2007. The seller challenged the competence of the court of arbitration with the argument that Chinese law would not allow for arbitration proceedings outside of the PRC in case of a dispute between two Chinese legal persons. The Arbitral Tribunal rejected the argumentation of the seller. The seller engaged in the proceeding, but brought a counterclaim. The Arbitral Tribunal rendered an arbitral award in which it rejected the claims of the purchaser and passed a judgment in favor of the seller. As purchaser did not fulfil his obligations from the arbitral award, the seller filed an application for recognition and enforcement of the arbitral award in Shanghai in 2013. The purchaser then brought the argument that the dispute would not contain a "foreign element" and since the law of the PRC would not allow for arbitration proceedings outside the PRC in the case that a foreign element is missing, the arbitral award would have to be set aside.

14 On November 27, 2015, the Intermediate People's Court, Shanghai No. 1, ruled that the dispute would be "foreign-related", recognized the arbitral award and ordered enforcement. The court accepted the dispute as "foreign-related" since both parties had foreign investors, were located in the free trading zone and that the free trading zone would expressly have the task to promote foreign trade.

15 Finally, the products in this case would have been imported from abroad and would have been stored in the zone duty-free; all this would make the dispute a "foreign-related dispute".

[11] [2013] Hu Yi Zhong Min Ren (Wai Zhong) Zi. No. 2; Bell/Chong/Sharp, The Golden Landmark Case.

B. Setting aside arbitral awards and rejection of enforcement in China

I. Setting aside arbitral awards

It is possible to set aside an arbitral award in China under particular conditions: 16

Article 58
PRC Arbitration Law
Application to set aside the Arbitral Award

(1) If a party produces evidence showing that one of the following circumstances exists, it may apply for the arbitral award to be set aside before the Intermediate People's Court at the seat of the arbitration commission:

1. There is no arbitration agreement;
2. Aspects of the arbitral award do not fall within the scope of the arbitration agreement or the arbitration institution was not authorized to carry out the arbitration proceedings;
3. The constitution of the Arbitral Tribunal or the arbitration proceedings are contrary to the statutory proceedings;
4. The arbitral award is based on incorrect evidence;
5. The opponent party has withheld evidence which sufficed to impact on the fairness of the decision;
6. During the arbitration proceedings on the respective dispute, an arbitrator asked for bribery or accepted bribery, acted in breach of duty for a personal benefit or bent the law when the arbitral award was rendered.

(2) [1]If a chamber of the People's Court finds after an examination and ascertainment of the facts that one of the circumstances described in the previous paragraph exists, it will decide to set aside the arbitral award. [2]If the People's Court comes to the conclusion that the enforcement of the arbitral award would conflict with the societal and public interests, it will decide to set aside the award.

Arbitral awards may be set aside by a state court, or enforcement may be rejected, 17 whereas the reasons are regulated differently depending on whether (i) this is a foreign arbitral award or (ii) a Chinese arbitral award, whereas in this case, another distinction has to be made as to whether the arbitral award concerned a national proceeding or a proceeding containing a "**foreign element**"[12] which may both be passed under CIETAC. This distinction again becomes very important in this case.[13]

Setting aside foreign arbitral awards is not possible due to lack of jurisdiction, but it is 18 possible to deny their recognition and enforcement (→ mn. 25 et seq.).

Merely national arbitral awards, on the other hand, may be set aside and their 19 enforcement may be rejected pursuant to Art. 248 PRC Civil Procedure Law, whereas in

[12] → mn. 25.
[13] → mn. 25.

particular no. 4 and no. 5 are decisive for the fact that here – however, to a much lesser extent than used to be the case – there may be a substantive review in the enforcement proceedings.

20 In a decision in 2019 the Shenzhen Intermediate Court emphasized that there is a fundamental difference between the judicial review of arbitral awards and the filing review (for enforcement of an award).[14] In enforcement cases [the court] generally does not judge the legality of the arbitral award itself, unless it belongs to the specific circumstances of prior arbitration. The court stated that the enforcement court substituted the judicial review of non-enforcement with the review of the filing of the enforcement case in this case, and the review procedure was improper.

21 Moreover, there is also the setting aside motion of the infringement of the *ordre public.*

22 The grounds from no. 4 and no. 5 were not adopted (Art. 291 PRC Civil Procedure Law) as an objection to the enforcement of an arbitral award **containing a foreign element**; consequently, a substantive review is not intended for arbitration proceedings containing a foreign element.

Article 59
PRC Arbitration Law
Deadline for Application

The Parties shall apply to set aside the arbitral award within 6 months after the deed of the arbitral award has been received.

Article 60
PRC Arbitration Law
Deadline for a Decision of the Arbitral Tribunal

The People's Court shall decide on the setting aside of the arbitral award or the rejection of the application within 2 months after the application to set aside an arbitral award has been accepted.

23 The **deadline for the application** to set aside an arbitral award is six months and the competent court for CIETAC awards is the Intermediate People's Court in Beijing. If the arbitral award was rendered by one of the CIETAC sub-commissions, the respective local Intermediate People's Courts are the competent courts. The respective People's Court then has two months to come to a decision about the application. There is no plea against the respective decision to set aside an arbitral award; this does not apply in the event of an unsuccessful application for annulment.

24 Furthermore; the People's Court may **refer** the matter **back to the Arbitral Tribunal** for another arbitration, subject to the approval of the higher court.[15]

[14] Civil Judgment of Shenzhen Intermediate People's Court, Yue Enforcement Review No. 912 (2019).
[15] Art. 61 PRC Arbitration Law.

Article 70
PRC Arbitration Law
Setting Aside the Arbitral Award

If a party produces evidence showing that one of the circumstances listed in Section 258 (1)[16] Civil Procedure Act exists in an arbitral award containing a foreign element, the chamber of the People's Court will decide to set aside the award after an examination and a collection of facts.

II. Rejection of enforcement

A rejection of enforcement is also possible under particular conditions: Recognition 25
and enforcement in China may only be denied for foreign arbitral awards if one of the grounds listed in Article V NYC exists.[17] In the case of national arbitral awards, a distinction again has to be made between merely national awards and those containing a foreign element.

The following applies to **arbitral awards containing a foreign element**: 28

Article 71
PRC Arbitration Law
Rejection of Enforcement

If the Respondent produces evidence showing that one of the circumstances listed in Section 258 (1)[18] Civil Procedure Act exists in an arbitral award containing a foreign element, the chamber of the People's Court will decide to reject enforcement after an examination and a collection of facts

Article 291
PRC Civil Procedure Law
Rejection of Enforcement

(1) If the Respondent produces evidence showing that one of the following circumstances exists in the case of an arbitral award rendered by an arbitration institution containing a foreign element of the People's Republic of China, a judge of a People's court will reject enforcement by court order after an examination:

1. The parties neither included an arbitration clause in the contract, nor subsequently reached an arbitration agreement;
2. The Respondent did not receive a notification on the appointment of the arbitrators or the execution of an arbitration, or was not able to submit its defense for reasons for which the Respondent is not responsible;
3. The constitution of the Arbitral Tribunal or the arbitration proceedings are not in accordance with the rules of arbitration;

---

[16] Now Art. 291 PRC Civil Procedure Law.
[17] Art V NYC.
[18] Now Art. 291 PRC Civil Procedure Law.

4. Aspects of the arbitral award do not fall within the scope of the arbitration agreement or the arbitration institution was not authorized to carry out the arbitration.

(2) If the People's Court rules that the enforcement of the arbitral award would be contrary to the societal and public interests, it will reject the enforcement by court order.

29 Other rules apply **for arbitration award containing merely national elements:**

Article 248
PRC Civil Procedure Law
Enforcement; Rejection of Enforcement; Consequences

(1) If a party does not implement an arbitration award rendered by a duly constituted arbitration institution, the Respondent may apply for enforcement to a competent People's Court. The People's Court that accepts the application has to carry out the enforcement.

(2) If the Respondent produces evidence showing that one of the following circumstances exists, a judge of a People's Court will reject the enforcement by court order after an examination:

1. The parties neither included an arbitration clause in the contract, nor subsequently reached an arbitration agreement;
2. Aspects of the arbitral award do not fall within the scope of the arbitration agreement or the arbitration institution was not authorized to carry out the arbitration proceedings;
3. The constitution of the Arbitral Tribunal or the arbitration proceedings are contrary to the statutory proceedings;
4. The essential evidence on which the fact-finding was based have been forged;
5. The other parties have withheld evidence from the Arbitral Tribunal that are sufficient to affect the impartiality of the arbitral award;
6. During the arbitration proceedings on the respective dispute, an arbitrator was open for bribery or accepted bribery, acted in breach of duty for a personal benefit or the benefit of a relative, or bent the law when the arbitral award was rendered.

(3) If a People's Court finds that the enforcement would be contrary to the social and public interests, it will reject enforcement by court order.

(4) The decision shall be delivered to both parties as well as the arbitration institution.

(5) If a People's Court passes the decision that an arbitral award will not be enforced, the parties may re-apply for arbitration proceedings pursuant to a written arbitration agreement or bring an action before a People's Court.

30 Consequently, the regulations of the Civil Procedure Law on the setting aside as well as on the non-enforcement that apply to national arbitral awards do not apply to arbitral awards in **proceedings containing a foreign element**.[19] Here, in addition to the reasons of lack of arbitration agreement, a subject matter of the dispute that is not covered by the arbitration agreement and the incorrect constitution of the Arbitral

[19] Art. 58 PRC Arbitration Law and Art. 248 PRC Civil Procedure Law.

Tribunal, one party has not been given sufficient **fair hearing**. However, the term of the infringement of the "social and public interests of China" is not defined in more detail. Experience has shown that this criterion is interpreted very strictly.[20]

Therefore, in the case of **CIETAC awards**, it also is to be expected that the **criteria rendering an arbitral award final** vary depending on whether it is a national award or an award containing foreign elements. 31

However, the setting aside of an arbitral award containing a foreign element and also any **non-enforcement** has to be authorized by the competent higher People's Court or the Supreme Court of the People's Republic of China; this is a regulation which was first introduced for the refusal of enforcement in 1995 and in 1998 also for the setting aside, after the non-recognition of foreign arbitral awards or arbitral awards containing a foreign element was subject to substantial complaints.[21] Since then, the situation has significantly improved as regards enforcement, since the courts pass more carefully considered decisions, also due to the review. 32

Article 292
PRC Civil Procedure Law
Consequences of the Rejection

If a People's Court passes the decision that an arbitral award will not be enforced, the parties may re-apply for arbitration proceedings pursuant to a written arbitration agreement or bring an action before a People's Court.

If a People's Court rejects the enforcement of an arbitral award, a party may **re-apply** for arbitration proceedings to the arbitration body on the basis of an arbitration clause or seize the state courts. 33

The wording is not clear: It seems to provide the option for a second proceeding, however, only if the arbitral award is not enforced. But it remains entirely unclear whether a new proceeding is possible here – also with regard to evidence, extent of the claim, material and legal submissions. 34

C. Current situation of enforcement in China

There exists a perception among foreign businessmen that arbitral awards are often not enforced in China. 35

Empirical studies over a time period of 20 years (1994 to 2015) on published judgments of the Chinese courts regarding the enforcement of foreign arbitral awards in China, however, show that the enforcement rate amounts to approx. 70 % of the 36

[20] In this regard see also *Fujian Across Express Information Technology Co., Ltd, Fujian Focus Media Co. Ltd, Cheng Zhen v. Starr Investments Cayman II Inc,* (2014) Rong Zhi Jian Zi No. 51, Civil Ruling by Fuzhou Intermediate People's Court of Fujian Province on November 5, 2014, cited in: Annual Report on International Commercial Arbitration in China (2014), pp. 85–86.

[21] Notification of the Supreme Court of the People's Republic of China on issues as to how the People's Courts should handle matters in connection with arbitration containing a foreign element and foreign arbitration, of August 28, 1995, Fa Fa (1995) no. 18, in German in: Kniprath, Die Schiedsgerichtsbarkeit der Chinese International Economic and Trade Arbitration Commission, p. 273, and Notification of the Supreme Court of the People's Republic of China on some issues of the setting aside of arbitral awards containing a foreign element by People's Courts – of April 23, 1998, Fa (1998) no. 40, in German in: Kniprath, pp. 265–266.

enforcements that were applied for.[22] It is also noteworthy that in particular in the years 2011–2015, the enforcement rate even amounted to 86.4 %. From 2019–2020 the People's Courts in Mainland China have handled 66 applications concering the recognition and enforcement of foreign arbitral awards. Among them were 62 applications for recongnition and enforcement and four applications for objections against the jurisdiction. All four applications for objection against the jurisdiction were rejected, meanwhile 40 applications for recognition and enforcement were permitted to be enforced, two were permitted to be partially enforced due to exceeding the arbitral agreement, while 11 applications were withdrawn by the party, three were solved in other ways and six were rejected.[23] The numbers vary from region to region, whereas the numbers in Tier 1 cities such as Beijing, Shanghai and Guangzhou amount to approx. 76 %, as opposed to only approx. 61 % in Tier 3 cities.[24] The main reasons for the rejection of enforcement were (i) invalid arbitration agreements; (ii) no constitution of an Arbitral Tribunal or the arbitration proceedings were not held in accordance with the agreement of the parties or the law applicable at the seat of the court of arbitration; and (iii) no valid notification of the unsuccessful party on the arbitrator who was appointed or the arbitration proceedings or insufficient fair hearing.[25]

37 An argument which was often brought in the past regarding the lack of enforcement was in particular local protectionism. However, this problem of local protectionism was acknowledged and already in August 1995, the Supreme Court submitted a notice to all Higher People's Courts "Regarding the Handling of the People's Courts of Issues on Foreign Arbitration Matters and Arbitration Matters containing a Foreign Element". Accordingly, a declaration of annulment or invalidity of an arbitration clause had to be reported to the higher courts by the lower courts, as well as also a rejection of enforcement. The same has applied since 1998 for the setting aside of an arbitral award. The introduction of such a reporting duty alone has proved to be a major contribution to promote objectivity. This has not only led to an improvement of the course of national proceedings, but also to a more competent handling of the obligations following from international conventions.

38 While the enforcement of arbitral awards has significantly improved, problems keep occurring in practice to identify the actual assets of the party against whom enforcement is sought, since Chinese companies frequently move or conceal their assets as a consequence of imminent enforcement. However, according to the observation of the author, the introduction of the Social Credit System in recent years has had some positive effects in this regard.[26]

---

[22] Utterback/Blackwell, Enforcing foreign arbitral awards in China.

[23] The Fourth Senate for civil proceedings of the Supreme People's Court, The annual report of the Supreme People's Court about the judicial examination of commercial arbitrations 2019, pp. 21, 24–25; The annual report of the Supreme People's Court about the judicial examination of commercial arbitrations 2020, p. 17.

[24] Utterback/Blackwell, Enforcing foreign arbitral awards in China.

[25] Utterback/Blackwell, Enforcing foreign arbitral awards in China.

[26] In one case a PRC party, which had lost an arbitration case in Singapore and the SIAC arbitration award was to be enforced intended to apply for an IPO in China (which would not be possible with negative entries in the Social Credit System). Therefore, the PRC party arranged for a rather quick payment of the debts owed to the foreign party.

Chapter 4
Summary assessment

In the past years, the arbitration environment in China has made some progress. Yet, for the time being there remain several particularities to be considered already at the level of the **shaping and negotiation of contracts** and the agreement on a CIETAC arbitration clause (→ Ch. 2 mn. 4–6). Further, an increasing tendency to align all legislation with the direction of the Chinese Communist Party can be observed. 1

In addition, as a result of the recession in recent years, the increasing economic pressure can also be felt in the area of arbitration. One example is the Revision of the Arbitration Law of the PRC, which had been listed in the Category 2 of the legislative plan of the Standing Committee of the 13th National People's Congress as early as 2018.[1] A draft from July 2021 which would have brought the PRC arbitration regime in line with international standards triggered substantial internal discussion and resistance from various circles within legislature and arbitral associations. Due to a series of sensitive issues, such as the *ad hoc* arbitration, which could lead to a substantial business loss for arbitration institutions, this draft finally failed to become law in the legislative period of the 13th National People's Congress (March 2018 to March 2023). Although the Revision of the PRC Arbitration Law is now listed in Category 1 of the legislative plan of the Standing Committee of the 14th National People's Congress[2], it seems unlikely that the draft will be adopted in its current "international" version. 2

[1] Available under http://www.npc.gov.cn (last visited January 2, 2024).
[2] Available under http://www.npc.gov.cn (last visited January 2, 2024).

PART II
ARTICLE-BY-ARTICLE COMMENTS

Chapter I
General Provisions

Article 1
Arbitration Commission

(1) The China International Economic and Trade Arbitration Commission ("CIETAC") originally named the Foreign Trade Arbitration Commission of the China Council for the Promotion of International Trade and later renamed the Foreign Economic and Trade Arbitration Commission of the China Council for the Promotion of International Trade, concurrently uses as its name the "Arbitration Institute of the China Chamber of International Commerce".

(2) Where an arbitration agreement provides for arbitration by the China Council for the Promotion of International Trade/China Chamber of International Commerce, or by the Arbitration Commission or the Arbitration Institute of the China Council for the Promotion of International Trade/China Chamber of International Commerce, or refers to CIETAC's previous names, it shall be deemed that the parties have agreed to arbitration by CIETAC.

Para. 1 reflects the **three names** which the CIETAC arbitration commission had in its 1 history of over 60 years, in addition to its **second name** "Arbitration Institute of the China Chamber of International Commerce" which is still in use today. CIETAC's original name shows its close ties to the CCPIT (→ Ch. 1 mn. 10). Still today, the parent organization CCPIT exercises influence over CIETAC by deciding on the choice of top employees of CIETAC. CIETAC keeps its main office in Beijing in the same building as the CCPIT.

Para. 2 provides for helpful **clarifications**. In practice, parties can act very creatively 2 when referring to an arbitration institution. Para. 2 clarifies that as long as the identity of the arbitration institution which was meant to be referred to is CIETAC (e.g., by using a former name of CIETAC), arbitration by CIETAC is **deemed to have been agreed.**[1] The underlying ***favor arbitri*** (i.e., to uphold an arbitration agreement) exists also on the sub-commission level in Art. 2(6) sent. 3–4. From a practical perspective, the assistance offered by the provision in para. 2 is helpful because parties negotiating arbitration agreements are often under extreme time pressure at the end of negotiations which can make them particularly prone to mistakes. Further, in international negotiations language barriers increase the risk of imprecise wording.

[1] Budke in Glöckner et al., Rechtliche Funktionsbedingungen, p. 200. For example, the Supreme People's Court upheld the validity of an arbitration agreement where the word "economic" was missing in the name of CIETAC (the reply of Supreme People's Court Re the Case Where Some Words Missing in Name of the Arbitration Institution Chosen by the Arbitration Clause Do Not Affect the Validity of the Arbitration Clause, Fa Jing (1998) No. 159, Supreme People's Court as reported by Wiegand/Ye in Balthasar, International Arbitration in China, p. 338 mn. 67); see also Yu/Cao, A Guide to the CIETAC Arbitration Rules and Practice, mn. 5.71 et seq. with two further case law examples.

Article 2
Structure and Duties

(1) The Chairman of CIETAC shall perform the functions and duties vested in him/her by these Rules while a Vice Chairman may perform the Chairman's functions and duties with the Chairman's authorization.

(2) CIETAC has an Arbitration Court ("Arbitration Court"), which performs its functions in accordance with these Rules under the direction of the authorized Vice Chairman and the President of the Arbitration Court.

(3) [1]CIETAC is based in Beijing. [2]It has sub-commissions or arbitration centers (Appendix I). [3]The sub-commissions/arbitration centers are CIETAC's branches, which accept arbitration applications and administer arbitration cases with CIETAC's authorization.

(4) A sub-commission/arbitration center has an arbitration court, which performs the functions of the Arbitration Court in accordance with these Rules under the direction of the president of the arbitration court of the sub-commission/arbitration center.

(5) Where a case is administered by a sub-commission/arbitration center, the functions and duties vested in the President of the Arbitration Court under these Rules may, by his/her authorization, be performed by the president of the arbitration court of the relevant sub-commission/arbitration center.

(6) [1]The parties may agree to submit their disputes to CIETAC or a sub-commission/arbitration center of CIETAC for arbitration. [2]Where the parties have agreed to arbitration by CIETAC, the Arbitration Court shall accept the arbitration application and administer the case. [3]Where the parties have agreed to arbitration by a CIETAC sub-commission/arbitration center, or have agreed to arbitrate or conduct the oral hearing in the province, autonomous region, or centrally-administered municipality where a CIETAC sub-commission/arbitration center is located, the arbitration court of that sub-commission/arbitration center shall accept the arbitration application and administer the case unless otherwise agreed by the parties. [4]The Arbitration Court may authorize and designate a sub-commission/arbitration center to administer relevant cases having regard to the circumstances of such cases.

[5]Where the sub-commission/arbitration center agreed upon by the parties does not exist or its authorization has been terminated, or where the agreement is ambiguous, the Arbitration Court shall accept the arbitration application and administer the case. [6]In the event of any dispute, a decision shall be made by CIETAC.

(7) Upon the agreement or request of the parties, CIETAC may provide administration and supporting services for ad hoc arbitration, including but not limited to offering guidance and consultation on the application of the arbitration rules, appointing arbitrators and deciding on the challenge of arbitrators, providing oral hearing services, scrutinizing draft awards, managing arbitrators' remuneration, etc., unless such agreement is inoperative or in conflict with a mandatory provision of the law applicable to the arbitral proceedings.

1 Para. 2 regulates **organizational questions** and **issues of competence**. Pursuant to para. 3, the **seat** of CIETAC is **Beijing**; in addition, CIETAC has **sub-commissions or arbitration centers** in Chengdu, Chongqing, Fuzhou, Hangzhou, Jinan, Nanjing,

Shanghai, Shenzhen, Tianjin, Wuhan and Xi'an (Appendix I) as well as an arbitration center in Hong Kong[2], Vancouver (Canada) and Vienna (Austria).[3]

Pursuant to para. 6 sent. 1, parties have the **choice** between the agreement on the competence of CIETAC or any of its sub-commissions/arbitration centers. The 2024 CIETAC Rules clarify in the third sentence that a **choice of a province** in which a sub-commission is located implies an arbitration under the auspices of such sub-commission. 2

Para. 6 provides in sentences 4 and 5 as a **general rule** for the principle that the Arbitration Court shall accept arbitration in case of **unclear arbitration agreements** or references to non-existing or unauthorized sub-commissions (an example was the termination of the competence of the sub-commission of CIETAC in Shanghai after its separation in 2013; → Ch. 1 mn. 28). The final decision shall lie with CIETAC. However, in case of a **subsequent procedure** of the recognition and enforcement of an arbitral award, the ultimate decision regarding the competence lies with the People's Courts (Art. 248(2) no. 1 PRC Civil Procedure Law). 3

The **Chairman of CIETAC** can delegate his tasks to his vice Chairman (para. 1). His tasks include, e.g., the admission of arbitrators outside CIETAC's panel of arbitrators (Art. 26(2)) and the decision on the challenge of an arbitrator (Art. 32(7)). Otherwise, its scope of competence has been amended considerably since the reorganization of CIETAC in 2015 by introduction of an Arbitration Court (para. 2). 4

The introduction of an **Arbitration Court** (para. 2), places CIETAC in line with widespread international practice. The Arbitration Court replaces the original secretariat to perform the case management duties and functions.[4] It will be represented by its President and its Vice-Chairman. The same **principle of representation** applies to the arbitration courts of the sub-commissions/arbitration centers (para. 4). The competent Arbitration Court shall decide on the **acceptance and administration** of an arbitration proceeding (para. 6 sent. 2–3). 5

Introduced in 2024, para. 7 provides the competence for CIETAC to support the parties in ***ad hoc*** **arbitration** upon agreement of the parties. The parties are free to decide the degree in which CIETAC will be involved in the arbitration, ranging from guidance and organizational support to scrutinizing draft awards. This provision connects to Art. 91, 93 of the 2021 Draft Revised PRC Arbitration law which **expressly allow** for *ad hoc* arbitration for foreign-related disputes (also → Ch. 1 mn. 34), whereby an *ad hoc* arbitration with support services by CIETAC provides an inventive middle ground. 6

Article 3
Jurisdiction

(1) CIETAC accepts cases involving economic, trade and other disputes of a contractual or non-contractual nature, based on an agreement of the parties.

(2) The cases referred to in the preceding paragraph include:

1. **international or foreign-related disputes;**
2. **disputes related to the Hong Kong Special Administrative Region, the Macao Special Administrative Region and the Taiwan region; [and]**
3. **domestic disputes.**

---

[2] Song/Yang/Chen, Commercial Dispute Resolution in China, p. 13 (at 4.b).

[3] Yu/Cao, A Guide to the CIETAC Arbitration Rules and Practice, mn. 2.44.

[4] Song/Yang/Chen, Commercial Dispute Resolution in China, p. 13 (at 1.).

1 While CIETAC was initially founded as the "foreign trade" arbitration commission of the CCPIT (Art. 1(1)), pursuant to para. 1, since 2005 CIETAC has been accepting not only international but all kinds of disputes of a contractual or non-contractual nature. However, with regard to **limitations of arbitrability**, in a recent case it was ruled "that the identification and treatment of monopoly acts are completely beyond the rights and obligations between the contractual counterparties".[5]

2 From a continental European perspective, the **distinction between "foreign related" disputes and "domestic" disputes** in para. 2 is important. The distinction has multiple impacts on the arbitration proceeding: (i) different criteria apply for the **annulment and the execution**;[6] (ii) the **fee structure** is different[7]; (iii) further, the nature of the dispute will have an impact on the decision by the Arbitral Tribunal and the President of the Arbitration Court (Art. 2(2)) **whether the place of the oral hearing may be moved to a place outside China** (Art. 36(2)).

3 An arbitration is **"foreign related"** if

1. one or both parties are foreigners, stateless persons, foreign enterprises or organizations;
2. the habitual residence of one party or both parties is outside PRC territory;
3. the subject matter is outside PRC territory;
4. the legal facts incurring, modifying or eliminating the civil relationship occur outside PRC territory;
5. other situations which can be recognized as a civil case involving foreigners or foreign affairs.[8]

4 In contrast, a dispute is **"domestic"** (para. 2 no. 3) if a Chinese legal party only has one foreign shareholder (e.g., from Germany) and the contract is subject to Chinese law.[9] This principle also applies when the dispute is between Chinese subsidiaries which are foreign controlled.[10] Therefore it is worth considering to add a further foreign element into the structure (e.g., by adding a foreign contract party) when planning the project in order to be able to use the advantages of a foreign-related arbitration. This option requires, however, that the foreign contractual element correlates with the reality and the real intention of the parties; otherwise the structure might be considered a circumvention of law.

---

[5] Civil Judgment of the SPC, (2021) Supreme Court Intellectual Civil Final No. 924.

[6] → Ch. 1 mn. 27 and 32, as well as Art. 248 PRC Civil Procedure Law and Art. 291 PRC Civil Procedure Law.

[7] Cf. for the various CIETAC Fee Schedules for national and foreign-related disputes → Appendix II.

[8] Art. 520 of the Interpretation of the Supreme People's Court concerning the "Civil Procedure Law of the People's Republic of China".

[9] Cf. Tevini, SchiedsVZ 2010, 25 (26).

[10] Cf. also Moser/Yuen in van den Berg, New Horizons in International Commercial Arbitration, p. 99, 103; see though in contrast the decision of the Middle People's Court of Shanghai, *Siemens International v. Golden Landmark* of November 27, 2015, where it was considered enough to accept an international element in case that a parallel seat was based in a free trade area and both the investors and beneficiaries of the parties were foreign (see → Ch. 3 mn. 12 et seq.); see also the overview and further case law provided by Burkardt/Zapletal/Guo in Respondek, Asia Arbitration Guide, pp. 55 et seq.

Article 4
Scope of Application

(1) These Rules uniformly apply to CIETAC and its sub-commissions/arbitration centers.

(2) Where the parties have agreed to refer their dispute to CIETAC for arbitration, they shall be deemed to have agreed to arbitration in accordance with these Rules.

(3) [1]Where the parties agree to refer their dispute to CIETAC for arbitration but have agreed on a modification of these Rules or have agreed on the application of other arbitration rules, the parties' agreement shall prevail unless such agreement is inoperative or in conflict with a mandatory provision of the law applicable to the arbitral proceedings. [2]Where the parties have agreed on the application of other arbitration rules, CIETAC shall perform the relevant administrative duties.

(4) Where the parties agree to refer their dispute to arbitration under these Rules without providing the name of the arbitration institution, they shall be deemed to have agreed to refer the dispute to arbitration by CIETAC.

(5) [1]Where the parties agree to refer their dispute to arbitration under CIETAC's customized arbitration rules for a specific trade or profession, the parties' agreement shall prevail. [2]However, if the dispute falls outside the scope of the specific rules, these Rules shall apply.

Art. 4 specifies the **scope of application** of the CIETAC Rules: Para. 1 underlines that the CIETAC Rules apply also to CIETAC's **sub-commissions/arbitration centers** (Art. 2(3) sent. 2). 1

Similar to the provisions in Art. 1(2) and Art. 2(6) sent. 3–4, para. 2 and para. 4 seek to clarify some uncertainties which may follow from the wording of the arbitration agreement: If the **CIETAC arbitration institution** is mentioned, this implies a choice of the CIETAC-Arbitration Rules; and *vice versa*. 2

Para. 3 sent. 1 guarantees **party autonomy** within the limits of mandatory law. The parties are therefore free to supplement the CIETAC model clauses (→ Ch. 2 mn. 7–9) as long as they do not infringe mandatory provisions of the law. More specific rules on party autonomy may be found in Art. 25(2), Art. 35(1) and (5). 3

Para. 3 sent. 2 provides the basis for conducting an arbitration in China with the **assistance of CIETAC** on the basis of **imported (foreign) arbitration rules** (e.g., the ICC Arbitration Rules; → Ch. 1 mn. 33).[11] 4

Para. 5 permits to agree on sector-specific **"customized" CIETAC Rules.** 5

[11] Johnston, J. Int. Arb. 2007, 565 (578). For example, the Supreme People's Court upheld an arbitration agreement that called for arbitral proceedings at CIETAC under the UNCITRAL Arbitration Rules in The Supreme People's Court Reply to the Inquiry regarding the Application of Zhejiang Yisheng Petrochemical Co. Ltd on the Validity of Arbitration Clause [2013] Min Si Ta Zi No. 60, December 18, 2013, as reported by Yu/Cao, A Guide to the CIETAC Arbitration Rules and Practice, mn. 3.12, 5.65; also → Ch. 3. mn. 10, 11.

Article 5
Arbitration Agreement

(1) An arbitration agreement means an arbitration clause in a contract or any other form of a written agreement concluded between the parties providing for the settlement of disputes by arbitration.

(2) [1]The arbitration agreement shall be in writing. [2]An arbitration agreement is in writing if it is contained in the tangible form of a document such as a contract, letter, telegram, telex, fax, electronic data interchange, or email. [3]An arbitration agreement shall be deemed to exist where its existence is asserted by one party and not denied by the other during the exchange of the Request for Arbitration and the Statement of Defense.

(3) Where the law applicable to an arbitration agreement has different provisions as to the form and validity of the arbitration agreement, those provisions shall prevail.

(4) [1]An arbitration clause contained in a contract shall be treated as a clause independent and separate from all other clauses of the contract, and an arbitration agreement attached to a contract shall also be treated as independent and separate from all other clauses of the contract. [2]The validity of an arbitration clause or an arbitration agreement shall not be affected by any modification, cancellation, termination, transfer, expiry, invalidity, ineffectiveness, rescission or non-existence of the contract.

1 **Art. 5** contains a **modern provision on the arbitration agreement** corresponding with international practice. Subject to prevailing provisions under the law applicable to the arbitration agreement (para. 3), para. 1 provides that an arbitration agreement can be concluded either in the contract ("*clause compromissoire*") or separately ("*compromis*") (correlating with international practice, see Art. II(2) NYC), and thereby also before or after the dispute arises.

2 Subject to the prevailing applicable law pursuant to para. 3, the arbitration agreement needs to be concluded **in writing** (para. 2 sent. 1). Para. 2 sent. 2 specifies that any "**tangible form of document**", including email, is sufficient.[12] An arbitration agreement may also be concluded by **incorporating** in the contract a reference to an arbitration agreement in another document.[13] The Beijing Fourth Intermediate Court held recently that a valid agreement to arbitrate exists between the parties when they agreed to submit the dispute to arbitration in the process of communication by WeChat, although they failed to reach a written contract.[14]

3 Para. 2 sent. 2 goes a step further and (again subject to the provision in para. 3) declares as sufficient if the defendant **omits to raise an objection** (which, from a German perspective, correlates with the German procedural instrument of "*rügelose Einlassung*" as known in German arbitration law pursuant to § 1032(1) ZPO). If a party intends to keep the option of executing an arbitration award, it should nonetheless bear

[12] See also Art. 11 PRC Civil Code and Art. 1 2006 SPC Interpretation (→ Ch. 1 mn. 34).

[13] Item 418 of the Supreme People's Court Decision on Abolishing Some Judicial Interpretations and Similar Documents Issued during the period from January 1, 1980, to June 30, 1997 (Ninth Batch), issued on January 14, 2013, and effective from January 18, 2013, as reported by Yu/Cao, A Guide to the CIETAC Arbitration Rules and Practice, mn. 5.11.

[14] Civil Judgment of the No. 4. Intermediate People's Court of Beijing, (2021) Beijing 04 Civil Special No. 715.

in mind the writing requirement in Art. II NYC and ensure that the competence of the Arbitral Tribunal is documented in the protocol to be signed by all parties (Art. 40(1) sent. 2). Although the protocol is mainly intended to serve as reference to the Arbitral Tribunal (Art. 40(2)), it makes sense that the parties also receive a copy of the protocol, which in practice does not represent a problem. Thereby, it is possible to organize a written confirmation of the arbitration agreement to avoid problems at the stage of execution of an arbitral award.

The provision on **priority of the applicable law** to the arbitration agreement in para. 3 for questions of form and validity documents the **independent qualification** of the arbitration agreement. In line with Art. 19 of the PRC Arbitration Law[15] and with Art. 10 of the 2006 Interpretation of the People's Supreme Court (→ Ch. 1 mn. 34), and further in line with international and comparative arbitration practice,[16] and against earlier Chinese jurisprudence,[17] para. 4 further specifies the **severability** of the arbitration agreement. The **validity of the arbitration clause** is therefore independent from the conclusion and validity of the main agreement (this becomes relevant for example, if the main agreement violates Chinese mandatory law)[18]. The decision about the **validity** of the arbitration agreement shall be taken **first by CIETAC** (→ Art. 6(1) and (2) sent. 2) and later – in case of an enforcement proceeding – by the competent court which decides about the enforcement of a CIETAC arbitration award (Art. 248(2) no. 1 PRC Civil Procedure Law; Art. V(1)(a) NYC). 4

Regarding the **determination of the law applicable to the arbitration clause** in the arbitration agreement, the 2006 Interpretation of the Supreme People's Court (→ Ch. 1 mn. 34) gives the following guidance: applicable is (i) the law chosen by the parties, (ii) otherwise the law at the place of the arbitration proceeding if the parties have agreed on the place of arbitration, (iii) otherwise, absent any agreement by the parties, the law at the seat of the court.[19] In practice, parties will have rarely made an explicit choice of the applicable law to the arbitration agreement (→ Ch. 2 mn. 7). Experience shows that merchants will rarely have an implicit intention to choose a specific law for an arbitration clause (of all topics). The **choice of law for the main contract** *can* imply the choice of law for the arbitration agreement.[20] 5

A clarification on the law applicable to the arbitration agreement avoids any discussion and uncertainty.

In light of the importance of the arbitration commission in China (→ mn. 5), the choice of such an arbitration commission *may* serve as an indication for an implicit choice of Chinese law also for the arbitration agreement. In practice, these questions may be left open (i.e., if the choice of the CIETAC Rules implies an implicit choice of 6

[15] Art. 23 Draft Revised PRC Arbitration Law (2021).

[16] See generally for the independent qualification of the arbitration clause Born, International Commercial Arbitration (2021), vol. I, § 3 pp. 375–505; Brödermann in Piltz, Münchener Anwaltshandbuch Internationales Wirtschaftsrecht, § 6 mn. 285.

[17] *China National Technical Import and Export Corp. v. Industrial Resources Co Inc*, (86) Hu Zhung Jing No 30 (October 11, 1988), cited according to Stricker-Kellerer/Moser in Schütze, Institutionelle Schiedsgerichtsbarkeit, Art. 5 (at fn. 10).

[18] See Stricker-Kellerer/Moser in Schütze, Institutionelle Schiedsgerichtsbarkeit, Art. 5 mn. 5 (with reference to the early cases of invalidity as a result of lacking competence in foreign trade according to Chinese foreign trade law).

[19] Art. 16 of the 2006 Interpretation of the Supreme People's Court (→ Ch. 1 mn. 34).

[20] Critical on this point Stricker-Kellerer/Moser in Schütze, Institutionelle Schiedsgerichtsbarkeit, Art. 5 mn. 3 ("the unlucky wording which leaves open whether the chosen substantive is directly applicable or whether the applicable law shall be determined according to the private international law").

Chinese law for the arbitration agreement) if all of the following possible connecting factors and indicators point towards concurrent choice of Chinese law: (i) choice of Chinese law for the main agreement, (ii) choice of the Chinese arbitration institution and (iii) choice of the seat of the Arbitral Tribunal in China.

7 Often, contracts contain **pathological arbitration clauses**. The 2006 Interpretation of the Supreme People's Court presents several examples in which the arbitration agreement is **invalid** (mostly relating to the requirement to designate a specific arbitration institution as set forth by Art. 16, 18 PRC Arbitration Law[21]).[22] However, more recently the Beijing Fourth Intermediate People's Court issued a ruling on the series of cases of *China Light & Power Sanlian International Trade Co. v. Tata International Metals (Asia) Co.* The arbitration agreement in the five sales contracts in question was held to be valid under Singaporean law even though the arbitration agreement contained a number of flaws:[23] (i) arbitration agreements **only defining the applicable arbitration rules** in case the institution cannot be derived from applicable arbitration rules;[24] (ii) arbitration agreements **naming two arbitration institutions** in case the parties are unable to reach a subsequent agreement on one institution;[25] (iii) arbitration agreements **violating the finality of arbitral awards**;[26] (iv) arbitration agreements **designating a non-existent arbitration institution** (and an existing institution remains unidentifiable);[27] (v) so-called **split clauses**, according to which one party may – depending on its own choice – either initiate an arbitration proceeding or bring the dispute before a state court are invalid because they lack a clear intent to arbitrate as required by Art. 16 PRC Arbitration Law.[28] However, there may be a possibility for a cure when the other party does not object to the choice of the initiating party according to Art. 7 SPC Interpretation (2006).[29]

---

[21] See, however, the proposed change in Art. 91, 93 Draft Revised PRC Arbitration Law (2021) (→ Ch. 1 mn. 15, 33).

[22] Art. 3 et seq. of the 2006 Interpretation of the Supreme People's Court, see also the enumeration in Yu/Cao, A Guide to the CIETAC Arbitration Rules and Practice, mn. 5.22–5.85.

[23] "The Tata Case: A New Development in the Value of Judicial Review of 'Sick Arbitration Agreements' by Chinese Courts, AnJie Broad Law Firm", March 25, 2019, reviewed at https://www.lexology.com.

[24] Art. 5 of the 2006 Interpretation of the Supreme People's Court. Parties that only choose the CIETAC Rules without specifying CIETAC as the competent institution thereby agree upon Art. 4.4 CIETAC Rules which stipulates that in such case the parties are "deemed to have agreed to refer the dispute to arbitration by CIETAC". Thus, the agreement is valid; see Yu/Cao, A Guide to the CIETAC Arbitration Rules and Practice, mn. 5.42.

[25] Art. 5 of the 2006 Interpretation of the Supreme People's Court; see also The Supreme People's Court Reply to the Inquiry regarding People's Court's Jurisdiction over the Case between *Rent Corporation and Complant Ningbo Import/Export Co. Ltd and Dongguan City Jianhua Construction Machinery Manufacturing Co. Ltd* [2008] Mi Si Ta Zi No. 4, March 18, 2008, as reported by Yu/Cao, A Guide to the CIETAC Arbitration Rules and Practice, mn. 5.58.

[26] The Supreme People's Court Reply to the Inquiry regarding the Validity of Arbitration Agreement between *Huzhou Second Resistant Refractory Materials Joint Management Factory and Minteq International Inc.* [2004] Min Si Ta Zi No. 42, November 30, 2004, as reported by Yu/Cao, A Guide to the CIETAC Arbitration Rules and Practice, mn. 5.61–5.62.

[27] Art. 3 of the 2006 Interpretation of the Supreme People's Court; see also The Supreme People's Court Reply to the Inquiry regarding the Validity of Arbitration Agreement between *Hangzhou Top Leader Textile Technology Co. Ltd. and Forward Machinery Industrial Corp.* [2005] Min Si Ta Zi No. 52, December 1, 2015, as reported by Yu/Cao, A Guide to the CIETAC Arbitration Rules and Practice, mn. 5.68.

[28] Art. 7 of the 2006 Interpretation of the Supreme People's Court; see also The Supreme People's Court Reply to the Inquiry regarding the Validity of Arbitration Agreement between *Nakajima and He Aibing et al.* [2004] Min Si Ta Zi No. 47, December 13, 2004, as reported by Yu/Cao, A Guide to the CIETAC Arbitration Rules and Practice, mn. 5.76.

[29] → Ch. 1 mn. 34.

Sometimes, the parties have chosen only the **place** of the arbitration and not a specific arbitration institution.[30] In a decision of 1998, the Supreme People's Court decided that such an arbitration clause shall be considered invalid if there is more than one arbitration institution at that location.[31] A draft of People's Supreme Court Interpretation of 2003 provided for the validity of such a clause.[32] However, the interpretation of 2006 (→ Ch. 1 mn. 34) reversed its position regarding the invalidity of such a simple arbitration clause with a mere reference to the place of arbitration,[33] thereby explicitly arguing against a decision of the Higher People's Courts in Shanghai of 2001.[34] **8**

Pursuant to Art. 5 PRC Arbitration Law,[35] a court may not accept a case if a valid arbitration agreement exists. This does not apply if the other party fails to object to the court's competence prior to the first hearing (Art. 26 PRC Arbitration Law[36]). **9**

Article 6
Objection to Arbitration Agreement and/or Jurisdiction

(1) [1]CIETAC has the power to determine the existence and validity of an arbitration agreement and its jurisdiction over an arbitration case. [2]Such power is delegated to the arbitral tribunal once it is formed.

(2) [1]Where CIETAC is satisfied by prima facie evidence that a valid arbitration agreement exists and decides that it has jurisdiction over the arbitration case, the arbitration shall proceed. [2]Such a decision shall not prevent the arbitral tribunal from making a new decision on jurisdiction based on facts and/or evidence it found during the arbitral proceedings that are inconsistent with the prima facie evidence.

(3) When deciding on jurisdiction, the arbitral tribunal may either make a separate decision on jurisdiction during the arbitral proceedings or incorporate the decision in the final arbitral award.

(4) [1]Any objection to an arbitration agreement and/or the jurisdiction over an arbitration case shall be raised in writing before the first oral hearing held by the arbitral tribunal. [2]Where a case is to be decided on the basis of documents only, such an objection shall be raised before the submission of the first substantive defense. [3]Where the law applicable to the arbitral proceedings provides otherwise, such provision shall prevail.

(5) The arbitration shall proceed notwithstanding an objection to the arbitration agreement and/or jurisdiction over the arbitration case.

(6) The aforesaid objections to and/or decisions on jurisdiction by CIETAC shall include objections to and/or decisions on a party's standing to participate in the arbitration.

---

[30] For an overview on the development on Chinese jurisprudence on this topic see Yu/Cao, A Guide to the CIETAC Arbitration Rules and Practice, mn. 5.27–5.38.

[31] Reported by Yu/Cao, A Guide to the CIETAC Arbitration Rules and Practice, mn. 5.29.

[32] Initially, the validity was foreseen in the draft provisions of the Supreme People's Court of December 31, 2003.

[33] Art. 6 SPC Interpretation (2006).

[34] Opinion of the Higher People's Court of Shanghai Municipality on Several Issues concerning the Application of the PRC Arbitration Law, January 3, 2001, as reported by Yu/Cao, A Guide to the CIETAC Arbitration Rules and Practice, mn. 5.33.

[35] Expected to remain unchanged in the new PRC Arbitration Law.

[36] Art. 40 Draft Revised PRC Arbitration Law (2021).

(7) [1]CIETAC or the arbitral tribunal shall decide to dismiss the case upon finding of lack of jurisdiction. [2]Where a case is to be dismissed before the formation of the arbitral tribunal, the decision shall be made by the President of the Arbitration Court. [3]Where the case is to be dismissed after the formation of the arbitral tribunal, the decision shall be made by the arbitral tribunal.

1 Art. 6 is concerned with mainly three subjects: the **competence of CIETAC** or of the Arbitral Tribunal to

1. **decide** about its own competence,
2. **conduct the arbitration procedure** irrespective of any objection against the validity of the arbitration agreement, and
3. **dismiss** an arbitration claim.

2 Para. 1 sent. 1 contains a Chinese *variation* of the international principle of **"competence-competence"** of the Arbitral Tribunal, according to which the Arbitral Tribunal is competent to decide about its own competence.[37] Pursuant to para. 1 sent. 1, it is **CIETAC** and not the Arbitral Tribunal which decides about its competence (Art. 13 (1)).[38] This is in line with Art. 20 PRC Arbitration Law. In this regard, the Draft Revised PRC Arbitration Law (2021) provides in its Art. 28 for a major change. Giving up the former Chinese approach on the question of competence, the draft law intends to recognize the international principle of "competence-competence" of the Arbitral Tribunal. In this regard, the 2024 CIETAC Rules take up this intention and quasi-implement it by replacing the former top-down rule, according to which CIETAC could empower an Arbitral Tribunal to decide about the validity of the arbitration agreement, with a standard rule whereby such power is generally **delegated** to the Arbitral Tribunal upon formation according to para. 1 sent. 2. The Arbitral Tribunal has a choice to decide about its own competence pursuant to para. 3 either separately or at the end of the arbitration procedure in the award.

3 If the **arbitration clause is unclear**, in practice it is advisable to informally liaise with CIETAC and have CIETAC determine if it will consider itself as competent in case of initiation of an arbitration proceeding.

4 Alternatively, it is possible to apply to a Chinese domestic Court for a **formal determination** about the competence of an arbitration commission (when the Shanghai International Arbitration Centre decided to separate from CIETAC in Beijing in 2013,[39] the Chinese arbitration community witnessed a series of litigation and court decisions about the competence of one or the other arbitration commission).[40] If, in a foreign related case, a court holds an **arbitration clause to be void**, it is obliged **to notify** this to **the next court level.**[41] If a party bound by an arbitration agreement files a claim with a **Chinese state court**, the court will decide on the matter if the respondent does not raise the defense of incompetence prior to the first oral hearing. The respondent is then deemed to have **waived** the **objection of incompetence.**[42]

5 Para. 2 provides the basis for a **two-pronged approach** of CIETAC and the arbital tribunal: (i) During a first review, CIETAC can decide on its jurisdiction ("*competence*")

[37] See also Born, International Commercial Arbitration, § 7.01 pp. 1141–1144 and 1162–1169.

[38] See also Öhlberger, Austrian Arbitration Yearbook 2009, p. 136 as well as Johnston, J. Int. Arb. 2007, 565 (573).

[39] → Ch. 1 mn. 28.

[40] See the short overview in Choong, The Asia-Pacific Arbitration Review 2014, 40 (41); see e.g. the Decision of SPC dated June 23, 2015, with comments from Neelmeier, SchiedsVZ 2015, 251–253.

[41] Art. 1 of the Circular of the Supreme People's Court on Issues in the People's Courts Handling of Foreign-related Arbitrations and Foreign Arbitrations.

[42] Art. 26 PRC Arbitration Law, Art. 40 Draft Revised PRC Arbitration Law (2021).

based on *prima facie* evidence. (ii) The arbitral tribunal **remains free** to decide again on the issue of competence and to **revise the initial decision** of CIETAC in light of the development of the arbitration proceedings, e.g., if new facts or evidence have or has been discovered.

Para. 4 seeks to ensure that **formal objections** against the arbitration agreement and/ or the jurisdiction ("*competence*") of CIETAC – including objections against **the other party's standing** to participate in the arbitration (para. 6) – are raised **early**: before the first oral hearing or – in case of written procedures – before the first defense on the subject matter itself (see also Art. 10) unless the law applicable to the arbitration provides otherwise. This exception is noteworthy because it presupposes that CIETAC arbitration may be conducted outside mainland China and that, in such case, the arbitration law at the seat of the arbitration shall apply. This is in line with the general concept that the arbitration law at the seat of the arbitration shall apply.[43] 6

Pursuant to para. 5, **formal objections** shall not prohibit the **proceeding** of the **arbitration**. Thereby, facts which need to be found or legal issues to be decided in order to decide about the validity of the arbitration agreement can be solved during the arbitration proceeding, and the decision on the formal objection does not cause a delay which is likely to impede upon the short time frame for rendering an award pursuant to Art. 51(1). This provision is helpful if the issues to be decided for the formal objection are also essential for the decision on the substance such as the legal existence or corporate identity of a contracting party[44] (see para. 6). 7

Pursuant to para. 7, **incompetence of a CIETAC Arbitral Tribunal** leads to a **dismissal** of the arbitration claim, to be pronounced (i) prior to the constitution of the Arbitral Tribunal (i.e., the receipt by the parties of the notice of formation of the Arbitral Tribunal as mentioned in Art. 32(3)) by the President of the Arbitration Court (Art. 2(2)), (ii) thereafter by the president of the Arbitral Tribunal. According to Art. 46 (4), the **seal** of CIETAC shall be affixed to the dismissal decision. 8

Article 7
Place of Arbitration

(1) Where the parties have agreed on the place of arbitration, the parties' agreement shall prevail.

(2) Where the parties have not agreed on the place of arbitration or their agreement is ambiguous, the place of arbitration shall be the domicile of CIETAC or its sub-commission/arbitration center administering the case. CIETAC may also determine the place of arbitration to be another location having regard to the circumstances of the case.

(3) The arbitral award shall be deemed as having been made at the place of arbitration.

Para. 1 grants **party autonomy** to the parties with respect to the place of arbitration (→ Ch. 2 mn. 4). This is the place in which the arbitration award shall be deemed as having been made pursuant to the "fiction" in para. 3. In this context it should be noted that pursuant to **Article 58 PRC Arbitration Law** – and different from Germany – not the place of arbitration but the **seat of the arbitration commission** administrating the 1

[43] Born, International Commercial Arbitration, vol. I, § 2.04, p. 371; vol. II, § 11.04, pp. 1669–1670.
[44] See Brödermann in FS Wegen, pp. 592–593.

arbitration serves as the connecting factor for the determination of the competent state court to decide upon the cancellation of an arbitral award. This, however, is expected to change with the new PRC Arbitration Law as Art. 77 Draft Revised PRC Arbitration Law (2021) now stipulates the **seat of arbitration** as the connecting factor for the determination of the competent state court.

2 Nonetheless, in case of a "foreign related" arbitration, it remains risky to choose a place outside of Mainland China. Even if CIETAC cooperates, there is the **residual risk of a local court proceeding** if one of the parties objects to jurisdiction and turns to a local court (e.g., in Seoul or Tokyo, if these places have been chosen as seat of arbitration); such local courts would not be bound by the PRC Arbitration Law. In case of the choice of a place of arbitration located in a **common law jurisdiction** such as Hong Kong (Art. 74) or Macao, there is the additional risk – from a civil law perspective – that then common law applies to the arbitration procedure and any arbitration related court litigation. Even if CIETAC is very co-operative, there may remain a residual risk that the opposing party – if things go wrong – turns to a local court; this may cost time and money.

3 If the parties have **not agreed** on the place of arbitration, **or** if the agreement is **unclear**, pursuant to para. 2 sent. 1 the place of arbitration will be the seat of CIETAC or its competent branch, unless CIETAC determines otherwise according to para. 2 sent. 2.

Article 8
Service of Documents and Periods of Time

(1) [1]All documents, notices and materials in relation to the arbitration ("arbitration documents") may be delivered in person or by registered or express mail, by fax, by electronic means or any other means of communication with a delivery record, or by any other means considered proper by the Arbitration Court or the arbitral tribunal. [2]Electronic means of delivery includes service of arbitration documents by electronic means to the email addresses or other electronic addresses agreed/designated by the parties, or via the digitalized information exchange system of CIETAC or other information system easily accessible to all parties, etc.

(2) Arbitration documents may be served by electronic means as a preferred way of delivery.

(3) [1]Arbitration documents shall be sent to the address provided by a party itself or by its representative(s), or to an address agreed by the parties. [2]Where a party or its representative(s) has not provided an address or the parties have not agreed on an address, the arbitration documents shall be sent to such party's address as provided by the other party or its representative(s).

(4) Any arbitration documents sent to a party or its representative(s) shall be deemed to have been properly served on the party if delivered to the addressee or sent to the addressee's place of business, place of registration, domicile, habitual residence or address of communication, or where, after reasonable inquiries by the other party, none of the aforesaid addresses can be found, the arbitration documents are sent by the Arbitration Court to the addressee's last known place of business, place of registration, domicile, habitual residence or mailing address by registered or express mail, or by any other means that can provide a record of the attempt at delivery, including but not limited to service by public notary, entrustment or retention.

(5) The periods of time specified in these Rules shall begin on the day following the day when the party receives or should have received the arbitration documents sent by the Arbitration Court.

Art. 8 regulates **service** of "documents, notices and written materials in relation to the arbitration" (hereinafter "arbitration materials") by the arbitration court or the Arbitral Tribunal (para. 1). 1

As part of the **digitalization effort** of the 2024 CIETAC Rules,[45] para. 1 now provides for the possibility to service arbitration materials by **electronic means** such as email or via the digitalized information exchange system provided by CIETAC. Documents may be sent to the (electronic) address which has been last communicated or agreed (para. 3). 2

When acting as a counsel or arbitrator out of Europe in a CIETAC arbitration, such liberal statement in the 2024 CIETAC Rules does not liberate from respecting any internationally mandatory law on **data protection**, such as notably the EU General Data Protection Regulation 2016/679, if the files contain personal data. 3

It is sufficient to **serve arbitration materials** at one of the places within the sphere of the addressee as set forth in para. 4, alternatively at the last such known place "or by any other means that can provide a record of the attempt at delivery". The concept of such "**other means**" is very broad and includes, e.g., the attempt of delivery by a notary or another person authorised to serve by CIETAC or by a provable "entrustment" of the Arbitral Tribunal (e.g., by video documentation or the retention of the arbitration material at the address of service in the presence of two witnesses). 4

Deadlines start to run on the **day following the service** (para. 4). 5

Article 9
Good Faith

Arbitration participants shall proceed with the arbitration in good faith.

Art. 9 emphasizes the procedural obligation of the parties to act in accordance with the principle of **good faith.** This principle can find expression, e.g., in (i) the **obligation to present the truth** in the pleadings (see the reference to the basis of "*true facts*" in Art. 7 PRC Arbitration Law[46]) or (ii) the **prohibition to influence the arbitrators** (see the reference to the **independence** of the "arbitration" in Art. 8 PRC Arbitration Law[47]). 1

In an international or foreign-related CIETAC arbitration with parties from different continents, it can be helpful from the perspective of the Arbitral Tribunal to commence the arbitration by **reminding of these general pillars** of a CIETAC arbitration and to thereby prepare the ground for efficient arbitration.

[45] See also the new Art. 52(7) and (10) as well as Art. 21 CIETAC Rules.

[46] Art. 7 Draft Revised PRC Arbitration Law (2021) now also references to transaction practices.

[47] Expected to remain unchanged in the Draft Revised PRC Arbitration Law (2021).

Article 10
Waiver of Right to Object

A party shall be deemed to have waived its right to object where it knows or should have known that any provision of, or requirement under, these Rules has not been complied with and does not promptly and explicitly submit its objection in writing to such non-compliance, yet participates in or proceeds with the arbitral proceedings or fails to participate in the hearing without a justifiable reason after being duly notified.

1 Art. 10 supplements and emphasizes the general thought underlying Art. 6(4) (→ Art. 6 mn. 5). As a **general rule**, it expresses the legal consequence of failing to object against a perceived violation of the CIETAC Rules or failing to participate in the hearing at all while this would be reasonably possible (arg. "where it knows or should have known").

2 A party who does not raise a formal **objection** against the arbitral proceeding **promptly** (i.e., without undue delay) **and explicitly**, **loses its right to object** because the behavior will be deemed to be a waiver of the objection. This waiver also extends to objections concerning the same matter in subsequent court proceedings.[48] The case category of "failing to participate in the hearing" has been added by the 2024 CIETAC Rules. It is a helpful tool to cope with obstructive defendants.

---

[48] The Beijing High People's Court Key Points of the Judicial Review of the Arbitral Awards of Domestic Commercial Arbitration, Jing Gao Fa Fa [2013] No. 65 (promulgated on, and effective from, March 7, 2013) as reported by Yu/Cao, A Guide to the CIETAC Arbitration Rules and Practice, mn. 3.70; see also *Beijing Guotou Investment Cooperation Equity Investment Fund (Limited Partnership) v. GFC Holding Co. et al.* [2016] Jing 04 Min Te No. 29, Beijing Fourth Intermediate People's Court, June 6, 2017, as reported by Yu/Cao at mn. 3.71.

Chapter II
Arbitration Proceeding

Section I
Request for Arbitration, Defense and Counterclaim

Article 11
Commencement of Arbitration

[1]The arbitral proceedings shall commence on the day on which the Arbitration Court receives a Request for Arbitration. [2]Where the Claimant submits a Request for Arbitration in writing and/or via CIETAC's online case filing system, the arbitral proceedings shall commence on the day when such Request is first received.

Art. 11 defines the **moment of receipt** of the Request for Arbitration by the Arbitration 1
Court as the **formal beginning** of the arbitration proceeding (sent. 2), whereby the new second sentence in the 2024 CIETAC Rules has added a reference to the possibility to file claims via the online case filing system which CIETAC set up as part of its digitalization effort. In contrast, the **time frame** of **six months** to conduct the arbitration and to render an arbitral award pursuant to Art. 51(1) starts **later** with the receipt of the Notice about the Formation of the Arbitral Tribunal mentioned in Art. 32(3).[1]

For the special case of a **joinder** of an additional party to the arbitration, Art. 18(1) 2
sent. 3 contains a parallel provision. It is submitted that the six month-period will then also start later and be calculated as of the receipt of service of the decision about the joinder pursuant to Art. 18(4).

Article 12
Application for Arbitration

(1) A party applying for arbitration under these Rules shall:

1. **Submit a Request for Arbitration in writing signed and/or sealed by the Claimant or its authorized representative(s), which shall, inter alia, include:**
   a. **the names and addresses of the Claimant and the Respondent, including the zip code, telephone, fax, email, or any other means of electronic telecommunications;**
   b. **a reference to the arbitration agreement that is invoked;**
   c. **a statement of the facts of the case and the main issues in dispute;**
   d. **the claim of the Claimant; [and]**
   e. **the facts and grounds on which the claim is based.**
2. **Attach to the Request for Arbitration the relevant documentary and other evidence on which the Claimant's claim is based.**

---

[1] Experienced practice, i.e., (i) by an information received from CIETAC during an arbitration proceeding and (ii) experienced consent of CIETAC to the calculation of a time-period in a request for prolongation of a deadline, cf. Art. 51(2).

3. Pay the arbitration fee in advance to CIETAC in accordance with its Arbitration Fee Schedule.

(2) [1]Where it is agreed in the arbitration agreement that negotiation or mediation shall be conducted before arbitration, the Claimant may apply for arbitration after conducting negotiation or mediation. [2]However, failure to negotiate or mediate shall neither prevent the Claimant from applying for arbitration nor prevent the Arbitration Court from accepting the case, unless the law applicable to the arbitral proceedings or the arbitration agreement expressly provides otherwise.

1 Art. 12 describes the **requirements for filing** an arbitration:

1. **A Request for Arbitration** which meets the requirements set forth in para. 1 (these are in line with international standards as known, e.g., from Art. 4(3) ICC Arbitration Rules);
2. attaching **documentation** as evidence;
3. **payment** of the fees as set forth in the CIETAC Arbitration Fee Schedule (whereby agreements with the arbitrators on their fee[2] may lead later to additional payments during the arbitration proceedings).

2 The **legal consequences** of failure – which apply if the formalities for the filing of a Request for Arbitration are not met – are governed by Art. 13(3). The conditions under 1. and 2. above reflect the provisions in Art. 23 no. 1 and 2 PRC Arbitration Law[3]. The requirement of a reference to the arbitration agreement in Art. 12(1) no. 1(b) correlates with Art. 22 PRC Arbitration Law[4]; the other conditions to be fulfilled by a Request for Arbitration find their basis in Art. 23 PRC Arbitration Law.

3 Where the arbitration agreement provides for a **multi-tired dispute resolution mechanism**, the **newly added para. 2** provides that arbitration may be initiated after negotiation or mediation. However, subject to express contrasting provisions in the applicable arbitration law, failure to do so does not limit the competence of CIETAC to accept the case (Art. 6(2)).

Article 13
Acceptance of a Case

(1) Upon the written application of a party, CIETAC shall accept a case in accordance with an arbitration agreement concluded between the parties either before or after the occurrence of the dispute, in which it is provided that disputes are to be referred to arbitration by CIETAC.

(2) [1]Upon receipt of a Request for Arbitration and its attachments, where after examination the Arbitration Court finds the formalities required for arbitration application to be complete, it shall send a Notice of Arbitration to both parties together with one copy each of these Rules and CIETAC's Panel of Arbitrators. [2]The Request for Arbitration and its attachments submitted by the Claimant shall be sent to the Respondent under the same cover.

(3) [1]Where the Arbitration Court, after examination, finds the formalities required for the arbitration application incomplete, it may request the Claimant to complete them within a specified time period. [2]The Claimant shall be deemed not to have

---

[2] On the one hand in the arbitrator's agreement and on the other hand in the payment agreements between the arbitration institution and arbitrators, → Ch. 1 mn. 14.

[3] Art. 37 Draft Revised PRC Arbitration Law (2021).

[4] Art. 36 Draft Revised PRC Arbitration Law (2021).

submitted a Request for Arbitration if it fails to complete the required formalities within the specified time period. [3]In such a case, the Claimant's Request for Arbitration and its attachments shall not be kept on file by the Arbitration Court.

(4) After CIETAC accepts a case, the Arbitration Court shall designate a case manager to assist with the procedural administration of the case.

Supplementing Art. 6(1) sent. 1, the provision in para. 1 (which was introduced in 2015) sets forth the **general rule** that CIETAC shall decide about the acceptance of a case if it considers itself competent. Pursuant to para. 2 sent. 2, the Arbitration Court of CIETAC decides if a Request for Arbitration meets the necessary **formal requirements** of an arbitration application. It follows from Art. 24 PRC Arbitration Law[5] that CIETAC has **five days** as of the receipt of the Request for Arbitration to make its decision. If the formal requirements (Art. 12) are not fully met, CIETAC can offer the Claimant to **complete the missing formalities** within a specified time period (para. 3 sent. 1). If the Claimant does not comply with such an offer in time, the Request for Arbitration is deemed not to have been submitted (para. 3 sent. 2–3). 1

Once the Arbitration Court is satisfied that the formalities have been complied with, pursuant to para. 2 sent. 1 it sends to **both parties**: 2

1. a notice about the commencement of an arbitration (**"Notice of Arbitration"**),
2. a copy of the CIETAC Rules, and
3. a list of CIETAC's Panel of Arbitrators.

For the **Respondent**, CIETAC will attach the Request for Application with enclosures (para. 2 sent. 2). 3

Para. 4 provides the legal basis for the **appointment of a CIETAC case manager** who will **support** the Arbitral Tribunal as of the acceptance of the arbitration by CIETAC (para. 1). In practice, the case managers will organize, for example, the **hearing room** at the CIETAC premises (including coping with conflicts of rooms). They will be **present at the hearings** (where they receive further support by employees helping with technical and IT questions), and they will contribute with hints meant to align the CIETAC's procedure with **standard forms**. Thus, they will prepare a short **formal protocol** limited to the essentials. In practice, – at least from the perspective of a foreign CIETAC arbitrator – the assistance by a case manager can be helpful. If an Arbitral Tribunal which includes a foreign arbitrator prepares itself a **more extensive protocol** in line with international practice (and/or the international expectation of the parties) – and which will be shared with the parties – the case managers tend to be flexible, not insisting on their own draft but rather changing their task to **control** that the Chairman's draft is in line with all formal requirements for a protocol, e.g. that all parties are mentioned correctly and that it is duly signed by the party representatives (Art. 40(1) sent. 2). 4

The case managers further organize the **financial matters** of the case, e.g. requesting advance payments of costs from the parties, supervising punctual payment (including crisis meetings prior to a hearing when a party missed to pay within the very short deadlines set by CIETAC which can be a challenge when paying from abroad), and concluding agreements on partial payment of the fees as agreed with the foreign arbitrators (based on hourly rates agreed with the parties and CIETAC). Further, the case managers can secure that **applications** for an extension of time pursuant to Art. 51(2) **reach the President** of the Arbitration Court (Art. 2(2)) in a timely manner (→ Art. 17 mn. 1). Also, they can arrange for **smooth and timely scrutiny** of the award (Art. 51). 5

[5] Art. 38 Draft Revised PRC Arbitration Law (2021).

Article 14
Multiple Contracts and Adding Contract(s) in Arbitration

(1) The Claimant may initiate a single arbitration concerning disputes arising out of or in connection with multiple contracts, provided that:

1. **such contracts consist of a principal contract and its ancillary contract(s), or such contracts involve the same parties as well as legal relationships of the same nature, or such contracts involve related subject matters;**
2. **the disputes in such contracts arise out of the same transaction or the same series of transactions; [and]**
3. **the arbitration agreements in such contracts are identical or compatible.**

(2) [1]If all of the circumstances set forth in the preceding Paragraph 1 Nr.1, 2, 3 are met, the Claimant may apply to add contract(s) during the arbitral proceedings. [2]However, such application may be denied if it is too late and may delay the arbitral proceedings.

(3) [1]The procedural matters in the preceding Paragraph 1 and 2 shall be decided by the Arbitration Court. [2]Where the application for adding contract(s) is made after the formation of the arbitral tribunal, such decision shall be made by the arbitral tribunal.

1 It can be often observed in practice that (main) contracts develop "a life of their own" over time with multiple supplements or ancillary agreements which often lack a proper coordination of the dispute resolution regime; as a result **"multiple contracts"** may govern the same legal and/or business relationship. In other scenarios, parties may conclude a multitude of contracts based on a framework agreement but without proper reference to it; or, for example, an exclusivity agreement can be misunderstood as a framework agreement and serve as the factual basis for a series of Chinese-German sale contracts.[6]

2 Para. 1 added in the 2015 version of the CIETAC Rules, enables a claimant to file a **Request for Arbitration** on the basis of multiple contracts as described in no. 1 and 2, as long as they have an **"identical or compatible" arbitration clause (no. 3)**. Considering the **arbitration friendly approach of CIETAC** (Art. 1(2) and Art. 2(6) sent. 3–4 for possible "repairs" of unclear arbitration clauses), these criteria should be considered as met where a difference in the arbitration agreements is merely textual or where one includes express provisions on certain legal aspects of the arbitration (like a designated place of arbitration) while the other is silent on the matter, provided the express provision yields the same result as the default provision of the CIETAC Rules,[7] or, under the circumstances of the case, compatibility appears to be the reasonable solution.[8]

3 Para. 2 added in the 2024 CIETAC Rules, extends the possibility to **add contract(s) to ongoing arbitral proceedings** having due regard to the state of proceedings and possible delays. In line with the new allocation of competence in Art. 6(1), para. 3 provides that applications to **add contract(s) before the formation** of the arbitral tribunal will be decided by the CIETAC Arbitration Court. After the formation of the arbitral tribunal, the competence lies with the arbitral tribunal. The addition of para. 2 is

[6] This example is drawn from experience in a CEAC (now ASEAC) case.

[7] See Yu/Cao, A Guide to the CIETAC Arbitration Rules and Practice, mn. 10.22.

[8] See also Yu/Cao, A Guide to the CIETAC Arbitration Rules and Practice, mn. 10.21 pointing at an examination on a case-by-case basis.

welcomed. It aligns with the international trend to allow multi-contract arbitration.[9] It is helpful to settle disputes regarding complex multi-contract long-term relationships.

Article 15
Statement of Defense

(1) [1]The Respondent shall file a Statement of Defense in writing within forty-five (45) days from the date of its receipt of the Notice of Arbitration. [2]If the Respondent has justified reasons to request an extension of the time period, the arbitral tribunal shall decide whether to grant an extension. [3]Where the arbitral tribunal has not yet been formed, the decision on whether to grant the extension of the time period shall be made by the Arbitration Court.

(2) The Statement of Defense shall be signed and/or sealed by the Respondent or its authorized representative(s), and shall, inter alia, include the following contents and attachments:

1. **the name and address of the Respondent, including the zip code, telephone, fax, email, or any other means of electronic telecommunications;**
2. **the defense to the Request for Arbitration setting forth the facts and grounds on which the defense is based; [and]**
3. **the relevant documentary and other evidence on which the defense is based.**

(3) The arbitral tribunal has the power to decide whether to accept a Statement of Defense submitted after the expiration of the above time period.

(4) Failure by the Respondent to file a Statement of Defense shall not affect the conduct of the arbitral proceedings.

Para. 1 and 2 stipulate the **formal conditions for a Statement of Defense**. Para. 1 sent. 1 determines the **time frame** for its submission: 45 days as of receipt of the Notice of Arbitration pursuant to Art. 13(2); the Arbitral Tribunal can grant an extension in case of "justified reasons" to be assessed with due regard to the circumstances according to para. 1 sent. 2. Prior to the constitution of the Arbitral Tribunal, the Arbitration Court is competent to take the decision on an **extension** under para. 1 sent. 3. Para. 2 determines the necessary **minimum contents**, including **documents** as proof (no. 3), if applicable. Like for all briefs, the **addressee** of the Statement of Defense is CIETAC or the acting sub-commission. 1

Para. 3 explicitly empowers the Arbitral Tribunal to accept a **belated Statement of Defense**. The provision contains no restriction or guidance for the Arbitral Tribunal. In practice, the Arbitral Tribunal will have due regard to (i) considerations based on its procedural obligation to respect the duty of good faith (Art. 9), (ii) any alleged "justified reasons" (as it would have considered in case of a timely request for a prolongation of time, para. 1 sent. 2–3) and (iii) the right to be heard and the prospects of enforcement (Art. 291(1) no. 2 PRC Civil Procedure Law; Art. V NYC). 2

Para. 4 regulates the case (occasionally relevant in practice) that the **Respondent does not participate** in the arbitration proceedings. In that case the arbitration procedure shall continue without the Respondent, as provided in Art. 25(2) PRC Arbitration Law.[10] 3

---

[9] Born, International Commercial Arbitration, vol. II, § 18.03, pp. 2815–2816.
[10] Art. 39 Draft Revised PRC Arbitration Law (2021).

Article 16
Counterclaim

(1) [1]The Respondent shall file a counterclaim, if any, in writing within forty-five (45) days from the date of its receipt of the Notice of Arbitration. [2]If the Respondent has justified reasons to request an extension of the time period, the arbitral tribunal shall decide whether to grant an extension. [3]Where the arbitral tribunal has not yet been formed, the decision on whether to grant the extension of the time period shall be made by the Arbitration Court.

(2) When filing the counterclaim, the Respondent shall specify the counterclaim in its Statement of Counterclaim and state the facts and grounds on which the counterclaim is based with the relevant documentary and other evidence attached thereto.

(3) When filing the counterclaim, the Respondent shall pay an arbitration fee in advance in accordance with the Arbitration Fee Schedule of CIETAC within a specified time period, failing which the Respondent shall be deemed not to have filed any counterclaim.

(4) [1]Where the formalities required for filing a counterclaim are found to be complete, the Arbitration Court shall send a Notice of Acceptance of Counterclaim to the parties. [2]The Claimant shall submit its Statement of Defense in writing within thirty (30) days from the date of its receipt of the Notice. [3]If the Claimant has justified reasons to request an extension of the time period, the arbitral tribunal shall decide whether to grant such an extension. [4]Where the arbitral tribunal has not yet been formed, the decision on whether to grant the extension of the time period shall be made by the Arbitration Court.

(5) The arbitral tribunal has the power to decide whether to accept a counterclaim or a Statement of Defense submitted after the expiration of the above time period.

(6) Failure of the Claimant to file a Statement of Defense to the Respondent's counterclaim shall not affect the conduct of the arbitral proceedings.

1 The **right to file a counterclaim** originates from Art. 27 sent. 2 PRC Arbitration Law[11]. Art. 16 transfers *in essence* the formal requirements known from Art. 12–13 and 15 for the Request for Arbitration and the Statement of Defense to the counterclaim:

2 Pursuant to para. 1 sent. 1, the same **time frame** applies as for the statement of defense (**45 days** as of receipt of the Notice of Arbitration pursuant to Art. 13(2)).

3 In case of "**justified reasons**", the Arbitration Court (para. 1 sent. 3) or, after its constitution (Notice of Formation as mentioned in Art. 32(3)), the Arbitral Tribunal (para. 1 sent. 2) is empowered to grant an **extension** (whereby practitioners report that, at least in the past, the time frame for a counterclaim was enforced more rigidly than the deadline for the Statement of Defense)[12].

4 Just like the Request for Arbitration and the Statement of Defense, the Counterclaim must contain **concrete claims, facts and grounds** on which it is based as well as the necessary **evidence** including documents (para. 2).

5 Like in the case of filing a Request for Arbitration (Art. 12(1) no. 3), the counter-claiming Respondent will have **to pay in advance**, at the time of filing (respectively the timeframe set by CIETAC), the Arbitration Fee pursuant to the Fee Schedule of

[11] Art. 41 Draft Revised PRC Arbitration Law (2021).

[12] Stricker-Kellerer/Moser in Schütze, Institutionelle Schiedsgerichtsbarkeit, Art. 14 mn. 1.

CIETAC (para. 3 sent. 1); otherwise the counterclaim will be deemed not to have been filed (para. 3 sent. 2).

Like in the case of a Request for Arbitration (Art. 13(2)), the Arbitration Court (Art. 2(2)) **examines** whether all **formal requirements** of filing are met. If so, the Court will serve the Counterclaim to the claimant together with a **Notice of Acceptance of Counterclaim** (addressed to both parties) (para. 4 sent. 1). If not (and if the 45 days pursuant to para. 1 have not expired in which case para. 5 will apply), CIETAC *is likely* to proceed in a pragmatic way in analogy to Art. 13(3) with due regard to the circumstances and will then give the Respondent a (short) time period to complete the missing formality, in particular if there is only a technical problem with the receipt of the advance payment. As para. 5 permits **leniency** even after expiry of the 45 days, it is likely that CIETAC will react flexibly as described above if the error concerning the formalities of a Counterclaim occurs before the 45 days have elapsed. 6

The deadline for the **Response to the Counterclaim** is **30 days** pursuant to para. 4 sent. 2. This shorter time limit (when compared to the Statement of Defense) makes sense because the situation is different. In contrast to a Respondent being served with a Request for Arbitration, the Claimant is already in an active dispute, so that it can be expected to react faster to the broadening of the subject matter of the dispute. 7

Para. 5 empowers the Arbitral Tribunal to admit a **delayed counterclaim or a Statement of Defense to such a counterclaim**. Like in the case of the Statement of Defense to the initial claim, as covered in Art. 15(3), one will expect that "justified reasons" are necessary (→ Art. 15 mn. 2) to convince the Arbitral Tribunal to exercise its discretion in admitting a delayed counterclaim or a Statement of Defense thereto. 8

A counterclaim is only **admissible** if it is based on the same arbitration agreement that has been invoked by the Claimant; otherwise, the Respondent needs to initiate separate proceedings and seek consolidation.[13] 9

Para. 6 covers the case of **silence** in reaction to a counterclaim. Like in the case of silence to a Request for Arbitration (Art. 15(4)), the arbitral procedure shall continue. 10

Article 17
Amendment to Claim or Counterclaim

[1]The Claimant may apply to amend its claim and the Respondent may apply to amend its counterclaim. [2]However, the arbitral tribunal may refuse any such amendment if it considers that the amendment is too late and may delay the arbitral proceedings.

With the consent of the Arbitral Tribunal, the Claimant or Respondent can **expand** or otherwise change their respective claim or counterclaim. The scope of discretion of the Arbitral Tribunal is broad. In addition to the general principles of arbitration management (such as the procedural duty to respect the principle of good faith in Art. 9), the Arbitral Tribunal will **consider the timing** within the context of the arbitration proceeding. A request to amend claims or counterclaims raised after the first substantive pleading will typically not be accepted.[14] An Arbitral Tribunal will also always have regard to the **six months' time limit** in Art. 51(1) and will want to **minimize the number of extensions** requiring approval by the President of the Arbitral 1

[13] This also applies in case of set-off if such is qualified as a counterclaim; see Yu/Cao, A Guide to the CIETAC Arbitration Rules and Practice, mn. 6.72, 6.76.

[14] Yu/Cao, A Guide to the CIETAC Arbitration Rules and Practice, mn. 6.106.

Court (Art. 51(2)), especially because, until an approval of a request for an extension, there is always a residual risk of enforcement pursuant to Art. 291 PRC Civil Procedure Law and Art. V no. 1(d) NYC: If the arbitration procedure surpasses the six month time limit (or a duly extended time limit, → Art. 51 mn. 2), it will not have been conducted "*in accordance with the agreement of the parties*" which includes the CIETAC Rules containing such time limit.

When **planning** an extension of claim or counterclaim, it can be helpful to bear in mind these kinds of considerations of an Arbitral Tribunal.

2 In case of extensions which are **reasonable under the circumstances** because they serve the solution of the dispute, the Arbitral Tribunal (depending, however, on its composition) is likely to endorse the extension or other change of the claim or counterclaim and prepare a reasoned request addressed to the President of the Arbitration Court in order to obtain an **extension of the total time period for the arbitration**. From the perspective of a foreign chairperson, the assigned CIETAC case manager (Art. 13(4)) can assist in organizing that the President of the Arbitration Court receives the request for an extension of time pursuant to Art. 51(2) in time. In case the Arbitral Tribunal accepts the amendment, the other party must be given reasonable time to raise a respond to the amended (counter-)claim.[15]

Article 18
Joinder of Additional Parties

(1) [1]During the arbitral proceedings, a party wishing to join an additional party to the arbitration may file the Request for Joinder with CIETAC, based on the arbitration agreement invoked in the arbitration that prima facie binds the additional party. [2]Where the Request for Joinder is filed after the formation of the arbitral tribunal, a decision shall be made by CIETAC after the arbitral tribunal hears from all parties including the additional party if the arbitral tribunal considers the joinder necessary.

[3]The date on which the Arbitration Court receives the Request for Joinder shall be deemed to be the date of the commencement of arbitration against the additional party.

(2) [1]The Request for Joinder shall contain the case number of the existing arbitration; the name, address and other means of communication of each of the parties, including the additional party; the arbitration agreement invoked to join the additional party as well as the facts and grounds the request relies upon; and the claim.

[2]The relevant documentary and other evidence on which the request is based shall be attached to the Request for Joinder.

(3) Where any party objects to the arbitration agreement and/or jurisdiction over the arbitration with respect to the joinder proceedings, the decision on jurisdiction shall be made in accordance with Article 6 of these Rules.

(4) After the joinder proceedings commence, the conduct of the arbitral proceedings shall be decided by the Arbitration Court if the arbitral tribunal is not formed, or shall be decided by the arbitral tribunal if it has been formed.

[15] Yu/Cao, A Guide to the CIETAC Arbitration Rules and Practice, mn. 6.108 with reference to *Shenyang Minxiang Technology Co. Ltd. v. Hanyu Information Technology et al.* [2016] Jing 04 Min Te No. 26, the Beijing Fourth Intermediate People's Court, December 22, 2016.

(5) [1]Where the joinder takes place prior to the formation of the arbitral tribunal, the relevant provisions on party's nominating or entrusting of the Chairman of CIETAC to appoint arbitrator under these Rules shall apply to the additional party. [2]The arbitral tribunal shall be formed in accordance with Article 29 of these Rules.

[3]Where the joinder takes place after the formation of the arbitral tribunal, the arbitral tribunal shall hear from the additional party of its comments on the past arbitral proceedings including the formation of the arbitral tribunal. [4]If the additional party requests to nominate or entrust the Chairman of CIETAC to appoint an arbitrator, both parties shall nominate or entrust the Chairman of CIETAC to appoint arbitrators again. [5]The arbitral tribunal shall be formed in accordance with Article 29 of these Rules.

(6) [1]The relevant provisions on the submission of the Statement of Defense and the Statement of Counterclaim under these Rules shall apply to the additional party. [2]The time period for the additional party to submit its Statement of Defense and Statement of Counterclaim shall start counting from the date of its receipt of the Notice of Joinder.

(7) CIETAC shall have the power to decide not to join an additional party where the additional party is prima facie not bound by the arbitration agreement invoked in the arbitration, or where any other circumstance exists that makes the joinder inappropriate.

The provision in Art. 18, added to the CIETAC Rules in 2015, provides a basis for integrating issues of joinder also in CIETAC arbitration clauses ("**arbitration clauses on joinder**" as mentioned in para. 1 → Ch. 2 mn. 11). Depending on whether the application is made prior or after the formation of the arbitral tribunal, **CIETAC** or the **Arbitral Tribunal** decides (Art. 6) about the **Request for Joinder** which is submitted **by a party** of the arbitration proceeding (not: by the possibly intervening party) pursuant to para. 1, to which the other party may oppose (para. 3). 1

According to para. 1 sent. 1, CIETAC can recognize an arbitration agreement that *prima facie* binds the additional party and **admit the Joinder or decline it** on the basis of para. 1 and 7; this set of rules is coherent with the regime in Art. 13 (1)–(3) on CIETAC's competence to find its own competence under an arbitration agreement. If the **Arbitral Tribunal is already formed** (i.e., after communication of the Notice of Formation mentioned in Art. 32(3)), para. 1 requires that (i) all parties including the potential additional party shall first be **heard** by the Arbitral Tribunal and (ii) the Arbitral Tribunal shall issue an **opinion** if it considers the joinder "necessary". To increase the chance of success, a well and clearly drafted **arbitration agreement** is necessary (→ Ch. 2 mn. 11). The **denial** pursuant to para. 7 is already possible when CIETAC finds the joinder to be "**inappropriate**".[16] 2

Para. 2 governs **formalities** including rules on the attachment of documents on which the claim is based; this regime correlates in essence with the requirements set forth in Art. 12(2) and 15(2) for a Request for Arbitration and a Statement of Defense.[17] 3

[16] Where the Arbitral Tribunal finds the joinder unnecessary in the first place, it is not obliged to hear from all parties, *see Brave Fortune Group Ltd v. Huaxing (H.K.) Real Estate Development Co. Ltd* [2018] Jing 04 Min Te No. 119, the Beijing Fourth Intermediate People's Court, as reported in Yu/Cao, A Guide to the CIETAC Arbitration Rules and Practice, mn. 10.31.

[17] The Arbitral Tribunal does not need to consider a Request for Joinder lacking the formal requirements of Art. 18.2, e.g.an oral request or mention in a written submission, see *Yang Jie v. Tianjin Skye Equity Investment Partnership* [2019] Jing 04 Min Te No. 60, Beijing Fourth Intermediate People's Court as reported by Yu/Cao, A Guide to the CIETAC Arbitration Rules and Practice, mn. 10.35.

4 In case of admission of the joinder, the Arbitral Tribunal, acting with the consent of CIETAC, – and prior to its formation with the consent of the Arbitration Court – will render a **Decision on Joinder** pursuant to **para. 4**. Nonetheless, the commencement of arbitration against the additional party is the date when the Request for Joinder is received (para. 1 sent. 3).

5 For a Request for Joinder **prior to the formation** of the Arbitral Tribunal (i.e., the service of the Notice of Formation mentioned in Art. 32(3)), the first subparagraph of para. 5 (= para. 5 sent. 1–2) governs the **formation of the Arbitral Tribunal** and **possible change** to the initial composition of the Arbitral Tribunal. In particular, pursuant to Art. 29(3), the party that stands alone against multiple parties may lose its right to appoint an arbitrator to the Arbitral Tribunal (→ Art. 29 mn. 2). Thereafter, the second subparagraph of para. 5 (= para. 5 sent. 3–4) requires that the parties are being **heard on the issue of composition** of the Arbitral Tribunal.

6 Para. 6 contains in essence a mere **reference** to the rules on the Statement of Defense and the Statement of Counterclaim (Art. 15, 16), whereby the **deadlines for the intervening party** should be calculated as of the receipt of the Notice of Joinder (by analogy to Art. 11).

Article 19
Consolidation of Arbitrations

(1) At the request of a party, CIETAC may consolidate two or more arbitrations pending under these Rules into a single arbitration if:

1. **all of the claims in the arbitrations are made under the same arbitration agreement;**
2. **the claims in the arbitrations are made under the arbitration agreements in multiple contracts that consist of a principle contract and its ancillary contract (s), or involve the same parties as well as legal relationships of the same nature, or involve related subject matters, and the arbitration agreements in such contracts are identical or compatible; [or]**
3. **all the parties to the arbitrations have agreed to the consolidation.**

(2) In deciding whether to consolidate the arbitrations in accordance with the preceding Paragraph 1, CIETAC shall take into account the opinions of all parties and other relevant factors such as the correlation between the arbitrations concerned, including the nomination and appointment of arbitrators in the separate arbitrations.

(3) Unless otherwise agreed by all the parties, the arbitrations shall be consolidated into the arbitration that was first commenced.

(4) After the consolidation of arbitrations, the conduct of the arbitral proceedings shall be decided by the Arbitration Court if the arbitral tribunal is not formed, or shall be decided by the arbitral tribunal if it has been formed.

1 Art. 19 (which was added to the CIETAC Rules in 2015) provides a basis for **combining arbitrations** that comply with any of the conditions set forth in para. 1. They relate, *firstly*, to the **same arbitration agreement** (no. 1).

2 They relate, *alternatively*, pursuant to para. 2, to arbitration agreements in **three scenarios**:

1. a **contract package** including **multiple contracts** defined as a principle contract (e.g., a framework contract) and ancillary contracts (repeating the definition in Art. 14(1) no. 1),

2. arbitration agreements between the **same parties** and bound by **legal relationships of the same nature** (example: many parallel orders with a CIETAC arbitration clause, while the framework contract, which the parties intended to conclude, was never properly concluded), or
3. contracts involving **related subject matters** (example from practice: a license and distribution agreement with multiple orders).

In addition to any of the three alternative conditions, the contracts need to contain **comparable or even identical claims.** The third case group was added by the 2024 CIETAC Rules and is welcomed to have, as demonstrated by the example from practice above. 3

Or, *thirdly*, all parties **solicit their consolidation** (no. 3). 4

Pursuant to para. 2, CIETAC takes the **decision** on the consolidation with due regard to all relevant circumstances. Subject to a deviating party agreement, CIETAC will consolidate the arbitration into the arbitration that was first commenced (para. 3). Thereafter, the Arbitral Tribunal manages the further proceedings (and, before its formation, the Arbitration Court) (para. 4). With this set of rules, CIETAC has regulated a modern[18] and internationally much debated topic in an adequate way and with due regard to the practical consideration. 5

Article 20
Submission and Exchange of Arbitration Documents

(1) All arbitration documents from the parties shall be submitted to the Arbitration Court.

(2) All arbitration documents to be exchanged during the arbitral proceedings shall be exchanged among the arbitral tribunal and the parties by the Arbitration Court unless otherwise agreed by the parties and with the consent of the arbitral tribunal or otherwise decided by the arbitral tribunal.

Art. 20 regulates practical questions of communication. Pursuant to the **basic rule** in **para. 1**, all written communication between the parties and from the parties to the Arbitral Tribunal shall be routed **via the Arbitration Court** of CIETAC. 1

Para. 2, added to the CIETAC Rules in 2015, provides by way of **two exceptions**: (i) that the parties may provide otherwise with the consent of the Arbitral Tribunal and (ii) the Arbitral Tribunal may decide otherwise. Thus, it has become possible to provide in a **procedural order** (with or without agreement of the parties) that a **deadline** shall be deemed to be **met** by submission of briefs in time with the Arbitral Tribunal (even upfront by email without attachment of briefs at that point in time, subject to meeting applicable standards of mandatory data protection law, especially if the Arbitral Tribunal operates out of the European Union). Art. 20 thereby grants a degree of **freedom** for the management of the arbitration proceeding by the Arbitral Tribunal which is in line with international arbitration practice. 2

CIETAC shall nonetheless receive a **copy** of the briefs, because a flexible mode of transmission is independent from the required number of copies (Art. 21). 3

[18] Cf., e.g., Art. 10 ICC Arbitration Rules 2021.

Article 21
Means of Submission and Copies of Arbitration Documents

(1) When submitting the Request for Arbitration, the Statement of Defense, the Statement of Counterclaim, evidence, and other arbitration documents, the parties may use electronic communication as a preferred means.

(2) [1]Where parties submit arbitration documents by electronic means, identical hard copies may be required if the Arbitration Court or the arbitral tribunal deems it necessary. [2]Where the electronic version is not identical with the hard copies, the electronic version shall prevail; unless otherwise agreed by the parties.

(3) [1]Where parties make their submissions in hard copies, such submissions shall be in quintuplicate. [2]Where there are multiple parties, additional copies shall be provided accordingly. [3]Where the party applies for conservatory measures, additional copies shall be provided accordingly. [4]Where the arbitral tribunal is composed of a sole arbitrator, the number of copies submitted may be reduced by two.

1 Art. 21 contains detailed, yet self-explanatory rules on the number of briefs and documents to be submitted. As part of the digitalization effort of the 2024 CIETAC Rules (Art. 8), para. 2 now provides rules in case the parties use **electronic communication** as their preferred means.

2 In practice, CIETAC accepts rules on service set forth in a **Procedural Order** of the Arbitral Tribunal which declare timely service of briefs by email (to the arbitrators with a copy to the CIETAC case manager (Art. 13(4)) without attachment of the annexes at that point in time as sufficient as long as all necessary copies are circulated thereafter with due regard to the requirements in Art. 20.

3 If the Arbitral Tribunal operates out of the Member States of the European Union, it should ensure compliance with the mandatory **data protection law** in the GDPR. From an arbitrator's perspective, it is advised to raise the requirements of mandatory data protection law early on in the case management. If the briefs or documents to be filed are likely to contain personal data which would need to be deleted or left out in the electronic submission under applicable data protection law, the parties should be invited to agree, in line with the last half-sentence of para. 2 sent. 2, that the hard copies shall prevail over conflicting electronic versions in order to comply with the relevant law. If the arbitrator issues a procedural order in this regard in an international arbitration proceeding, without prior agreement of the parties, CIETAC is likely to respect such order as a matter of practice.

Article 22
Representation

(1) [1]A party may be represented by its authorized Chinese and/or foreign representative(s) in handling matters relating to the arbitration. [2]In such a case, a Power of Attorney shall be submitted to the Arbitration Court by the party or its authorized representative(s), and the Arbitration Court shall forward such Power of Attorney to the other parties and the arbitral tribunal.

(2) If a party changes or adds representative(s) after the arbitral tribunal is formed, the President of the Arbitration Court may take necessary measures to prevent the occurrence of conflicts of interest on the arbitrator(s) as a result of the

change including exclusion of the new representative(s) from participating in the arbitral proceedings, having regard to factors such as the parties' opinions made within a reasonable time on the challenge of arbitrator(s) and the progress of the arbitral tribunal's hearing of the case.

Art. 29 PRC Arbitration Law[19] enshrines the right to appoint "**lawyers or other agents**" for an arbitration proceeding. Pursuant to **Art. 22**, the parties are free to appoint a Chinese or a foreign attorney. In practice, foreign related and international CIETAC arbitrations are also handled by mixed teams from several nations. 1

For **foreign lawyers** it must be noted that Chinese regulations contain the **restriction** that they may not advise on Chinese law.[20] To the extent that **Chinese law** is applicable, of relevance and/or to be interpreted (e.g., for issues which go beyond the applicable contract law in the arbitration; → Ch. 1 mn. 16 et seq.), the parties will have to rely on a co-counsel who is admitted as attorney in law in China or they must work with an expert on Chinese law.[21] These restrictions need to be respected, even in an international arbitration with foreign arbitrators. It may be noted that there will always be Chinese competent persons in the room who will be aware of the restrictions (e.g., the CIETAC case manager and possibly further employees of CIETAC who are all aware of local regulations; Art. 13(4)). 2

According to **para. 1 sent. 2**, the 2024 version of the CIETAC Rules has supplemented an obligation of the Arbitration Court to forward received powers of attorney to the other parties and the Arbitral Tribunal. It is very helpful in practice if this happens in the background. 3

Para. 2 has been added in the 2024 version of the CIETAC Rules and gives The President of the Arbitration Court (Art. 2(2)) the power to intervene where a change in party representation after formation may lead to a conflict of interest on the Arbitral Tribunal. This modern rule is consistent with efforts in other arbitration institutions to ensure the efficient work of the arbitrator(s) after formation.[22] 4

Article 23
Conservatory Measures and Interim Measures

(1) [1]Where a party applies for conservatory measures, CIETAC shall forward the party's application to the competent court designated by that party.

[2]Upon the request of a party, CIETAC may forward its application for conservatory measures to such court in advance of issuing the Notice of Arbitration.

(2) [1]In accordance with the applicable law or the agreement of the parties, a party may apply to the Arbitration Court for emergency relief pursuant to the CIETAC Emergency Arbitrator Procedures (Appendix III). [2]The emergency arbitrator may decide to order or award necessary or appropriate emergency measures. [3]The decision of the emergency arbitrator shall be binding upon both parties.

---

[19] Art. 42 Draft Revised PRC Arbitration Law (2021).

[20] See Art. 15 of the Regulations on the Administration of Foreign Law Firms' Representative offices in China of December 22, 2001 (Order of the PRC State Council No. 338) (which prohibits the activities of foreign lawyers in "affairs on Chinese law") in connection with Art. 32 of the Provisions of the Ministry of Justice on the Execution of the Regulations on the Administration of Foreign Law Firms' Representative Offices in China of July 4, 2002 (which defines "affairs on Chinese law"); Brödermann in FS Elsing, p. 68; Yu/Cao, A Guide to the CIETAC Arbitration Rules and Practice, mn. 6.122–6.123.

[21] Laprès, China Business Review 2009, 46 (48).

[22] Cf. e.g.Art. 17(2) ICC Arbitration Rules 2021.

(3) At the request of a party, the arbitral tribunal may decide to order or award any interim measure it deems necessary or proper in accordance with the applicable law or the agreement of the parties and may require the requesting party to provide appropriate security in connection with the measure.

1 Para. 1 contains the basic principle according to which **applications for injunctive relief** have to be forwarded to the courts as a matter of principle in arbitration proceedings in China that are governed by the laws of the People's Republic of China.

2 Para. 2 now contains regulations on **emergency arbitrators**. However, these regulations do not apply to arbitration proceedings seated in the People's Republic of China, since the PRC Arbitration Law stipulates that the Chinese courts are responsible for injunctive relief (see Art. 28 PRC Arbitration Law, however, only for measures taken after the arbitral award has been passed, as well as Art. 103, Art. 104 and Art. 289 PRC Civil Procedure Law).[23]

3 Due to this situation, there are also very few cases of emergency arbitrator cases in China. SIAC had in September 2019 initiated a case of emergency arbitrator proceedings in Shanghai. In that case, the parties, both of whom were natural persons from Taiwan, had a dispute over the transfer of an equity interest in an enterprise registered in Hong Kong, and the parties agreed to submit any dispute to arbitration by SIAC and to apply the laws of the Hong Kong SAR. At the same time as filing the arbitration with SIAC, the claimant submitted an application for interim measures and requested the appointment of an emergency arbitrator to freeze the disputed shareholding in the Hong Kong enterprise. After organizing a hearing and reviewing the case, the Emergency Arbitrator issued a Decision of the Emergency Arbitrator to freeze the disputed shareholding in the Hong Kong enterprise in accordance with Article 22 B(2) of the Arbitration Ordinance (Chapter 609 of the Laws of Hong Kong) and the Arbitration Rules of the arbitration, which was ultimately endorsed by the High Court of Hong Kong. Apart from that, there appears at present to be no case of enforcing the Emergency Arbitrator's Decision in Mainland China.

Section II
Arbitrators and the Arbitral Tribunal

Article 24
Duties of Arbitrator

(1) An arbitrator shall not represent either party, and shall be and remain impartial and independent of the parties and treat them equally.

(2) Upon acceptance of appointment/nomination, the arbitrator shall perform his/her duties in accordance with these Rules and carry out the arbitral proceedings diligently and efficiently.

1 Art. 24 emphasizes **three duties**, which from an international arbitration perspective are inherent to the position of an arbitrator:[24] (i) the obligation and the commitment to **impartiality and independence** (as set forth already in Art. 8 PRC

---

[23] Also → Annex 3 regulations on emergency arbitrators.

[24] Art. 11(1) ICC Arbitration Rules, Art. 9.1 DIS Arbitration Rules; cf. also Art. 12(1) UNCITRAL Arbitration Rules.

Arbitration Law[25] and also emphasized since 2015 in Art. 49 (1)), (ii) the **obligation to treat the parties equally**, and (iii) the obligation to carry out the arbitral proceedings with **diligence and efficiency** in accordance with the CIETAC Rules in para. 2 which has been added in 2024. Further obligations are summarized in the **CIETAC Code of Conduct for Arbitrators**[26] and in the **CIETAC Rules for Evaluating the Behavior of Arbitrators.**[27]

In the PRC Arbitration Law, the obligation to act independently and to remain 2
independent roots not only in **Art. 8 PRC Arbitration Law** ("free from interference of administrative organs, social organisations or individuals"). It is also inherent to **Art. 34 PRC Arbitration Law**, which provides for the possibility to apply (in CIETAC arbitrations by an application to CIETAC) for a **withdrawal of an arbitrator** from an arbitration under any of the following circumstances: (i) if the arbitrator is a **party** to the case or a **relative of the parties or their attorneys** (no. 1) **or** has **other relations** with the parties or their attorneys involved in the case that might affect the fair ruling of the case (no. 3); (ii) if the arbitrator has vital **personal interests** in the case (no. 2); or (iii) if the arbitrator **meets the parties** concerned **or their attorneys in private** or has **accepted gifts** or **attended banquets hosted by the parties concerned or their attorneys** (no. 4). This latter provision is part of China's fight against corruption. In practice, it requires caution in case of contacts, which, from a European perspective, may be socially adequate. In an international CIETAC arbitration, this rule may require from the arbitrators not to accept certain invitations expressed at the occasion of large international legal events (e.g., the annual meeting of the International Bar Association), such as an invitation to a reception of a large law firm which is representing one of the parties.

Pursuant to Art. 35 PRC Arbitration Law, the **withdrawal** shall be requested **before** 3
the first hearing (with an exception in case of later knowledge). The Chairman of CIETAC shall decide over the application (Art. 36 PRC Arbitration Law, unless he himself is concerned).

According to Art. 37 PRC Arbitration Law, a **replacing arbitrator** shall be selected or 4
appointed and the Arbitral Tribunal shall decide about whether to have a "re-start" of the arbitration procedure. Pursuant to Art. 38 PRC Arbitration Law, severe cases of no. 4 shall further be prosecuted otherwise, as well as active or passive corruption or "perversion of the law" under Art. 58 no. 6 PRC Arbitration Law; the arbitrator shall be removed from the panel of arbitrators (Art. 38 PRC Arbitration Law, last alternative).

Article 25
Number of Arbitrators

(1) The arbitral tribunal shall be composed of one or three arbitrators.

(2) Unless otherwise agreed by the parties or provided by these Rules, the arbitral tribunal shall be composed of three arbitrators.

Para. 1 repeats the provision in Art. 30 sent. 1 PRC Arbitration Law, according to 1
which Arbitral Tribunals can be composed of a sole arbitrator or a decision body of **three arbitrators**. The latter alternative is the rule pursuant to para. 2. A **deviating**

[25] Expected to remain unchanged also in the future (with regard to the Draft Revised PRC Arbitration Law (2021)).

[26] Dated April 6, 1993, amended on April 27, 2021, available at http://www.cietac.org/.

[27] Available at http://www.cietac.org/.

party agreement in favor of a sole arbitrator will be implemented according to the provision in Art. 28.

2 In ordinary Chinese domestic arbitration procedure there exist no cost incentives to agree on a sole arbitrator because the **arbitrator fees** are part of the lump sum costs. This is different if the parties are prepared to pay hourly rates to the arbitrator(s) in order to secure a higher level of choice of arbitrators, including arbitrators from outside the CIETAC List of Arbitrators (Art. 26(2)). Then, of course, it makes a difference to pay one arbitrator or three arbitrators.

To reduce arbitration costs, it is quite common in international practice to agree on one arbitrator for disputes up to a certain threshold and on three arbitrators as of that threshold. Para. 2 suggests that such agreement would be recognized by CIETAC

Article 26
Nomination or Appointment of Arbitrator

(1) [1]CIETAC maintains a Panel of Arbitrators which uniformly applies to itself and all its sub-commissions/arbitration centers. [2]The parties shall nominate arbitrators from the Panel of Arbitrators provided by CIETAC.

(2) Where the parties have agreed to nominate arbitrators from outside CIETAC's Panel of Arbitrators, an arbitrator so nominated by the parties or nominated according to the agreement of the parties may act as arbitrator subject to the confirmation by the Chairman of CIETAC.

(3) The arbitral tribunal shall be formed in accordance with these Rules, unless otherwise agreed by the parties.

(4) If the procedure of forming the arbitral tribunal agreed by the parties is manifestly unfair or unjust, or if a party abuses its rights in a way that results in undue delay of the arbitral proceedings, the Chairman of CIETAC may determine the procedure of formation of the arbitral tribunal or appoint any member of the arbitral tribunal.

1 Para. 1 emphasizes the importance of the **Panel of Arbitrators**. Pursuant to para. 1 sent. 1, CIETAC maintains such a list for all of its arbitration centers (→ Art. 2 mn. 1). CIETAC updates the list every three years. It mentions jurists which, pursuant to the assessment of CIETAC, are apt to conduct CIETAC arbitrations. As per January 1, 2024, it mentions 1016 Chinese and 409 foreign arbitrators.[28] Para. 1 sent. 2 indicates that usually arbitrators will be appointed from that panel list.

2 As an alternative, para. 2 provides for the possibility **to agree** (→ Ch. 2 mn. 6 et seq.) on **arbitrators** who are **not listed on the CIETAC panel**. The only condition for their appointment is the **confirmation** by **the Chairman of CIETAC**. Usually, CIETAC will request a *curriculum vitae* from the proposed arbitrator and take an autonomous decision. The Chairman of CIETAC is likely to accept the proposed arbitrator if he does not see an obstacle. Hints from the opposing party which raise doubts about the independence of the arbitrator candidate from a Chinese perspective (e.g., references to private meetings between the arbitrator candidate and the party representative which, from a European perspective, may be assessed as "socially adequate") may cause the

[28] See http://www.cietac.org.

Chairman of CIETAC to refuse confirmation without further ado, probably with regard to Art. 34 no. 4 PRC Arbitration Law; → Art. 24 mn. 2).

3 Like in any other arbitration, the **composition of the Arbitral Tribunal** is of **prime importance**: Arbitration awards of CIETAC are binding (Art. 49(9)); there is principally no appeal or recourse to a state court (except to avoid execution in case of a violation of the arbitration rules and/or the arbitration agreement). Art. 70–71 PRC Arbitration Law read in conjunction with currently Art. 291(1) PRC Civil Procedure Law[29]). The rules on setting aside and enforcement of foreign-related arbitrations are expected to change under the Draft Revised PRC Arbitration Law (2021); Art. 70–71 on setting aside and enforcement of foreign-related arbitrations will be deleted, subjecting them to the same provisions as chinese arbitrations: Art. 77 Draft Revised PRC Arbitration Law (2021) provides a unitary standard for setting aside proceedings, extending the grounds formally listed in Art. 58 PRC Arbitration Law. Art. 82 Draft Revised PRC Arbitration Law (2021) provides that enforcement shall be rejected where it is contrary to social and public interest. Whether these changes will come into force needs to be seen.

4 The **choice of the presiding arbitrator** (referred to in China often as the "**Chairman**") is particularly important. His or her decision is decisive pursuant to **Art. 49(6) sent. 1**, as long as the two party appointed arbitrators[30] do not unite themselves against the Chairman, which is a very rare exception in practice. As a party of European origin or its counsel, one may have an interest in "**sensed neutrality**".[31]

To obtain such sensed neutrality (e.g., a Chair from a neutral jurisdiction) in the context of agreeing on a CIETAC arbitration clause, one is well advised to provide for **supplements to the standard CIETAC arbitration clause** on the composition and the qualification of the Arbitral Tribunal (→ Ch. 2 mn. 7). Otherwise there is a high probability that, e.g., in a Chinese-German arbitration, a Chinese arbitrator and not an arbitrator of a neutral jurisdiction will be appointed as a Chairman because CIETAC is located in China and the venue of the arbitration is usually in China (over the last 20 years, many Chinese lawyers have received excellent comparative legal education and are well qualified to arbitrate cross-border cases).

5 In taking its decision, the Chairman of CIETAC receives guidance from **Art. 30** but is otherwise **free** in its assessment unless the arbitration clause provides for more concrete guidance. Such clause might also consider the need to circumvent the short time limits in Art. 27. In contrast, the constitution of an Arbitral Tribunal on the basis of an agreement which deviates from the CIETAC standard clause can take **substantially more time** if it contains requirements which are difficult to meet (e.g., up to ten months).

6 According to **para. 3**, added in 2024, the CIETAC Rules provide, first of all, the default procedure for the formation of the Arbitral Tribunal (Art. 27). Second, by providing the default rules, the CIETAC Rules 2024 explicitly recognize the possibility for the parties to choose their own rules on nomination and appointment of arbitrators. Parties wishing to deviate by amending the standard arbitration clause (→ Ch. 2 mn. 7) are advised to provide for a fair system and consider the new **para. 4** which gives the Chairman of CIETAC the power to intervene in case the agreement is manifestly unfair, or if one party abuses its rights thereunder.

---

[29] This replaces the outdated Art. 258 2007 PRC Civil Procedure Law (→ Ch. 1 mn. 18) which is still mentioned in Art. 70–71 PRC Arbitration Law (the reference to Art. 281 PRC Civil Procedure Law will change to Art. 291 when the new PRC Civil Procedure Law comes into force).

[30] Appointed each by one or several parties, see Art. 27(1) and 29(1).

[31] See Beneyto/Brödermann/Meyer/Zhao, RIW 2011, 12 (15–16).

Article 27
Three-Arbitrator Tribunal

(1) Within fifteen (15) days from the date of receipt of the Notice of Arbitration, the Claimant and the Respondent shall each nominate, or entrust the Chairman of CIETAC to appoint, an arbitrator, failing which the arbitrator shall be appointed by the Chairman of CIETAC.

(2) Within fifteen (15) days from the date of the Respondent's receipt of the Notice of Arbitration, the parties shall jointly nominate, or entrust the Chairman of CIETAC to appoint, the third arbitrator, who shall act as the presiding arbitrator.

(3) [1]The Claimant and the Respondent may agree that the arbitrators they each nominate shall jointly nominate the presiding arbitrator, and the two arbitrators so nominated shall jointly nominate, or entrust the Chairman of CIETAC to appoint the presiding arbitrator within seven (7) days from the date of their acceptance of the nomination. [2]Failing such joint nomination or entrustment within the above time limit, the presiding arbitrator shall be appointed by the Chairman of CIETAC.

(4) [1]The parties may each recommend one to five arbitrators as candidates for the presiding arbitrator and shall each submit a list of recommended candidates within the time period specified in the preceding Paragraph 2. [2]Where there is only one common candidate on the lists, such candidate shall be the presiding arbitrator jointly nominated by the parties. [3]Where there is more than one common candidate on the lists, the Chairman of CIETAC shall choose the presiding arbitrator from among the common candidates having regard to the circumstances of the case, and he/she shall act as the presiding arbitrator jointly nominated by the parties. [4]Where there is no common candidate on the lists, the presiding arbitrator shall be appointed by the Chairman of CIETAC from outside the lists.

(5) [1]In accordance with the parties' agreement or upon the parties' joint requests, the Chairman of CIETAC may provide a list of three candidates for the parties to nominate the presiding arbitrator within seven (7) days upon receipt of such list.

[2]In such case, unless otherwise agreed by the parties, the presiding arbitrator shall be appointed/nominated in the following manner:

1. **Each party may exclude one or more candidates to whom it objects and submit the list of remaining candidates to the Arbitration Court.**
2. **[1]Where there is only one common candidate on the lists of remaining candidates submitted by the parties, such candidate shall be the presiding arbitrator jointly nominated by the parties. [2]Where there is more than one common candidate on the lists, the Chairman of CIETAC shall choose the presiding arbitrator from among the common candidates having regard to the circumstances of the case, and he/she shall act as the presiding arbitrator jointly nominated by the parties. [3]Where there is no common candidate on the lists, the presiding arbitrator shall be appointed by the Chairman of CIETAC from outside the lists.**

(6) Where the parties have failed to jointly nominate the presiding arbitrator according to the above provisions, the presiding arbitrator shall be appointed by the Chairman of CIETAC.[32]

---

[32] Art. 27(6) appears in the version published by CCPIT on September 5, 2023, but not in the version published by CIETAC on its website. CCPIT is the Chinese organisation in charge of CIETAC, the authors assume therefore that the CCPIT version should be the governing version.

Art. 27 provides for a system of appointment of arbitrators which allocates a **central position to the Chairman** of the arbitral institution, i.e., CIETAC, but it has been substially amended in 2024 to give the parties more influence on the nomination of the presiding arbitrator. As to the details: 1

A. The importance of the first 15 days (including special seven-day periods)

As of the **receipt of the Notice of Arbitration** pursuant to Art. 13(2) sent. 1 (→ Art. 13 mn. 2), para. 1 sent. 1 provides **for both parties** a **15-day period** to nominate a party appointed arbitrator or to entrust the choice to the Chairman of CIETAC. If the **deadline** is not met, pursuant to para. 1 last half sentence (which mirrors Art. 32 PRC Arbitration Law[33]), it is also the Chairman of CIETAC who will act and appoint an arbitrator for the defaulting party. In practice, time zone differences, the need to liaise with the client and possibly also its Asian or, e.g., US mother company as well as different bank holidays can become a challenge for meeting the short deadline from an intercontinental European perspective. However, the parties may request for an **extension** of that short time period which will usually be granted.[34] 2

During the same time period, pursuant to para. 2 **parties** shall agree on **a presiding arbitrator**[35] or to entrust the Chairman of CIETAC to make the selection. The parties may agree on **three different procedures** set forth in para. 3 (added in 2024), para. 4 (formerly para. 3) and para. 5 (added in 2024). 3

Under para. 3, the parties may agree (i) that their **party appointed arbitrators jointly nominate** (thereby the party appointed arbitrators operate quasi as a filter in the process of selection of the presiding arbitrator) or (ii) **entrust the Chairman of CIETAC to nominate** the presiding arbitrator within a short period of **seven days** from the date of their acceptance of nomination; (iii) **failing to do so** within the time limit, the Chairman of CIETAC will appoint the presiding arbitrator. This newly added mechanism is in line with international practice. 4

As the presiding arbitrator has a particularly important role in a CIETAC procedure (Art. 49(6) sent. 1), it is worth from the perspective of a continental European party – often obliged to accept arbitration in far distant China (→ Ch. 1 mn. 1 et seq.) – to insist on an **amendment of the standard arbitration clause** (possibly combined with a provision on the origin or qualification of the presiding arbitrator; → Ch. 2 mn. 7).

The addition of para. 3 ratifies a previous practice. Even before the introduction of para. 3, CIETAC has honored agreements of the parties by which the **co-arbitrators were asked to select the presiding arbitrator** (subject to the confirmation by the Chairman of CIETAC pursuant to Art. 26(2) if the presiding arbitrator is not listed on the CIETAC panel).[36] This approach costs time, but it avoids that the decision is made entirely by a third party (while, in case of a choice made by party appointed co-arbitrators, each party has actively chosen at least one of the brains making the decision). 5

---

[33] Art. 51 Draft Revised PRC Arbitration Law (2021), now stipulating that the arbitration institution shall make the appointment.

[34] Assessment of Yu/Cao, A Guide to the CIETAC Arbitration Rules and Practice, mn. 7.54.

[35] See also Art. 30 sent. 2 PRC Arbitration Law, Art. 50(1) sent. 2 Draft Revised PRC Arbitration Law (2021).

[36] Such agreements are valid pursuant to Art. 4(3) CIETAC Rules as Art. 31 PRC Arbitration Law is not binding; see Yu/Cao, A Guide to the CIETAC Arbitration Rules and Practice, mn. 7.52.

6 The detailed (and self-explanatory) procedure set forth in para. 4 – with each party submitting up to five proposals on a **list of recommended candidates** – will rarely function in Chinese-European (or other intercontinental) disputes. In view of the great distance between the parties or their lawyers, the different study and working backgrounds of the lawyers representing the parties and the cultural diversity which tend to become more visible in case of dispute (→ Ch. 1 mn. 3 et seq.), it is unlikely that the parties will find consent in such a short time period. In such a case, without an explicit and communicated agreement of the parties on a deviating procedure such as the one in para. 3, the presiding arbitrator will be determined by the Chairman of CIETAC from outside the list of candidates (para. 4). A non-Chinese party may not feel comfortable with such a solution, especially as there is no obligation that the presiding arbitrator comes from a neutral jurisdiction.

7 As a third possible mechanism, **para. 5** allows the parties to request a **list of three recommended candidates** from which the parties shall choose the presiding arbitrator within **seven days**, whereas the Chairman of CIETAC will, as under the mechanism in para. 4, choose the presiding arbitrator where there is no or more than one common candidate. If no common candidate emerges, **para. 6** applies.

8 In summary, despite the opening to party autonomy in para. 3, the entire provision including the short deadlines still **reflects the Chinese *"top down" approach*** of (administrated) arbitration (→ Ch. 1 mn. 12) and deviates from the European/American approach to arbitration.[37] The possibilities of the parties to influence the process are somewhat limited from a continental European perspective, especially if there is no good understanding between the lawyers representing the opposing parties.

9 In the process applied by CIETAC for the determination of the presiding arbitrator (which reflects the legal requirements in the PRC Arbitration Law[38]), the co-arbitrators are not yet officially appointed when the choice of the presiding arbitrator needs to be made. In case of an international dispute (or a national Chinese dispute in which the legal department of the European mother company of one of the involved Chinese entities wants to take the decisions), the Chinese approach **reduces the chances to find an agreement** on the selection of the presiding arbitrator within the short time frame. The Chinese CIETAC approach in Art. 27 is understandable in the context of a nation with approx. 1.5 billion people and the huge volume of arbitration procedures to administer (→ Ch. 1 mn. 21); from the perspective of a European mother company needing to supervise the activities of a subsidiary in one of the world's most important markets, the approach may not be perceived as the most adequate.

B. The time thereafter

10 Unless the arbitration agreement explicitly states otherwise by changing the CIETAC standard arbitration clause (which is possible by agreement of the parties even after the dispute occurs within the 15-day period of para. 1), the Chairman of CIETAC will determine the presiding arbitrator pursuant to para. 6 once the 15-day period in para. 2 has elapsed. The provision in para. 6 correlates with Art. 32 PRC Arbitration Law.

---

[37] Art. 12(5) ICC Arbitration Rules (30 days); Art. 12.2 DIS Arbitration Rules (21 days).
[38] See also already in Art. 30–32 PRC Arbitration Law.

Article 28
Sole-Arbitrator Tribunal

Where the arbitral tribunal is composed of one arbitrator, the sole arbitrator shall be nominated pursuant to the procedures stipulated in Paragraphs 2, 4, 5 and 6 of Article 27 of these Rules.

In case the arbitration agreement provides for a sole arbitrator (i.e. the exception; Art. 25(2)), Art. 28 refers to the rules on the selection of the presiding arbitrator in case of a three-arbitrator-tribunal, which entails the strong position of the Chairman of CIETAC: including (i) the possibility to delegate the decision to him (Art. 27(2)); (ii) limited chances of a *matching* of the parties' proposals of a sole arbitrator in case of a single chance to compare up to five proposals with subsequent appointment by the Chairman of CIETAC; (iii) right and obligation to appoint the sole arbitrator after the short 15-days period has expired (Art. 27(4) in conjunction with (2)). The comments made on the amendment of the standard CIETAC arbitration clause in the context of Art. 27 (→ Art. 27 mn. 4) apply by analogy. 1

Article 29
Multiple-Party Tribunal

(1) Where there are two or more Claimants and/or Respondents in an arbitration case, the Claimant side and/or the Respondent side, following discussion, shall each jointly nominate or jointly entrust the Chairman of CIETAC to appoint one arbitrator.

(2) [1]The presiding arbitrator or the sole arbitrator shall be nominated in accordance with the procedures stipulated in Paragraphs 2, 4, 5 and 6 of Article 27 of these Rules. [2]When making such nomination pursuant to Article 27 of these Rules, the Claimant side and/or the Respondent side, following discussion, shall each submit a list of their jointly agreed candidates.

(3) Where either the Claimant side or the Respondent side fails to jointly nominate or jointly entrust the Chairman of CIETAC to appoint one arbitrator within fifteen (15) days from the date of its receipt of the Notice of Arbitration, the Chairman of CIETAC shall appoint all three members of the arbitral tribunal and designate one of them to act as the presiding arbitrator.

Regarding **multi party arbitration**, Art. 29 modifies the procedure for the appointment of a party-appointed arbitrator, a chairperson or a sole arbitrator pursuant to Art. 27(2) to (4) by requiring that the side with multiple parties shall reach an agreement on a **joint execution of its rights** (including more concretely the right to appoint an arbitrator (para. 1) or to submit a joint proposal of candidates (para. 2 in conjunction with Art. 27(3)). 1

With its revision of para. 3 in 2015,[39] CIETAC has followed an **international trend**[40] on how to regulate multi party arbitration: In case the two sides do not reach an 2

---

[39] Originally introduced as Art. 27(3) in 2012, now contained in Art. 29(3) with minor changes regarding the wording; see Yu/Cao, A Guide to the CIETAC Arbitration Rules and Practice, mn. 7.71.

[40] Cf. e.g. Art. 12(8) ICC Arbitration Rules; Art. 20.3 and 20.4 DIS Arbitration Rules.

agreement within the short **15-day period** (which is also contained in Art. 27(1) sent. 1), **CIETAC will determine** all three arbitrators (a three-arbitrator panel being provided by the default rule in Art. 25(2)). The competence lies with the **Chairman of CIETAC**. If more than one party acts on the other side (e.g., for internal reasons of a group of companies), the risk increases that CIETAC decides alone on the composition of the Arbitral Tribunal. The party which faces alone multiple parties thereby bears an organizational risk and a risk that the other side will not reach agreement. Under such circumstances, it is even more important that the arbitration clause contains clear conditions with respect to the qualification and/or nationality of the arbitrators (→ Ch. 2 mn. 7).

Article 30
Considerations in Appointing Arbitrators

When appointing arbitrators pursuant to these Rules, the Chairman of CIETAC shall take into consideration the law applicable to the dispute, the place of arbitration, the language of arbitration, the nationalities of the parties, the type of dispute, and any other factor(s) the Chairman considers relevant.

1 Introduced in 2015, Art. 30 provides an open list of criteria to be used by the Chairman of CIETAC in making its decision on appointment (Art. 27–29; 33(3)). For example, the reference to "the **nationalities of the parties**" may inspire the Chairman of CIETAC to consider appointing one of the international arbitrators on the CIETAC panel from a neutral jurisdiction if one of the parties is Chinese and the other party is foreign. The consideration of the "**law applicable to the dispute**" is meant to ensure the quality in the application of the law by choosing an arbitrator with training and experience in the applicable law. Considering "**the type of dispute**" may call for candidates with experience in a certain industry or a certain kind of dispute (like post M&A disputes).

2 In case of a conflict between the different factors to consider, the Chairman will have to use its best discretion under the circumstances (e.g., in case of conflict between the search for a neutral arbitrator and the necessity of knowing the applicable law or rules of law, → Art. 52 mn. 8 et seq.). **Other factors** may include experience of arbitrator candidates in cross cultural arbitrations. For foreign-related and international arbitration procedures, this rule provides a **modern and state of the art basis** for an arbitrator selection which is responsive to the circumstances of the case.

Article 31
Disclosure

(1) An arbitrator nominated by the parties or appointed by the Chairman of CIETAC shall sign a Declaration and disclose any facts or circumstances likely to give rise to justifiable doubts as to his/her impartiality or independence.

(2) If facts or circumstances that need to be disclosed arise during the arbitral proceedings, the arbitrator shall promptly disclose such facts or circumstances in writing.

(3) The Declaration and/or the disclosure of the arbitrator shall be submitted to the Arbitration Court to be forwarded to the parties and other members of the arbitral tribunal.

To secure their **independence** (Art. 24 as well as Art. 8 PRC Arbitration Law[41]), in the interest of transparency, and in line with internationally established practice,[42] para. 1 requires that the arbitrators **need to disclose** all facts and circumstances which may "give rise to justifiable doubts as to his/her impartiality or independence". When deciding which facts and circumstances require disclosure, the **criteria of Art. 34 PRC Arbitration Law** (discussed in → Art. 24 mn. 2) as well as the essentially parallel requirements enumerated in Art. 5 of the Code of Conduct and Art. 7 of the Evaluation Rules need to be considered.[43] In practice, CIETAC requires arbitrator candidates to sign a "Declaration of Acceptance and Statement of Independence" with a modern, extensive and state of the art wording. 1

Para. 2 extends the obligation to disclosure facts and circumstances which may give 2 doubts about the arbitrator's **independence** to the time period **during the arbitration**.

Para. 3 provides for an **organizational duty** to submit the declaration via the 3 Arbitration Court (Art. 2(2)) to the parties and other members of the Arbitral Tribunal. **Art. 32–34** govern the consequences if the declaration gives rise to doubt with respect to the independence of the arbitrator.

Article 32
Challenge to Arbitrator

(1) [1]Upon receipt of the Declaration and/or the written disclosure of an arbitrator, a party wishing to challenge the arbitrator on the grounds of the disclosed facts or circumstances shall forward the challenge in writing within ten (10) days from the date of such receipt. [2]If a party fails to file a challenge within the above time period, it may not subsequently challenge the arbitrator on the basis of the matters disclosed by the arbitrator.

(2) A party having justifiable doubts as to the impartiality or independence of an arbitrator may challenge that arbitrator in writing and shall state the facts and reasons on which the challenge is based with supporting evidence.

(3) [1]A party may challenge an arbitrator in writing within fifteen (15) days from the date it receives the Notice of Formation of the Arbitral Tribunal. [2]Where a party becomes aware of a reason for a challenge after such receipt, the party may challenge the arbitrator in writing within fifteen (15) days after such reason has become known to it, but no later than the conclusion of the last oral hearing.

(4) The challenge by one party shall be promptly communicated to the other party, the arbitrator being challenged and the other members of the arbitral tribunal.

(5) [1]Where an arbitrator is challenged by one party and the other party agrees to the challenge, or the arbitrator being challenged voluntarily withdraws from his/her office, such arbitrator shall no longer be a member of the arbitral tribunal. [2]However, in neither case shall it be implied that the reasons for the challenge are sustained.

(6) In circumstances other than those specified in the preceding Paragraph 5, the Chairman of CIETAC shall make a final decision on the challenge with or without stating the reasons.

---

[41] Expected to remain unchanged in the Draft Revised PRC Arbitration Law (2021).

[42] Cf. only the IBA Guidelines on Conflicts of Interest in International Arbitration, Guideline 3, at https://www.ibanet.org/resources (last visited July 19, 2023).

[43] Yu/Cao, A Guide to the CIETAC Arbitration Rules and Practice, mn. 7.81–7.83.

(7) An arbitrator whose challenge has been applied shall continue to serve on the arbitral tribunal until a final decision on the challenge has been made by the Chairman of CIETAC.

1 Para. 1 sent. 1 offers to each party the possibility to **challenge** an arbitrator **without giving any further reason** on the grounds disclosed by the arbitrator within a short time frame of **ten days** from the date of receipt of the facts as circumstances of a notice pursuant to Art. 31(3). Thereafter, the right to challenge on the basis of any disclosed facts is **forfeited** (para. 1 sent. 2). The rule has the same effect as an (implicit) waiver under the IBA Guidelines on Conflicts of Interest in International Arbitration[44].

2 Pursuant to para. 2 – and within a short deadline (para. 3) – each party can also challenge an arbitrator **upon its own initiative**. Such challenge needs to be properly founded. In such a case, the reasons do not follow from the declaration provided by the arbitrator himself. Pursuant to para. 3, the **15-day period** starts with the **receipt** of the **Notice of Formation of the Arbitral Tribunal** (which is mentioned by the CIETAC Rules for the first time here in this context), which also triggers the six-month period for the arbitration procedure as a whole pursuant to Art. 51(1). If the party gains knowledge of the circumstances which can serve as a ground for a challenge **later**, i.e., after the receipt of the Notice of Formation, the challenge needs to be filed within 15 days as of acquisition of such knowledge, "but no later than the conclusion of the last oral hearing".

3 **Para. 4** deals with organizational obligations of **communications**.

4 Pursuant to para. 5 sent. 1, an arbitrator will **no longer be a member** of the Arbitral Tribunal either (i) by consent of the other party to the challenge of the first party, or (ii) if the arbitrator voluntarily **withdraws** from his/her office, **without** this implying a recognition of the reasons (sent. 2)[45]. This may be considered an expression of the goal of living in universal harmony (he *wei gui*: 和为贵; → Ch. 1 mn. 2).

5 If the **challenged arbitrator does not withdraw** on its own initiative pursuant to para. 5, the Chairman of CIETAC will decide pursuant to para. 6 without giving any reason. Until such a decision, the arbitrator is obliged to continue working pursuant to para. 7. The Chairman's decision is final.[46]

Article 33
Replacement of Arbitrator

(1) [1]In the event that an arbitrator is prevented de jure or de facto from fulfilling his/her functions, or fails to fulfill his/her functions in accordance with the requirements of these Rules or within the time period specified in these Rules, the Chairman of CIETAC shall have the power to replace the arbitrator. [2]Such arbitrator may also voluntarily withdraw from his/her office.

(2) The Chairman of CIETAC shall make a final decision on whether or not an arbitrator should be replaced with or without stating the reasons.

(3) [1]In the event that an arbitrator is unable to fulfill his/her functions due to challenge or replacement, a substitute arbitrator shall be nominated or appointed within the reasonable time period specified by the Arbitration Court according to the same procedure that applied to the nomination or appointment of the arbitrator

[44] See IBA Guidelines on Conflicts of Interest in International Arbitration, Guideline 4.
[45] Similar: § 1038(2) German Code of Civil Procedure.
[46] Yu/Cao, A Guide to the CIETAC Arbitration Rules and Practice, mn. 7.102.

being challenged or replaced. [2]If a party fails to nominate or appoint a substitute arbitrator accordingly, the substitute arbitrator shall be appointed by the Chairman of CIETAC.

(4) After the replacement of an arbitrator, the arbitral tribunal shall decide whether and to what extent the previous proceedings in the case shall be repeated.

Para. 1 regulates the replacement of arbitrators with some "**Chinese particularities**": a mixture between a *top-down approach* and the possibility of face saving for the challenged arbitrator (also → Art. 32 mn. 4): (i) On the one hand, the Chairman of CIETAC can **replace** the arbitrator because of non-performance of his or her duties (for any reason whatsoever: factual or legal ones; also in case of a violation of the CIETAC Rules or in case of failure to meet deadlines (*top-down approach*, → Ch. 1 mn. 14). (ii) On the other hand, the arbitrator may also **withdraw upon his own initiative**; this face-saving alternative for the arbitrator serves the goal of acting "in accordance with the principle of universal harmony" (*he wei gui*: 和为贵; → Ch. 1 mn. 4), as also observed in the context of Art. 32(5). 1

Pursuant to para. 2, absent a voluntary withdrawal, the Chairman of CIETAC takes the final decision. The CIETAC Rules do not provide concrete rules on how to determine non-performance of an arbitrator. The criteria of Art. 34 PRC Arbitration Law as discussed at → Art. 24 mn. 2 can provide some guidance but the reference to non-performance within the applicable time limits in para. 1 goes beyond these criteria. According to the wording, any **substantial violation** of a duty might serve as a basis for a replacement of an arbitrator, whereby, due to the impact of a replacement on the arbitration procedure, one may assume that CIETAC will carefully consider the concrete circumstances of the case. Possible grounds for a replacement can be: illness or injury of an arbitrator, imprisonment, issuance of new regulations that prohibit certain persons from acting as arbitrator, violations of the regulations in the CIETAC Code of Conduct for Arbitrators or the CIETAC Rules for Evaluating the Behavior of Arbitrators (Amendment).[47] The CIETAC rules do not require a "reasoned" decision (in practice, according to information received from colleagues, CIETAC does not give reasons). 2

Pursuant to para. 3, the replacement arbitrator will be determined according to the same rules which also apply to the arbitrator whose position has become vacant (Art. 27–29); **CIETAC will set deadlines** (which are again likely to be reasonably short). 3

After the appointment of the replacement arbitrator, the **Arbitral Tribunal will decide if and to what extent** the arbitration procedure needs to be **repeated** (para. 4). 4

Article 34
Continuation of Arbitration by Majority

[1]After the conclusion of the last oral hearing, if an arbitrator on a three-member tribunal is unable to participate in the deliberations and/or to render the award owing to his/her demise or to his/her removal from CIETAC's Panel of Arbitrators, or for any other reason, the other two arbitrators may request the Chairman of CIETAC to replace that arbitrator pursuant to Article 33 of these Rules. [2]After consulting with the parties and upon the approval of the Chairman of CIETAC, the

[47] Yu/Cao, A Guide to the CIETAC Arbitration Rules and Practice, mn. 7.107–7.110. Available under http://www.cietac.org.

other two arbitrators may also continue the arbitral proceedings and make decisions, rulings, or render the award. [3]The Arbitration Court shall notify the parties of the above circumstances.

1 Art. 34 regulates the extreme case that, in an Arbitral Tribunal consisting of three arbitrators, one of them becomes unavailable: due to death, illness or another reason, be it "his/her removal from CIETAC's Panel of Arbitrators". The explicit reference to the latter reason documents (i) the importance of the Panel of Arbitrators as anchored in Art. 13(2), 26(1) sent. 2 and in Art. 38 PRC Arbitration Law (→ Art. 24 mn. 4) and (ii) the strong position of CIETAC which administers that list (→ Ch. 1 mn. 14).

2 The remaining arbitrators may either request the **replacement** of the missing arbitrator (sent. 1) **or continue** the arbitration proceeding and render a decision (sent. 2), provided that (i) they have **consulted** with the parties and (ii) obtained the **consent of the Chairman of CIETAC**. In some circumstances, this latter alternative can be appropriate (e.g., if the taking of evidence took substantial efforts and time and the arbitrators have all been appointed by CIETAC; Art. 29(3)). Pursuant to sentence 3, the Arbitration Court will **inform** the parties, in particular regarding the result. In case of a continuation of the proceeding, the parties will be particularly interested in the result since they would learn about the problem at the latest by the consultation of the Arbitral Tribunal pursuant to sentence 2.

Section III
Hearing

Article 35
Conduct of Hearing

(1) [1]The arbitral tribunal shall examine the case in any way it deems appropriate unless otherwise agreed by the parties. [2]Under all circumstances, the arbitral tribunal shall act impartially and fairly and shall afford a reasonable opportunity to both parties to present their case.

(2) [1]The arbitral tribunal shall hold oral hearings when examining the case. [2]However, the arbitral tribunal may examine the case on the basis of documents only if the parties so agree and the arbitral tribunal consents or the arbitral tribunal deems that oral hearings are unnecessary and the parties so agree.

(3) Unless otherwise agreed by the parties, the arbitral tribunal may adopt an inquisitorial or adversarial approach in hearing the case having regard to the circumstances of the case.

(4) The arbitral tribunal may hold deliberations at any place or in any manner that it considers appropriate.

(5) [1]Unless otherwise agreed by the parties, the arbitral tribunal may, if it considers it necessary, issue procedural orders or question lists, produce terms of reference, or hold pre-hearing conferences, etc. [2]With the authorization of the other members of the arbitral tribunal, the presiding arbitrator may decide on the procedural arrangements for the arbitral proceedings at his/her own discretion.

1 **Subject to overriding party agreement**, Art. 35 grants considerable **freedom** to the Arbitral Tribunal with respect to the conduct of the arbitral proceeding, as long as it respects the principles of fairness and due process (para. 1) which is in line with the

foundations of modern international arbitration law[48] and paramount to the Chinese approach goal to act "in accordance with the principle of universal harmony" (*he wei gui:* 和为贵; → Ch. 1 mn. 4).

2 Pursuant to para. 3, the Arbitral Tribunal has **a choice between an inquisitorial and an adversarial approach**. From a party autonomy driven perspective to arbitration, this may appear at first surprising from a continental European, African or American perspective because the CIETAC rule is so explicit with regard to the existing options. However, for example in essence the German law is not different, as evidenced by Art. 28.2 DIS Arbitration Rules 2018. At least as important as the rule is its application in practice. A Chinese arbitrator with mainly domestic experience is likely to apply the rule differently and less cautiously than an internationally experienced (Chinese or foreign) arbitrator. Again, the freedom of choice for the arbitrator demonstrates that the composition of the Arbitral Tribunal is of fundamental importance for the arbitration (→ Art. 26 mn. 2–3). In domestic CIETAC arbitrations, the **inquisitorial approach appears to be more current**,[49] while, from an international perspective, the focus rather lies on an adversarial approach with limited questioning of the Arbitral Tribunal to key issues.

3 Para. 5 sent. 1 enumerates several **tools for conducting an arbitration**: procedural orders, lists with questions, pre-hearing conferences, preliminary hearings, even the agreement on terms of reference (as known notably from the ICC practice). Usually, a domestic CIETAC arbitration procedure is likely to be quite **streamlined** (e.g., a pre-deliberation of the arbitrators, a relatively short oral hearing (in which the protocol shall be made for the mere documentation for the Arbitral Tribunal and for CIETAC, Art. 40 (2)), as the **establishment of the relevant facts** is the key goal. If, however, the parties do wish an international style arbitration (possibly with a court reporter, Art. 40(3)) and if they express this in the arbitration agreement or indirectly by their choice of arbitrators, **CIETAC** is **flexible**. The competent CIETAC case manager (Art. 13(4)) will support such **international conduct of the arbitration** and merely oversee that the Arbitral Tribunal observes the formalities which are relevant from a CIETAC perspective.

4 Pursuant to para. 5 sent. 2, the co-arbitrators can entrust the **Presiding Arbitrator** with the freedom of **determining the procedural details**. This is not mandatory; by doing so, one relinquishes essential possibilities of a dialogue, which the parties probably wanted, as expressed by their decision for a three-arbitrator-tribunal. An efficient and practically proven compromise (between the solution in para. 5 sent. 2 and "no delegation") consists in empowering the Presiding Arbitrator to issue alone procedural orders decided by the Arbitral Tribunal.

5 Para. 2 sent. 1 requires an **oral hearing**. This rule implements the right of each party "to debate during the process of hearing" in Art. 47 sent. 1 PRC Arbitration Law. However, a **decision on the basis of documents**, without a hearing, is possible when the parties agree (sent. 2; Art. 39 PRC Arbitration Law), but it is rare. At the end of the oral hearing, the parties are entitled to a **final statement** (Art. 47 sent. 2 PRC Arbitration Law). If the Arbitral Tribunal proposes at the end of an oral hearing that the parties comment merely in writing on an additional claim which was accepted under the circumstances due to its close connection with the claim (Art. 17) and only one party objects, an additional oral hearing needs to take place.

6 Para. 4 underlines the freedom of the Arbitral Tribunal to determine the **place** of the hearing; however, practical hurdles can hinder its implementation (→ Ch. 2 mn. 3).

---

[48] See the due process requirement in Art. V(1)(b) NYC.

[49] See already the assessment of the author team in the pre-edition: Stricker-Kellerer/Moser in Schütze, Institutionelle Schiedsgerichtsbarkeit, Art. 29 mn. 4.

Everybody who agrees on a CIETAC arbitration clause should be prepared **to travel to China several times** for the arbitration proceeding. However, the openness to video-conferencing under the 2024 amendment of the CIETAC Arbitration Rules can attenuate the connected risk of travel costs.

7 When deciding on how to conduct proceedings under the CIETAC Rules, the Arbitral Tribunal now has increasing options to rely on **virtual technology** (→ Art. 37 mn. 4 et seq.). For example, the Arbitral Tribunal can order fully virtual or hybrid hearings. This, however, is subject to the consent of all parties involved.[50] Additionally, CIETAC now offers an electronic portal for arbitrators and digital access to file documents (→ Art. 37 mn. 5).[51] In the future, CIETAC may well make this portal also accessible to the parties.

Article 36
Place of Oral Hearing

(1) Where the parties have agreed on the place of an oral hearing, the case shall be heard at that agreed place except in the circumstances stipulated in Paragraph 3 of Article 85 of these Rules.

(2) Unless otherwise agreed by the parties, the place of oral hearings shall be in Beijing for a case administered by the Arbitration Court or at the domicile of the sub-commission/arbitration center administering the case, or if the arbitral tribunal considers it necessary and with the approval of the President of the Arbitration Court, at another location.

1 In accordance with international practice, Art. 36 grants the parties the **right to choose another place** than the seat (or "*venue*") of the arbitration for the oral hearing. Pursuant to para. 1, this freedom is subject to an advance payment of a security for related costs (Art. 82(3)) within the (usually short) deadlines set by CIETAC (often, e.g., one week). In addition, if the agreed place is outside of China, there may be practical issues like the issuance of a visa for the CIETAC case manager (→ Ch. 2 mn. 5) and, if the parties jointly decide to have a hearing outside of China during an on-going arbitration, the necessity for the arbitrators to liaise with CIETAC on such change of the place of the hearing.

2 Pursuant to para. 2, unless otherwise agreed by the parties, the place of the hearing will be **Beijing** (1st alternative) or, as applicable, the **seat of the sub-commission in charge** (2nd alternative), i.e. presently Chengdu, Chongqing, Fuzhou, Hangzhou, Jinan, Nanjing, Shanghai, Shenzhen, Tianjin, Wuhan, Xi'an, Hong Kong, Vancouver, and Vienna (→ Art. 2 mn. 1).

3 For **deviations** from these two alternatives, para. 2 sets forth **two conditions**: (i) the Arbitral Tribunal must consider the choice of another location as "necessary" (i.e., at the place of a construction site to take evidence); (ii) the President of the Arbitration Court needs to approve the change of the place of arbitration.

4 It is not mandatory to actually conduct an **oral hearing** (→ Art. 35 mn. 5).

---

[50] Anecdotally, the author has heard of at least one CIETAC Arbitration where no virtual hearing was conducted due the lack of consent of one party. The Arbitral Tribunal decided that it could not impose a virtual hearing to a party and in its reasoning referenced Chinese jurisprudence on virtual hearings in litigation.

[51] Regarding data protection, CIETAC states that digital access via the electronic portal is safer than normal distribution of documents via email.

Article 37
Notice of Oral Hearing

(1) [1]Where a case is to be examined by way of an oral hearing, the parties shall be notified of the date of the first oral hearing at least twenty (20) days in advance of the oral hearing. [2]A party having justified reasons may request a postponement of the oral hearing. [3]However, the party shall communicate such request in writing to the arbitral tribunal within five (5) days of its receipt of the notice of the oral hearing. [4]The arbitral tribunal shall decide whether or not to postpone the oral hearing.

(2) Where a party has justified reasons for its failure to submit a request for a postponement of the oral hearing in accordance with the preceding Paragraph 1, the arbitral tribunal shall decide whether or not to accept the request.

(3) A notice of a subsequent oral hearing, a notice of a postponed oral hearing, as well as a request for postponement of such an oral hearing, shall not be subject to the time periods specified in the preceding Paragraph 1.

(4) [1]Where a case is to be examined by way of an oral hearing, the parties and their authorized representative(s) shall have the right to participate in the oral hearing. [2]The arbitral tribunal shall decide whether other relevant participants to the arbitration may participate in the oral hearing. [3]Unless otherwise agreed by the parties and the arbitral tribunal, persons other than the participants to the arbitration may not participate in the oral hearing.

(5) After consultation with the parties and taking into consideration of the circumstances of the case, the arbitral tribunal may, at its own discretion, decide to conduct the oral hearing in person, by remote virtual conference, or by other appropriate means of electronic communication.

(6) The Arbitration Court provides oral hearing facilities as well as administrative and logistical support for remote virtual hearings.

Para. 1–3 have been fully revised in 2015 and para. 4–6 were added in 2024. Pursuant 1
to para. 1 sent. 1, the Arbitral Tribunal needs to give **notice** to the parties of the first oral hearing at least **20 days** prior to the hearing. Within **five days** as of receipt of the notice **(para. 1 sent. 3),** the parties may submit a **reasoned request to postpone the hearing** (para. 1 sent. 2). The Arbitral Tribunal will decide about such a request (para. 1 sent. 4). If the **request** is **submitted late**, the Arbitral Tribunal must first decide whether to accept it (para. 2).

With regard to **subsequent** or postponed **hearings**, the short notice and application 2
periods set forth in para. 1 do not apply (**para. 3**).

Para. 4 sent. 1 documents the **rights of the parties** and their **authorized representa-** 3
tives to participate in the oral hearing. From a practical perspective, this clarification – which was added in 2024 – avoids discussions about the right of directors, who represent a party under the applicable company law, to participate. As the directors will often also be a witness in the arbitration, their right under sentence 1 will often impact the management of the arbitration and in particular the **sequence in which witnesses are heard** (it may be necessary to hear them first before they hear what other witnesses are saying). Pursuant to para. 4 sent. 2, the Arbitral Tribunal has discretion to limit the participants of oral hearings to the parties and their authorized representatives (Art. 22), absent a deviating party agreement.

4 Para. 5 now provides the Arbitral Tribunal with the discretion to conduct **remote hearings** virtually while CIETAC provides the necessary support as per para. 6.

5 As with other arbitration institutions during COVID-19, arbitration hearings have increasingly taken place online. CIETAC has issued special rules for online hearings.[52] Further, since January 1, 2019, a CIETAC online case filing system has been put into use to improve the efficiency of the case filing procedures. On January 28, 2020, CIETAC published the "Urgent Notice on Work Arrangements during the Prevention and Control of the COVID-19", encouraging the parties to file their arbitration applications through its online case filing system.

6 In principle, the arbitral tribunal can decide to hold online hearings, even if one party opposes. However, in practice online hearings have not taken place if one party opposes. There is in particular a decision by the Supreme Court of the PRC stating that an online hearing cannot be held if one party does not agree to such hearings. Irrespective of COVID-19, a considerable number of hearings will be conducted online in the future and CIETAC is gearing up to ensure a secure and reliable platform for such online hearings. There remain obstacles for foreign related arbitrations as sometimes CIETAC is not as "international" as it claims, as some features are offered only in Chinese.

Article 38
Confidentiality

(1) [1]Hearings shall be held in camera. [2]Where both parties request an open hearing, the arbitral tribunal shall make a decision.

(2) For cases heard in camera, the parties and their representatives, the arbitrators, the witnesses, the interpreters, the experts consulted by the arbitral tribunal, the appraisers appointed by the arbitral tribunal and other relevant persons shall not disclose to any outsider any substantive or procedural matters relating to the case.

1 Art. 38 is based on a moderate approach to **confidentiality:** (i) In principle, the oral hearing will take place pursuant to para. 1 *in camera*, i.e., behind closed doors. (ii) All participants in the hearing (as enumerated in para. 2) are obliged not to disclose "to any outsider **any substantive or procedural matter** relating to the case".[53] The reference to "other relevant persons" was added with the revision of the CIETAC Rules in 2015. This relates to **case managers** (Art. 13(4)) and **technical support staff** of CIETAC, **court reporters** (Art. 40(3)) or a **Tribunal Secretary** appointed with the consent of the parties (not provided for in the CIETAC Rules but accepted in practice) or a **protocol keeper** (i.e., a "minute keeper" pursuant to Art. 48(2) PRC Arbitration Law[54]). This can also relate to **parties and their organs** participating at the oral hearing; with agreement of the CIETAC Rules, they accept the **obligation of confidentiality** pursuant to the standards of the CIETAC Rules.

2 Para. 1 (sent. 2) provides for the possibility **to agree** on an "open" (i.e., **public**) hearing. In such case, it is still up to the Arbitral Tribunal to decide if it will respect the parties' decision (→ Ch. 1 mn. 14 on the *"top-down" approach*).

[52] CIETAC Guidelines on Proceeding with Arbitration Actively and Properly during the COVID-19 Pandemic issued on April 28, 2020.

[53] The obligation to keep the proceedings confidential also extends to the Arbitral Award. For example, confidentiality prohibits the parties to publish the award on social media (as happened in a CIETAC case the author has anecdotally heard of).

[54] Art. 65 Draft Revised PRC Arbitration Law (2021).

The parties may also agree **to increase** the level of confidentiality, e.g., to not even disclose the existence of an arbitration proceeding.[55] 3

As Chinese law does not respect contracts to the detriment of third parties,[56] such additional duties agreed between the parties do not extend to **CIETAC employees** und the arbitrators (unless they agree to increased confidentiality obligations). 4

Article 39
Default [in Hearing]

(1) [1]If the Claimant fails to appear at an oral hearing without a justifiable reason, or withdraws from an on-going oral hearing without the permission of the arbitral tribunal, the Claimant may be deemed to have withdrawn its application for arbitration. [2]In such a case, if the Respondent has filed a counterclaim, the arbitral tribunal shall proceed with the hearing of the counterclaim and make a default award.

(2) [1]If the Respondent fails to appear at an oral hearing without a justifiable reason, or withdraws from an on-going oral hearing without the permission of the arbitral tribunal, the arbitral tribunal may proceed with the arbitration and make a default award. [2]In such a case, if the Respondent has filed a counterclaim, the Respondent may be deemed to have withdrawn its counterclaim.

Art. 39 provides for a strict and draconic regime for any "**no show" of the Claimant** (para. 1) or **of the Respondent** (para. 2). It correlates with Art. 42 PRC Arbitration Law[57]. **"Without showing sufficient cause"** (to be accepted by the Arbitral Tribunal), the Arbitral Tribunal may consider a party's "no show" as an **implicit declaration of withdrawal** of its claim or counterclaim and decide on the petitions of the other (present) party by **default award** (i.e., in the absence of the defaulting party) with due regard to the facts and the submitted evidence.[58] 1

Article 40
Record of Oral Hearing

(1) [1]The arbitral tribunal may arrange for a written and/or an audio-visual record to be made of an oral hearing. [2]The arbitral tribunal may, if it considers it necessary, take minutes of the oral hearing and request the parties and/or their representatives, witnesses and/or other persons involved to sign and/or affix their seals to the written record or the minutes.

(2) [1]Where the parties and other relevant participants to the arbitration believe there is an omission or error in the written record of their statements, they may apply for correction. [2]Such application shall be kept in the record if denied by the arbitral tribunal.

(3) The written record, the minutes and the audio-visual record of an oral hearing shall be available for use and reference by the arbitral tribunal.

---

[55] Cf. e.g., the model wording in (e) of the ASEAC Arbitration Clause, available at https://www.aseac-arbitration.com/arbitration/model-arbitration-clause/.

[56] Ling, Contract Law in China, mn. 5.056 (p. 258).

[57] Art. 60 Draft Revised PRC Arbitration Law (2021).

[58] Similar, e.g., Art. 26(2) ICC Rules; R-32 AAA Commercial Arbitration; Art. 29(2) ICDR Arbitration Rules; Art. 30(2) ASEAC Arbitration Rules; Art. 30 DIS Arbitration Rules; § 1048 ZPO.

(4) At the request of a party, the Arbitration Court may, having regard to the specific circumstances of the arbitration, decide to engage a stenographer to make a stenographic record of an oral hearing, the cost of which shall be advanced by the parties.

1 Art. 40 grants freedom to the Arbitral Tribunal with regard to the keeping of the **record** which is required **(i)** by Art. 48(1) sent. 1 PRC Arbitration Law[59], **(ii)** under the 2021 Draft Revised PRC Arbitration Law, for national disputes and international disputes.[60] It can choose between various forms (dictation; taking notes; or dictation to a "minute keeper"[61]). The Arbitral Tribunal shall also require – in line with the provision in Art. 48(2) PRC Arbitration Law[62] – that the "people participating in the hearing" **sign the record**.

2 Introduced in 2024, para. 2 gives a right to the parties to **request correction** of the record if something is stated incorrectly or missing (or to record the application for correction if it was not granted) and is thereby in line with Art. 48 sent. 2 PRC Arbitration Law[63]. In the practice of a foreign-related or an international CIETAC arbitration, the case manager (Art. 13(4)) will ensure that the protocol is signed (whereby the draft of the Arbitral Tribunal will have priority over the draft prepared by the case manager, → Art. 13 mn. 4).

3 Introduced in 2015, para. 4 (former para. 3) regulates the use of **court reporters** (which were admitted in practice even before that change). The Arbitral Tribunal can request the parties to deal with certain organizational tasks, such as getting hold of court reporters. It may however be sensible (i) that the Arbitral Tribunal **keeps the record itself**, (ii) admitting the *verbatim* record of the court reporter only for essential parts of the procedure (opening statements, closing statements, questioning of witnesses and experts) and (iii) to attach the *verbatim* record only to the record as an integral annex to the extent that it covers these parts. CIETAC – represented by the CIETAC case manager – also endorses such creative solutions which are covered by para. 1 and by Art. 35(1) sent. 1 (which does not only grant more control of the record to the Arbitral Tribunal but also, if both parties so wish, the possibility to talk "off the (*verbatim*) record" in an appropriate way about possible issues of settlement; Art. 47(5)). Last, but not least, such organization considerably reduces the number of pages of the *verbatim* record to be agreed by the parties as being correct and thereby **contributes to saving costs** (of lawyers reviewing the *verbatim* record).

The review of the record directly at the seat of the arbitration proceeding (e.g., within short deadlines until the next morning or noon) and then signing it at the end of the oral hearing or the next morning (prior to traveling home) avoids lengthy future briefs about the correctness of the *verbatim* protocol prepared by the court reporters (para. 4). The court reporters are often native English speakers who must listen to non-native (e.g., Chinese or European) speakers with different accents participating in the hearing, which can be a reason for substantial errors and needs for correction. Organizing that objections are raised while the international teams involved in an international CIETAC arbitration are still all present at the venue, requires appropriate management of the timetable and may require an additional (short) meeting of the parties on the day after the (last day of the) main hearing.

[59] Art. 65 2021 Draft Revised PRC Arbitration Law (2021).

[60] According to Art. 69 PRC Arbitration Law, which the Draft Revised PRC Arbitration Law (2021) intends to delete, such protocol is not mandatory in foreign-related arbitrations, even though it is advisable already today as a matter of state-of-the-art arbitration procedure.

[61] Art. 48(2) PRC Arbitration Law, Art. 65 Draft Revised PRC Arbitration Law (2021).

[62] Art. 65 sent. 4 Draft Revised PRC Arbitration Law (2021).

[63] Art. 65 sent. 2 Draft Revised PRC Arbitration Law (2021).

Pursuant **to para. 3,** "[t]he written record, the minutes and the audio-visual record" serve only as confidential, internal documents not giving any right to review to the parties or their representative (other than at the drafting stage prior to signing, Art. 48 sent. 2 PRC Arbitration Law)[64]. In practical reality, CIETAC has no objection if the Arbitral Tribunal distributes copies of the signed protocol to the parties and later refers to it in the Arbitral Award (based on practical experience under Art. 51 on Scrutiny). 4

Article 41
Evidence

(1) Each party shall bear the burden of proving the facts on which it relies to support its claim, defense or counterclaim and provide the basis for its opinions, arguments and counter-arguments.

(2) [1]The arbitral tribunal may specify a time period for the parties to produce evidence and the parties shall produce evidence within the specified time period. [2]The arbitral tribunal may refuse to admit any evidence produced after that time period. [3]If a party experiences difficulties in producing evidence within the specified time period, it may apply for an extension before the end of the period. [4]The arbitral tribunal shall decide whether or not to extend the time period.

(3) If a party bearing the burden of proof fails to produce evidence within the specified time period, or if the produced evidence is not sufficient to support its claim or counterclaim, it shall bear the consequences thereof.

(4) [1]Unless otherwise agreed by the parties,. the arbitral tribunal may decide to apply in whole or in part the CIETAC Guidelines on Evidence ("Guidelines on Evidence") to hear the case. [2]However, the Guidelines on Evidence do not constitute an integral part of these Rules.

Art. 41 provides details with regard to the principle in Art. 43 PRC Arbitration Law[65] according to which, like under German and many other laws, **each party shall produce evidence** for the facts underlying its position. 1

The rule on **burden of proof** in para. 1 mentions only the facts underlying the claim, the defense and the counterclaim, but the principle applies to all briefs if the Arbitral Tribunal admits further briefs (Art. 35(1) sent. 1). Para. 2 regulates **time periods** (setting of time periods, prolongation of time periods for the production of evidence, exclusion of evidence which is produced belatedly and the competence of the Arbitral Tribunal to decide on such issues). Para. 3 underlines that each party bears the **consequences** of belated and/or insufficient proof. 2

The arbitral procedural rules on **burden of proof** in Art. 41(1) – to be read with the background of Art. 43 PRC Arbitration Law – correlate with Art. 67(1) PRC Civil Procedure Law. It follows from the procedural origin of the rule that Chinese law qualifies the burden of proof as a **procedural question**. This procedural qualification applies in case of CIETAC arbitration in China as Chinese private international law[66] – as, e.g., German private international law – requires the qualification of questions 3

[64] Art. 65 sent. 2 Draft Revised PRC Arbitration Law (2021).

[65] Art. 61 Draft Revised PRC Arbitration Law (2021).

[66] Art. 8 of the Law of the People's Republic of China on the Laws Applicable to Foreign-related Civil Relations (I).

according to the law of the (arbitral) forum (*lex fori* qualification). For example, pursuant to the Chinese qualification as procedural, Chinese procedural law on burden of proof applies to a German-Chinese contract with choice of German law and a CIETAC arbitration clause and trumps German law on burden of proof as well as the European qualification in Art. 18 Rome I Regulation on the law applicable to contractual obligations.

4 As to **establishment of the evidence**, a binding interpretation of the Supreme People's Court refers to the **"rule of thumb"**,[67] which so far has not been subject of intensive and detailed debate.[68] However, from a German perspective, the historical similarity of German and Chinese civil and civil procedure law may be recalled. Discussions with Chinese practitioners suggest that the lead sentences of the German Federal Court of Justice on the assessment of evidence (*"freie Beweiswürdigung"*)[69] have been perceived as a proper description also of the Chinese rule of thumb.[70] It requires determining **facts to the free conviction of the Arbitral Tribunal without necessarily fully excluding any remaining doubts.**

5 Introduced in 2024, para. 4 prescribes that, unless the parties have otherwise agreed, the Arbitral Tribunal may apply the **CIETAC Guidelines on Evidence** which have come into force with effect as of March 1, 2015. In essence, they correlate with the IBA Rules on the Taking of Evidence. They **limit the effect of the distribution of the burden of proof**. In particular, they contain in their Art. 7.1 a rule according to which each party can request from the other side the production of specified documents which are "material and relevant".[71] They introduce the international compromise between *common* and *civil law* parties into the Chinese legal system which is civil law based. The parties are free to **explicitly exclude** the application of the CIETAC Guidelines on Evidence in the **arbitration clause** (→ Ch. 2 mn. 7).

> The parties may wish to consider this if they all come from civil law jurisdictions which are generally hostile to disclosure. In contrast, in case of a contract between a **party from a common law jurisdiction** and a Chinese party, the parties may be well advised to consider the opposite and to explicitly agree on the compromise between civil and common law which is contained in the "relevant and material test" und the CIETAC Guidelines on Evidence. If they make such an agreement, they may wish to also include the **IPBA Guidelines on Privilege and Attorney Secrecy in International Arbitration** in order to level the playing field between the parties on these issues.[72]

[67] Art. 10(1) no. 4 of the Provisions by the Supreme People's Court on Evidence in Civil Procedures.

[68] In practice, many Chinese arbitrators will follow the Provisions by the Supreme People's Court on Evidence in Civil Procedures as a complete set of evidentiary rules compatible with Chinese legal culture and tradition (assessment of Yu/Cao, A Guide to the CIETAC Arbitration Rules and Practice, mn. 8.79).

[69] BGH 17.2.1970 – III ZR 139/67, NJW 1970, 946; see only the summary by Laumen/Prütting/Gerhlein, § 286 mn. 4 which can be translated as follows: "According to the constant German jurisprudence, judicial conviction requires no absolute or irrevocable certainty and also no utmost probability, but only a level of certainty which can be applicable in practical life and which silences doubt without completely eliminating it."

[70] Legal discussion with James Wu, Wu Luan Zhao Yan law firm, Beijing, Leader of a delegation of 40 lawyers of the All China Lawyers Association, during four weeks of internship in 2013, first referred to in Brödermann in FS Elsing, p. 56 (at fn. 13).

[71] Whereby the Arbitral Tribunal has discretion to dismiss the request to produce at the request of the other party pursuant to Art. 7.3.

[72] Available at: https://ipba.org/publications/.

Article 42
Examination of Evidence

(1) Unless otherwise agreed by the parties, where a case is examined by way of an oral hearing, the evidence shall be produced at the oral hearing and may be examined by the parties.

(2) [1]Where a case is to be decided on the basis of documents only, or where the evidence is submitted after the hearing and both parties have agreed to examine the evidence by means of writing, the parties may examine the evidence in writing. [2]In such circumstances, the parties shall submit their written opinions on the evidence within the time period specified by the arbitral tribunal.

1 The rules in Art. 42, adapted in 2015, make a distinction for the examination of evidence depending on whether the arbitration procedure includes an **oral hearing** (→ Art. 35 mn. 5). If so, the evidence will be examined in the oral hearing unless the parties agree otherwise (para. 1). Otherwise, the examination of evidence will take place **in writing** (para. 2). This applies also – in case of a correlating party agreement (which is likely to be rare; → Art. 35 mn. 4) – for evidence submitted **after** the oral hearing if the Arbitral Tribunal admits it (Art. 35(1) sent. 1).

Article 43
Investigation and Evidence Collection by the Arbitral Tribunal

(1) The arbitral tribunal may undertake investigation and collect evidence as it considers necessary.

(2) [1]When investigating and collecting evidence, the arbitral tribunal may notify the parties to be present. [2]In the event that one or both parties fail to be present after being notified, the investigation and collection of evidence shall proceed without being affected.

(3) Evidence collected by the arbitral tribunal through its investigation shall be forwarded to the parties for their comments.

1 Art. 43–44 implement the **principle of (possible) investigation** in Art. 43 sent. 2 PRC Arbitration Law[73] and Art. 67(2) PRC Civil Procedure Law into CIETAC arbitrations. Art. 43(1) enables the Arbitral Tribunal to research the facts. In practice, this occurs by: (i) **hearing expert evidence**; according to Art. 44(1) PRC Arbitration Law[74], the Arbitral Tribunal has discretion to either listen to a party appointed expert or to appoint itself an expert; or (ii) by **examining with its own eyes** (e.g., of goods, machines or equipment in case of claims relating to alleged quality deficiencies). It is also possible that (iii) the Arbitral Tribunal requests a party to **produce a certain document**.

2 For evidence collecting, the Arbitral Tribunal has a large room of **discretion** ("*as it considers necessary*"; also → Art. 35(1)).[75] In practice, evidence collection by the Arbitral Tribunal (*ex officio*) can make sense under the special circumstances of the case and

[73] Art. 61 Draft Revised PRC Arbitration Law (2021).

[74] Art. 62 Draft Revised PRC Arbitration Law (2021).

[75] See e.g., *Shaanxi Changsheng Industrial Group Co. Ltd. v. Mafagrobotic* [2013] Yi Zhong Min Te Zi No. 6539, Beijing First Intermediate People's Court, December 20, 2013 (as reported by Yu/Cao, A Guide to the CIETAC Arbitration Rules and Practice, mn. 8.122), where one party tried to set aside the award

help to save costs. For example, in an international arbitration with relations to both civil and common law jurisdictions, to avoid lengthy and expensive discovery of documents which might contain certain contractual language in other similar contracts, an Arbitral Tribunal ordered the preparation of a document integrating, in an anonymous way, certain clauses from certain contracts which might or might not contain the language of relevance. How careful the Arbitral Tribunal will use its discretion and thereby interfere into the burden of proof depends on the discretion of the Arbitral Tribunal (→ Ch. 2 mn. 7; → Art. 26 mn. 3). For a Chinese lawyer, the investigation of evidence *ex officio* may be slightly more natural than for a German lawyer in a German procedure; but Art. 28.2 of the DIS Arbitration Rules also permits the collection of evidence *ex officio*. Differences between Chinese and German arbitrators in applying the discretion of the Arbitral Tribunal is not rooted in different rules, they are rather rooted in a slightly different ***mind-set*** and slight differences regarding the perception ("*Leitbild*") of a trial first encountered during their respective legal educations.

3 Para. 2 and 3 regulate the ***ex officio* collection of evidence** by the Arbitral Tribunal: The parties shall be given an opportunity to comment on any collected evidence (para. 3). Further, the parties shall receive an opportunity to be present at the investigating and collecting of evidence *if* the Arbitral Tribunal considers this **appropriate** ("may notify the parties to be present"; "可以通知当事人到场" in para. 2). In short, the Arbitral Tribunal has a **large degree of discretion** when collecting evidence *ex officio*.

Article 44
Expert's Report and Appraiser's Report

(1) [1]The arbitral tribunal may consult experts or appoint appraisers for clarification on specific issues of the case. [2]Such an expert or appraiser may be a Chinese or foreign institution or natural person.

(2) The arbitral tribunal has the power to request the parties, and the parties are also obliged, to deliver or produce to the expert or appraiser any relevant materials, documents, property, or physical objects for examination, inspection or appraisal by the expert or appraiser.

(3) [1]Copies of the expert's report and the appraiser's report shall be forwarded to the parties for their comments. [2]Upon the application of either party or the request of the arbitral tribunal, the expert or appraiser shall participate in an oral hearing and explain the report when the arbitral tribunal considers it necessary.

1 Art. 44 contains a self-explanatory **special rule** on *ex offico* collection of evidence **from experts**. Pursuant to para. 1, the Arbitral Tribunal exercises discretion in appointing experts or appraisers. The rule has such a broad wording that it can even serve as a basis for an international CIETAC Arbitral Tribunal consisting solely of foreign arbitrators to appoint a **Chinese expert on procedural issues of law**; while the competence for such an appointment may also be found in Art. 35(1) and/or – best – in the consent of the parties.

2 Pursuant to para. 2, the Arbitral Tribunal can request from the parties the production of **documents** (or to provide objects for inspection) directly to the tribunal appointed expert.

alleging that the Arbitral Tribunal had not legally conducted the investigation. The court upheld the award by referencing to the tribunal's broad discretion regarding investigation.

Para. 3 adapts, in essence, the general rule in Art. 43(2)-(3) to the *ex officio* taking of evidence via experts: (i) It provides for a **possibility** for the parties to **comment** on the expert's or appraiser's report. (ii) It gives **discretion** to the Arbitral Tribunal with respect to the decision whether or not the expert shall be present in the oral hearing ("*when the Arbitral Tribunal considers it necessary*"). Prior to the amendment of para. 3 in 2024, the participation of experts or appraisers was subject to the approval of the Arbitral Tribunal and thereby deviated slightly from Art. 44(2) PRC Arbitration Law[76]: According to that provision, the Arbitral Tribunal needs to appoint an appraiser at the request of a party or at its own discretion and to examine him or her at the hearing; deleting the consent requirement of the Arbitral Tribunal put Art. 44 in line with this provision. The new rule in para. 3 sent. 2 leaves it to the parties (or their representatives), when making the tactical choices, to decide if they want their expert present in the room. 3

Article 45
Suspension of the Arbitral Proceedings

(1) Where the parties jointly or separately request a suspension of the arbitral proceedings, or under circumstances where such suspension is necessary, the arbitral proceedings may be suspended.

(2) The arbitral proceedings shall resume as soon as the reason for the suspension disappears or the suspension period ends.

(3) [1]The arbitral tribunal shall decide whether to suspend or resume the arbitral proceedings. [2]Where the arbitral tribunal has not yet been formed, the decision shall be made by the President of the Arbitration Court.

Art. 45, introduced in 2015, governs a possible **suspension of the proceedings**, either (i) **upon request** by a party or (ii) ***ex officio***, i.e. upon the initiative of the Arbitral Tribunal, with due regard to the circumstances if it considers the suspension "*necessary*" (para. 1 and para. 3 sent. 1). 1

Many reasons may give **grounds** for a suspension: For example, granting a limited suspension can be the less perturbing measure (*minor*) to the arbitration as compared to the replacement of an arbitrator pursuant to Art. 33 in case of a sudden surgery of an arbitrator which is likely to delay the arbitration only by a few months (this will require liaison with CIETAC as the Chairman of CIETAC controls the decision of replacement, → Art. 33 mn. 2). Another obvious reason is a natural disaster preventing any of the parties, the arbitrators or CIETAC from acting. The decision will have to consider all circumstances, such as who needs to act with possible distinctions if the event occurs after the oral hearing and the parties are no longer allowed to submit any further briefs. Further scenarios include parties requesting a suspension to have time for settlement negotiations, ongoing proceedings before a state court regarding the validity of the arbitration agreement or ongoing parallel proceedings that potentially have an impact on the arbitral proceedings.[77] According to para. 3 sent. 1, the Arbitral Tribunal shall take the decision; before its formation the President of the Arbitration Court is in charge (para. 3 sent. 2). 2

Pursuant to para. 2, the arbitral proceeding shall **continue** as soon as any of the two events mentioned therein occur (expiration of the time period set for the suspension; disappearance of the circumstances on which the suspension is founded). 3

[76] Art. 62 Draft Revised PRC Arbitration Law (2021).

[77] Yu/Cao, A Guide to the CIETAC Arbitration Rules and Practice, mn. 8.135.

4 For the **competence** regarding the decision to resume, the same rules in para. 3 apply as are applicable to the decision to suspend (Arbitral Tribunal or, prior to its formation, President of the Arbitration Court).

Article 46
Withdrawal and Dismissal

(1) [1]A party may withdraw its claim or counterclaim in its entirety. [2]In the event that the Claimant withdraws its claim in its entirety, the arbitral tribunal may proceed with its examination of the counterclaim and render an arbitral award thereon. [3]In the event that the Respondent withdraws its counterclaim in its entirety, the arbitral tribunal may proceed with the examination of the claim and render an arbitral award thereon.

(2) A party may be deemed to have withdrawn its claim or counterclaim if the arbitral proceedings cannot proceed for reasons attributable to that party or due to relevant provisions of law.

(3) [1]A case may be dismissed if the claim and counterclaim have been withdrawn in their entirety. [2]Where a case is to be dismissed prior to the formation of the arbitral tribunal, the President of the Arbitration Court shall make a decision on the dismissal. [3]Where a case is to be dismissed after the formation of the arbitral tribunal, the arbitral tribunal shall make the decision.

(4) The seal of CIETAC shall be affixed to the Dismissal Decision referred to in the preceding Paragraph 3 and Paragraph 7 of Article 6 of these Rules.

1 Art. 46 governs the **withdrawal of a claim or a counterclaim** and the legal consequences of such withdrawal. Pursuant to para. 1, the withdrawal of a claim does not affect the arbitration about any (counter-)claim filed by the other side. Pursuant to para. 3, in case of withdrawal of all claims and counterclaims, if any, the Arbitral Tribunal or, prior to its constitution, the President of the Arbitral Tribunal will dismiss the case. Pursuant to para. 4, CIETAC shall affix its seal to such a dismissal.

2 Pursuant to para. 2, introduced in 2015 and amended in 2024, any **behavior** of a party or **relevant provisions of law** that prohibit the continuation of the arbitration proceedings (e.g., obstructive omission to comply with an order) can be assessed as a withdrawal of a claim or counterclaim brought by that party. In the rare situation that parties are trying to misuse an arbitral tribunal for money laundering purposes by faking a dispute, the discovery of such facts during the arbitration might fall under this provision. In the same vein, para. 2 covers cases in which a natural person dies without heirs or a company is dissolved with no successor in rights and obligations.[78]

Article 47
Combination of Conciliation with Arbitration

(1) [1]Where both parties wish to conciliate, or where one party wishes to conciliate and the other party's consent has been obtained by the arbitral tribunal, the arbitral tribunal may conciliate the dispute during the arbitral proceedings. [2]The parties may also settle their dispute by themselves.

[78] Yu/Cao, A Guide to the CIETAC Arbitration Rules and Practice, mn. 8.140.

(2) With the consents of both parties, the arbitral tribunal may conciliate the case in a manner it considers appropriate.

(3) During the process of conciliation, the arbitral tribunal shall terminate the conciliation proceedings if either party so requests or if the arbitral tribunal considers that further conciliation efforts will be futile.

(4) The parties shall sign a settlement agreement where they have reached settlement through conciliation by the arbitral tribunal or by themselves.

(5) Where the parties have reached a settlement agreement through conciliation by the arbitral tribunal or by themselves, they may withdraw their claim or counterclaim, or request the arbitral tribunal to render an arbitral award or a conciliation statement in accordance with the terms of the settlement agreement.

(6) [1]Where the parties request for a conciliation statement, the conciliation statement shall clearly set forth the claims of the parties and the terms of the settlement agreement. [2]It shall be signed by the arbitrators, sealed by CIETAC, and served upon both parties.

(7) Where conciliation is not successful, the arbitral tribunal shall resume the arbitral proceedings and render an arbitral award.

(8) Where the parties wish to conciliate their dispute but do not wish to have conciliation conducted by the arbitral tribunal, CIETAC may, with the consents of both parties, assist the parties to conciliate the dispute in a manner and procedure it considers appropriate.

(9) Where conciliation is not successful, neither party may invoke any opinion, view or statement, and any proposal or proposition expressing acceptance or opposition by either party or by the arbitral tribunal in the process of conciliation as grounds for any claim, defense or counterclaim in the subsequent arbitral proceedings, judicial proceedings, or any other proceedings.

(10) [1]Where the parties have reached a settlement agreement by themselves through negotiation or conciliation before the commencement of an arbitration, either party may, based on an arbitration agreement concluded between them that provides for arbitration by CIETAC and the settlement agreement, request CIETAC to constitute an arbitral tribunal to render an arbitral award in accordance with the terms of the settlement agreement. [2]Unless otherwise agreed by the parties, the Chairman of CIETAC shall appoint a sole arbitrator to form such an arbitral tribunal, which shall examine the case in a procedure it considers appropriate and render an award in due course. [3]The specific procedure and time period for rendering the award shall not be subject to other provisions of these Rules.

1 Art. 47 regulates **different variations** of combining arbitration and conciliation/mediation (MedArb/ArbMed): (i) ArbMed **with or without support** of the Arbitral Tribunal (para. 1–9), **with or without success**; as well as (ii) **settlement by negotiation or conciliation/mediation** prior to the commencement of the arbitral proceedings (para. 10). The level of detail exhibited by the rules shows the extent to which conciliation and mediation match with the search for harmony (*he wei gui*: 和为贵, → Ch. 1 mn. 4).[79] As to the details, upfront a note on language: The notions of conciliation and mediation cut across each other and are used here jointly in a smooth way without a clear demarcation, which could be either a proposal made pursuant to para. 8, or simply the facilitation of a consent of the parties (*mediation*) possibly as a result of a proposal of the Arbitral Tribunal or any other third party determined by

[79] See also Yu/Cao, A Guide to the CIETAC Arbitration Rules and Practice, mn. 8.145.

CIETAC (*conciliation*). From a Chinese perspective – and with regard to the wide wording of para. 2 – both forms of reaching a settlement are covered by Art. 47:[80]

2 Coherent with the civil law tradition, para. 1 provides the basis that (i) the **Arbitral Tribunal** may conciliate/mediate during the arbitration proceeding or, according to an addition of 2015, (ii) the **parties** may settle the matter by themselves. Furthermore, (iii) para. 8 provides for a possibility that **CIETAC** assists in a conciliation/mediation without the involvement of the Arbitral Tribunal.

3 Para. 2 grants a **high degree of discretion** to the Arbitral Tribunal in conducting conciliation/mediation.

4 Para. 4–6 provide rules for a **successful conciliation/mediation**. A successful conciliation/mediation which is conducted pursuant to para. 1 sent. 1 and para. 2 upon **request of both parties** (possibly after some "influence" of the Arbitral Tribunal upon the other party which initially does not want to conciliate/mediate) is terminated by a **written settlement** (para. 4).

5 Pursuant to para. 5, the parties wishing to terminate the arbitration have a choice between a **withdrawal** of the claim or the **application for an award** (or a conciliation settlement) which reflects the contents of their settlement.

6 Para. 6 regulates the conditions for such an award on agreed terms (hereinafter referred to as **"Settlement Arbitration Award")** (clear conditions; signature, seal of CIETAC; service upon the parties). In case of a settlement which is favorable to the Respondent, the option to apply for a "Settlement Arbitration Award" needs to be balanced against the option to simply withdraw the claim. An award has the advantage that it develops *res iudicata* (i.e., the force of a judgment) while, in case of a withdrawal, this will only be the case if, pursuant to Art. 46(3), the Arbitral Tribunal formally dismisses the claim, which is not mandatory (*"may"*). Without *res iudicata*, the claimant might later file a new claim pursuant to Art. 50 PRC Arbitration Law[81] (e.g., after collecting more evidence for the same claim).

7 The rules in Art. 47 provide details to the provisions in **Art. 51–52 PRC Arbitration Law**[82], but the latter also supplement the rules. Thus, Art. 52(3) PRC Arbitration Law regulates the case that after a settlement one of the parties changes its mind and **refuses to sign the settlement agreement**; in that case the Arbitral Tribunal shall issue a 'timely' award.

8 Para. 3, 7 and 9 govern the case of an **unsuccessful conciliation/mediation**. If a conciliation/mediation conducted pursuant to para. 1 sent. 1 and para. 2 upon **request of both parties** is unsuccessful and/or leads to its termination, be it upon the decision of a party or pursuant to the impression of the Arbitral Tribunal (para. 3), the arbitration procedure shall be continued, thus leading to an arbitral award (para. 7). The **opinions, views or statements** expressed during the conciliation/mediation process remain **confidential** and cannot be used in the ongoing arbitration procedure (para. 9). It may be doubted (and is to be decided by counsel from case-to-case) if, during the conciliation/mediation all parties will fully discuss their weaknesses with the conciliator/mediator in the knowledge of a possible subsequent continuation of the arbitration procedure. The task of the arbitrator-conciliator/mediator will be to ensure that the conciliation/mediation does not unduly influence the arbitration or is perceived as such and that the parties do not use the conciliation/mediation as a "testing ground" for their argumentation in the (potentially) ensuing arbitration.[83] In practice, even if the legal hurdles for either party are

---

[80] Yu/Cao, A Guide to the CIETAC Arbitration Rules and Practice, mn. 8.149.
[81] Art. 67 Draft Revised PRC Arbitration Law (2021).
[82] Art. 68, 71 Draft Revised PRC Arbitration Law (2021).
[83] See Yu/Cao, A Guide to the CIETAC Arbitration Rules and Practice, mn. 8.158.

clear after the exchange of the main briefs (statement of claim, statement of defense and rebuttal), prior to the taking of evidence there remains often considerable room to reach agreement within a "corridor" of possible agreements when the results of such taking of evidence are unknown.

Para. 10 offers CIETAC services in situations in which the **parties have reached agreement** by themselves "*before the commencement of an arbitration*". This includes both consent **by negotiation** (para. 1 sent. 2) or by **successful conciliation** prior to the commencement of an arbitration which leads to a settlement (para. 4, 2nd alternative). 9

In contrast, the settlement reached without participation of an Arbitral Tribunal **after** the commencement of an arbitration proceeding (para. 1 sent. 2; para. 8) is governed by para. 5 (→ mn. 5). In these two case scenarios, para. 10 empowers CIETAC to **appoint a sole arbitrator** at the **request of a party**. The sole arbitrator will then conduct an **abbreviated arbitration procedure** organized in his or her sole discretion (e.g., without an oral hearing) which leads to an arbitral award including the contents of the settlement agreement ("Settlement Arbitration Award"; → mn. 4 for the advantages as compared to a withdrawal of a claim). For such a short (mini) arbitration, the other provisions in the CIETAC Rules do not apply as clarified by para. 10 sent. 3. It is estimated that approximately 20–30 % of the cases are settled by conciliation. 10

Article 48
Third-Party Funding

(1) [1]Once a third-party funding agreement is concluded, the funded party shall communicate to the Arbitration Court, without any delay, the existence of the third-party funding arrangement, the financial interest therein, the name and address of the third party funder and other relevant information. [2]The Arbitration Court shall forward such information to the other parties and the arbitral tribunal. [3]The arbitral tribunal may order the funded party to disclose other relevant information of the funding if it deems necessary.

(2) When deciding the costs of arbitration and other fees in the award, the arbitral tribunal may take into account of the existence of the third-party funding arrangement and the fact whether the requirements set forth in the preceding Paragraph 1 are complied with by the funded party.

Art. 48 imposes a **disclosure obligation** upon those parties, who receive third-party funding. Third-party funding has now been for the first time addressed in the CIETAC Arbitration Rules. Prior to that only the Hong Kong Arbitration Center of CIETAC, had released in 2017 Guidelines for Third Party Funding,[84] According to the Guidelines, the "funding" here should not be limited to the financial funding but includes all kinds of material support to a party in arbitration. Therefore, also a provider of pure services could also be regarded as a funder according to Art. 48. 1

The scope of disclosure under Art. 48 includes the basic relevant information, such as the **existence of the third-party funding arrangement**, the **involved financial interest**, the **name and address of the third-party funder**. Through that information not only the funder but also the conditions of funding and the influence of the funder on the arbitration proceedings can be identified. 2

[84] https://hkarbitration.files.wordpress.com/2017/09/cietac-hk-tpf-guidelines.pdf.

3 In the first place the obligation of disclosure of third-party funding is with the party who receives funding.

4 However, whether and to which extent an **arbitrator should also disclose his relationship with the third-party funder** in accordance with Art. 31, is still an open question. On the one hand, the wording of Art. 31 requires an arbitrator to disclose all "*facts or circumstances likely to give rise to justifiable doubts as to his/her impartiality or independence*". Considering that an economic or personal relationship between the arbitrator and the third party could give rise to an unjustified favor to the funded party, the relationship with the third party is a fact that likely gives rise to justifiable doubts as to his impartiality and therefore should be disclosed.[85] On the other hand, according to another view, the conflict of interest as to the arbitrator refers mainly to the close economic or personal relationship with a party of the case, which could not directly be applied on the relationship between the arbitrator and the funder of a party.[86] It must be taken in to account that "in certain types of arbitration, such as maritime, sports or commodities arbitration, arbitrators have to be drawn from a smaller or specialized pool of individuals"[87]. Under these circumstances the high flexibility of the modern economic and the widely defined "funding" make a complete and entire disclosure of the relationships with the funder almost impossible. Otherwise, the arbitration proceeding would be exposed to the danger of delay if the arbitrator must always keep an eye on the funder behind the party instead of the party itself.

5 Due to the "**doctrine of maintenance and champerty**" in common law jurisdictions third-party funding was until recently prohibited. This doctrine was originally determined in the case of *British Cash & Parcel Conveyors Ltd v. Lamson Store Service Co Ltd*· which defined "**maintenance**" as an intervention which "was directed against wanton and officious intermeddling with the disputes of others in which the intervenor has no interest whatever, and where the assistance he renders to the one or the other party is without justification or excuse" and **"champerty"** as an "aggravated form of maintenance, in which the maintainer receives something of value for the assistance given."[88]

6 However, during the last decade **third-party funding has now become legitimate** in international commercial arbitration both in the common law jurisdictions in Singapore[89] and in Hong Kong.[90]

7 In Mainland China, third-party funding developed **in a different way**. The question, how a party receives his money for the proceeding, has always been regarded to be beyond the concern of the Arbitration Tribunal and the Court. Thus, third-party funding has been a reality in the arbitration practice of Mainland China. In 2022, an intermediate a court of Jiangsu Province determined for the first time in a resolution that the disclosure of the third party **violates neither the confidentiality nor the justice of the arbitral award**,[91] which can be regarded as the **official recognition of third-party funding in arbitration cases**.

8 As the consequence of a violation of the disclosure obligation, para. 2 gives the arbitral tribunal leeway to decide the costs of arbitration and other fees in the award. It

---

[85] Zhou/Cheng, Chinese Journal of Maritime Law 2018, 44–55.

[86] Holtzmann/Neuhaus, A guide to the UNCITRAL Model Law on International Commercial Arbitration, p. 389.

[87] International Bar Association, Guidelines on Conflicts of Interest in International Arbitration 2014, 3.1.3 (at fn. 5).

[88] *British Cash & Parcel Conveyors Ltd v. Lamson Store Service Co Ltd* [1908] 1 K.B. 1006, 1014.

[89] The new sections 5A and 5B of the Civil Law Act, which came into force on March 1, 2017, abolish the common law torts of maintenance and champerty.

[90] Part 10A Arbitration Ordinance.

[91] (2022)苏02执异13号.

is not clear whether the other party can in this case apply for a revocation of the award according to Art. 58(1) no. 3 PRC Arbitration Law.

Article 49
Interim Award

(1) Where the arbitral tribunal deems necessary, or where a party requests and the arbitral tribunal approves, the arbitral tribunal may render an interim award on any issue in the case before rendering the final award.

(2) Failure of either party to perform an interim award shall neither affect the arbitral proceedings nor prevent the arbitral tribunal from making the final award.

Art. 49 on interim awards was added in 2024. Reading Art. 49 both in the context of the CIETAC Rules and the arbitration practice in mainland China in the past, its impact is potentially limited mainly to awards on issues of jurisdiction or the applicable law whereby the language of Art. 49 would allow to make an award under Art. 49 also in any other scenario which is not covered by Art. 53, Art. 23 or Art. 80. 1

A. Distinctions

To determine the purpose of Art. 49 on interim measures, it is helpful to distinguish it from Art. 53 (Partial Awards) and Art. 23 and Art. 80 (Interim Measures). 2

I. Partial award

Art. 49 largely repeats the wording of Art. 53 on partial awards. Whereas under **Art. 53**, interim awards are not expressly addressed, **para. 1** now allows the Arbitral Tribunal to render an interim award. Especially in complex and lengthy arbitrations, it is helpful to **bifurcate the proceedings** and to render a partial award which is fully enforceable, e.g. on the foundation of a claim as opposed to its amount or *quantum* (→ Art. 53 mn. 2). The purpose of Art. 49 is different and does not relate to such examples of bifurcation. 3

The **biggest difference** between an Interim Award and a Partial Award lies in their **binding effect**. 4

On one side, a **Partial Award** under Art. 53, despite its incompleteness regarding the scale of claims in question, usually states explicitly that it is "**final and binding** upon both parties". Therefore, it is qualified as binding on the parties and can be recognized and enforced under the New York Convention (if the other criteria are fulfilled). 5

On the other side, the binding effect of an **Interim Award** is heavily **disputed**, since it is normally not explicitly regulated in arbitration rules. 6

Some opinions argue in favor of a binding effect also of Interim Awards. They base their view on the wording of Art. 2 no. v ICC-Arbitration Rules (2021).[92] According to this view, since the Interim Award, like the Final Award, is defined as another subclass of the award, it should have the same legal effect, namely *res iudicata*, as the Final Award (→ Art. 47 mn. 6). Hence the decisions, which are made in an Interim Award, 7

[92] Wang, Beijing Arbitration Law 2017, 31–48; Yang, The Effect of International Commercial Arbitral Award, p. 16.

cannot be revoked by the arbitration tribunal itself without justified reasons. An Interim Award should be also binding on the parties. Furthermore, the wording of the New York Convention mentions only "the Award" and does not distinguish between an Interim and a Final Award. As a result, an Interim Award should not be seen as excluded by Art. V(1)(e) NYC, which requires no finality of an award.

8 **Other opinions** reject such binding effect.[93] According to their view, an Interim Award as designed to "**decide an issue** (e.g., choice of law, liability) relevant to disposing of a claim, but does not finally dispose of the claim." Thus, it cannot be regarded as "having become binding on the parties" in terms of Art. V(1)(e) NYC. Furthermore, an **Interim Award** (e.g., on the determination of the applicable law) **may lack a content of obligation or right**, which is enforceable.

9 The **PRC Arbitration Law** does not recognize the legal instrument of an Interim Award. Therefore, although Art. 248(1), 290 PRC Civil Procedure Law do not explicitly require legal effectiveness for the enforcement of a domestic arbitral award, it is submitted that the **application for the enforcement of a domestic Interim Award** has most likely no chance of success.

10 For a **foreign Arbitral Award**, whose recongnition and enforcement is applied for in a court of the PRC, Art. 304 Civil Procedure Law requires explicitly that it must have "legal effectiveness" (发生法律效力, *res judicata*). In accordance with Art. 158 Civil Procedure Law, those judgments and rulings, which are made by the Supreme People's Court and which may not be appealed against or have not been appealed against within the prescribed time limit, will acquire the "legal effectiveness". From this definition it can be derived that "legal effectiveness" means to be final and binding. For instance, the only application for recongnition and enforcement, which was rejected by the People's Court in 2019, was due to the reason that it could not be determined, whether it had already acquired "legal effecctiveness" abroad[94].

11 However, a **foreign Interim Award** could lead to a **legal effect regarding the evidence**. According to Art. 10(1) no. 5 Provisions by the Supreme People's Court on Evidence in Civil Procedures a fact, which has been determined by an effective award (生效), does not need to be proven again. Therefore, the parties do not have to prove a fact which has been determined by a foreign Interim Award.

II. Distinction between Art. 23 and Art. 80.

12 In line with the international practice, the CIETAC Rules address specifically in Art. 80 the issue of interim and emergency matters. Art. 80 permits the Arbitral Tribunal (**only at CIETAC HK**) to issue an **order** in emergency cases and conservatory measures which require attention before a final award can be rendered in view of a **time element** suggesting some urgency.

13 From an **international perspective**, such **conservatory and emergency matters** are often handled through an interim award. For example, the ICC Arbitration Rules offer in their Art. 28 the option to decide on the issue either through an award or by an order. Examples for such interim awards include, e.g., (i) whether parties shall be requested to protect perishable goods to prevent further losses, (ii) whether parties shall be requested to allow for tests to be conducted on machines or equipment; or (iii) whether parties shall

[93] Born, International Commercial Arbitration, p. 3015; Song, Arbitration Law, p. 143.
[94] The Fourth Senate for civil proceedings of the Supreme People's Court, The annual report of the Supreme People's Court about the judicial examination of commercial arbitrations 2019, p. 24.

be requested to appoint a liquidation committee, e. g., in order to liquidate a joint venture; or (iv) to inhibit a party to transfer money from a specific account.

Under Art. 80, the normal form to address such emergency scenarios is an **order**. For **14** example, in one of the first cases known under Art. 80, the emergency arbitrator, acting during the COVID-19 pandemic, had to decide on ordering the transfer of certain bills of lading to enable the transfer of goods to subsequent buyers along the chain of sales.[95] In light of the existence of Art. 80 as the core instrument to cope with emergency situations in the CIETAC Rules, an Interim Award under Art. 49 will have its role only in scenarios in which an order under Art. 80 is not sufficient under the specific circumstances of a case (→ mn. 15).

B. Interim Measures – arbitration practice in Mainland China

Although the Interim Award has been generally established in the practice of **15** international commercial arbitration,[96] it has so far **not** been formally recognized by the **PRC Arbitration Law**. Due to a lack of a uniform legal regulations, the role of an Interim Award is handled and interpreted differently within the arbitration practice in Mainland China.

Three types of approaches towards Interim Awards could be observed during **16** the past years (whereby Art. 49 follows the third approach set forth here and in the following).

The **first** can be found in the **SHIAC-Arbitration Rules** (2015) and SCIA-Arbitra- **17** tion Rules (2019), which, following Art. 55 PRC Arbitration Law, only regulate a Partial Award and do not deal with an Interim Award. In these cases, an Arbitral Tribunal is consequently unable to render an Interim Award as Interim Awards do not have a distinct function as compared to Partial Awards.

The **second approach** is based on the view of the academic circles[97] according to **18** which an Interim Award can be rendered and is deemed to focus mainly on the procedural issues, such as jurisdiction and evidence, while a Partial Award should mainly deal with the substantial questions relating to the claims or counterclaims. This view was once adopted in Art. 49 **SCIA-Arbitration Rules (2016)**. Under such circumstances it depends on the legal nature of the faced questions, whether an Interim or a Partial Award is issued, but both types of awards are permitted.

The newly added Art. 49 follows a **third type** which was initially developed by the **19** **BIAC-Arbitration Rules** (2015), which set the criterion on the object and content of awards itself. As far as **claims or counterclaims** are concerned, a Partial Award may be issued. This includes all scenarios where an issue relating to a claim or counterclaim can be bifurcated. **For all other legal questions,** whether they are procedural or substantial, an **Interim Award** shall be rendered. This includes namely issues of **jurisdiction or the determination of the applicable law** and has been proven as a more pragmatic method to differentiate between these two types of awards.

---

[95] See Meng, China Business Law Journal 2022, available at https://law.asia/cietacs-latest-emergency-arbitration/.

[96] See for example Art. 2 no. v ICC-Arbitration Rules (2021).

[97] Jiang/Xiao, Arbitration Law, p. 207.

C. Options

20 As a result, whenever an issue is (i) not a mere issue of emergency covered by an order under Art. 23 or Art. 80, and (ii) no issue for which bifurcation and therefore an enforceable partial award under Art. 53 is possible, the Arbitral Tribunal may issue an Interim Award, and the parties may request it. This includes decisions on **jurisdiction**, on the **applicable law** (if that is a disputed topic, e.g., due to an unclear choice of law), or on a **preliminary question** for the dispute for which the issuance of an award makes sense, e.g. in case of a dispute under a paramount clause of a global framework contract the issue whether a country agreement which is relevant for the decision of the arbitration has been validly terminated.

21 Furthermore, if it is important to overcome any issue on bindingness, recognition and enforceability of a **decision on jurisdiction** of the Arbitral Tribunal abroad (e.g., to avoid or counter anti-suit injunction situations), it is submitted that nothing prevents an Arbitral Tribunal to alternatively issue a decision on jurisdiction in the form of a binding partial award under Art. 53 instead of an interim award under Art. 49 which has more of an effect limited to the arbitral proceeding itself, when the determination of the jurisdiction is a part of the claims of a party.

Article 50
Early Dismissal

(1) A party may request for the early dismissal of a claim or counterclaim in whole or in part on the ground that the claim or counterclaim is manifestly without legal merit, or is manifestly outside the jurisdiction of the arbitral tribunal ("Request for Early Dismissal").

(2) [1]A Request for Early Dismissal shall be in writing and shall state the facts and legal basis supporting the application. [2]In order to prevent the abuse of the request to delay the arbitral proceedings, the arbitral tribunal may require the requesting party to provide justifiable grounds for the request and to demonstrate that the early dismissal process will expedite the overall proceedings. [3]A Request for Early Dismissal by the parties shall not prevent the arbitral tribunal from proceeding with the arbitration.

(3) Unless otherwise decided by the arbitral tribunal, a Request for Early Dismissal shall be made as early as possible and no later than the submission of the Statement of Defense or the Reply to the Counterclaim.

(4) The arbitral tribunal shall have the power to decide on whether to accept and consider a Request for Early Dismissal after inviting the parties to express their views.

(5) [1]The arbitral tribunal shall render a decision or an award on the request for early dismissal with reasons stated within sixty (60) days from the date on which such request is made. [2]At the request of the arbitral tribunal, the President of the Arbitration Court may extend the time period if he/she considers such extension justified and necessary.

(6) Where the arbitral tribunal renders an award granting the Request for Early Dismissal, in whole or in part, such award shall not prevent the arbitral tribunal from continuing the hearing of other claims or counterclaim.

A. Introduction

I. Function

Art. 50 was introduced in 2024. Para. 1 gives any party the chance to **request for a rejection of a claim or counterclaim within 60 days**, when it holds the Arbitral Tribunal for manifestly incompetent or the claim or counterclaim for manifestly legally unfounded. The Arbitral Tribunal has discretion to accept such application and to **dismiss claims or counterclaims** early on if they are **manifestly** outside the jurisdiction of the Arbitral Tribunal or without legal merit. The goal is to **expedite** the arbitral process and to spare the time and costs of lengthy arbitral proceedings (of six months in an ideal case, see Art. 51(1)). In case of **multiple claims** or counterclaims, the early dismissal can help to **streamline** an arbitration by quasi striking out a manifestly unfounded claim or counterclaim within a bundle of claims. Especially in complex (e.g., multi-party or multi contract) arbitrations, it can be helpful to determine early on the relevant issues of law and fact and the sorting out of irrelevant, unmeritorious, or frivolous claims. 1

II. Background and comparative experience

The legal instrument of early dismissal is firstly initiated by Rule 41(5) of the Rules of Procedure for Arbitration Proceedings of International Centre for Settlement of Investment Disputes (ICSID Arbitration Rules 2006)[98]. Within the last decade it has been accepted by the arbitral practice in some common law countries, such as the 2016 Arbitration Rules of the Singapore International Arbitration Center[99], Art. 43 of the 2018 Administered Arbitration Rules of the Hong Kong International Arbitration Centre[100] and Art. 22.1 (viii) of the 2020 Arbitration Rules of the London Court of International Arbitration[101]. 2

From a **civil law perspective**, such power of the Arbitral Tribunal does not warrant an explicit provision (e.g. no such provision is found in the 2021 Arbitration Rules of the International Chamber of Commerce[102] or the 2021 Swiss Rules of International Arbitration[103]). An Arbitral Tribunal would be free to issue a partial award under Art. 53 if it wishes to dispose separately of a specific claim or counterclaim within a bundle of claims. Compared to that option, issuing a decision or an award to dispose of a request for early dismissal may provide only a gradually different instrument for the Arbitral Tribunal (→ mn. 8). 3

[98] See www.icsid.worldbank.org.

[99] https://siac.org.sg/siac-rules-2016.

[100] https://www.hkiac.org/arbitration/rules-practice-notes/hkiac-administered-2018.

[101] https://www.lcia.org/Dispute_Resolution_Services/lcia-arbitration-rules-2020.aspx.

[102] https://iccwbo.org/dispute-resolution/dispute-resolution-services/arbitration/rules-procedure/2021-arbitration-rules/. The ICC has added explanatory language for early dismissal to their Note to Parties and Arbitral Tribunals on the Conduct of the Arbitration of January 1, 2021, available at https://iccwbo.org/news-publications/arbitration-adr-rules-and-tools/note-parties-arbitral-tribunals-conduct-arbitration/, paras. 109–114.

[103] https://www.swissarbitration.org/resources/swiss-rules-2021/.

B. Conditions and procedure

4 Para. 2 to 5 aim to ensure the parties request for early dismissal does **not unduly delay or hinder the main proceedings**. Para. 2 sent. 1 calls for submitting a well-founded request in writing, stating the facts and legal basis supporting the application. If the Arbitral Tribunal is not satisfied, it may request the submitting party to provide justifiable grounds that the early dismissal will expedite the overall proceeding (para. 2 sent. 2). The request must be made at an **early stage of the proceedings** (para. 3), and no later than the submission of the **Statement of Defense** or the Reply to the Counterclaim (para. 3), and the Arbitral Tribunal will decide within 60 days of the day on which the request was made (para. 5). This time period must include the **right to be heard** of the other party or parties (para. 4). In parallel, the Arbitral Tribunal may **continue with the arbitration** according to the timetable of the arbitration (para. 2 sent. 3).

5 In accordance with ICSID arbitration practice, where the early dismissal was first developed in 2006, the **standard for a request for early dismissal is set high**. It demands, the party requesting an early dismissal must (i) establish its objection to the claim clearly and obviously; (ii) with relative ease and (iii) the claim is so obviously defective from a legal point of view (of the applicable law) that it can properly be dismissed outright.

C. Decision making

6 When deciding on the request for early dismissal, the Arbitral Tribunal has a choice between rendering a **decision or an award** on the matter of the request. Depending on the circumstances, an award will thus be either final; or it may be partial (i.e., an enforceable partial award → Art. 53 mn. 2) if other claims or counterclaims are also pending to be addressed in the further main proceedings (para. 6).

D. Application in a general or summary arbitration procedure

7 An early dismissal can be applied for not only in a general procedure but also in a summary procedure for cases below RMB 5,000,000 (Art. 59). The period of application coincides with the period of the submission of the Defense or the Reply to the Counterclaim (para. 3). In case of a general procedure, it will be 45 days for the Respondent and 30 days for the Claimant and in case of a domestic arbitration or a summary procedure 20 days for both sides.

E. Limited impact on the arbitration

8 From a practical perspective, the impact of a decision or award on early dismissal is likely to be limited. By the time the Arbitral Tribunal can decide on an application for early dismissal (i.e., after reading both the request for early dismissal and the views of the other party or parties pursuant to para. 4), it will often have seen already enough submissions to hold the oral hearing and then to write an award. It may make sense to operate with an early dismissal if the arbitration is complex including **multiple claims**. In that case, an Arbitral Tribunal will have to balance the burden of writing an

additional decision against (i) the efficiency gained by issuing an additional decision and (ii) the advantage of avoiding future time (and cost) for the parties and the arbitrators to read additional submissions on claims which are obviously unfounded. It is in this context that a **decision** pursuant to para. 4 may provide a practical compromise road. It may be less work than a full award and address the request sufficiently.

In contrast, in **simple cases** with only one – manifestly unfounded – claim, operating with an early dismissal will often not save time. As the Arbitral Tribunal will decide on the early dismissal only after hearing the other party or parties to express their views (para. 4), it may often as well write the award early. The only advantage of early dismissal would be to avoid an oral hearing without the consent of the parties (Art. 35(2)). 9

From the **perspective of counsel in an arbitration**, it is advisable to step back and critically assess from a bird's eye perspective of a judge, if the circumstances of the case really justify a request for early dismissal. If it is not well founded, it will fail and thereby cost time and money. For example, SIAC has received 55 requests for early dismissal from 2016 to 2022, among which 28 were allowed to proceed and finally just 10 early dismissals were granted.[104] Thus, almost half of the requests for early dismissal ended up with not being accepted by the Arbitral Tribunal.

To sum up: The early dismissal is designed to accelerate the procedure, so that the Arbitral Tribunal and parties can spare the 3, 4 or 6 months for the proceedings. On the one hand, the party, which requests an early dismissal, must have a justifiable ground and take the burden of proof of the fact that the early dismissal process could expedite the overall proceedings. On the other hand, the Arbitral Tribunal can also decide not to accept the request for early dismissal if it considers the request as unfounded and the proceeding will therefore be **delayed**. Thus, a request for early dismissal bears the risk of bouncing back and annoying the Arbitral Tribunal through additional workload (not reflected in the payment scheme if the Arbitral Tribunal is paid on the basis of a payment scheme and not on an hourly basis). 10

F. Cost issues

If a request for early dismissal is unsuccessful, let alone manifestly abusive, the Arbitral Tribunal can consider these circumstances in its decision on the allocation of fees under Art. 55. 11

Article 51
Time Period for Rendering Award

(1) The arbitral tribunal shall render an arbitral award within six (6) months from the date on which the arbitral tribunal is formed.

(2) Upon the request of the arbitral tribunal, the President of the Arbitration Court may extend the time period if he/she considers it truly necessary and the reasons for the extension truly justified.

(3) Any suspension period shall be excluded when calculating the time period in the preceding Paragraph 1.

[104] https://siac.org.sg/annual-reports.

1 Para. 1 provides for an extendible **six-month deadline** for the making of an arbitral award calculated by CIETAC practice **as of the Notice of Formation** of the Arbitral Tribunal mentioned in Art. 32(3). Pursuant to para. 3, which was supplemented in 2015, **suspension periods** (Art. 45) are to be deducted. The deadline needs to be taken seriously in order to maintain the chances of enforcement. Both Art. V(1)(d) NYC (for recognition and execution abroad) and Chinese legislation (Art. 281(1) no. 3 PRC Civil Procedure Law (for foreign-related arbitrations → Ch. 1 mn. 8) and Art. 248(2) no. 3 PRC Civil Procedure Law) require that the arbitration must have been conducted in compliance with the arbitration agreement which is supplemented by the agreed arbitral rules. Thus, a transgression of the six-month deadline is not in the interest of the arbitration (but likely to be invoked by the losing party).

2 Pursuant to para. 2, the President of the Arbitration Court (Art. 2(2)) **can prolong** the time period for the making of an award. In practice, this requires a **reasoned application by the Arbitral Tribunal** (another example of the *top-down approach* in Chinese arbitration, → Ch. 1. mn. 14).

> Such an application should be filed in time; here, the cooperation with the CIETAC case manager, appointed pursuant to Art. 13(4), is helpful. The case manager can organize within CIETAC that the application reaches the competent president or his deputy (→ Art. 2 mn. 4) promptly.

Chapter III
Arbitral Award

Article 52
Making of Award

(1) The arbitral tribunal shall independently and impartially render a fair and reasonable arbitral award based on the facts of the case and the terms of the contract, in accordance with the law, and with reference to international practices.

(2) [1]Where the parties have agreed on the law applicable to the merits of their dispute, the parties' agreement shall prevail. [2]In the absence of such agreement or where such agreement is in conflict with a mandatory provision of the law, the arbitral tribunal shall determine the applicable substantive law or principles of law.

(3) [1]The arbitral tribunal shall state in the award the claims, the facts of the dispute, the reasons on which the award is based, the result of the award, the allocation of the arbitration costs, and the date on which and the place at which the award is made. [2]The facts of the dispute and the reasons on which the award is based may not be stated in the award if the parties have so agreed, or if the award is made in accordance with the terms of a settlement agreement between the parties. [3]The arbitral tribunal has the power to fix in the award the specific time period for the parties to perform the award and the liabilities for failure to do so within the specified time period.

(4) The seal of CIETAC shall be affixed to the arbitral award.

(5) [1]Where a case is examined by an arbitral tribunal composed of three arbitrators, the award shall be rendered by all three arbitrators or a majority of the arbitrators. [2]A written dissenting opinion shall be kept with the file and may be appended to the award. [3]Such dissenting opinion shall not form a part of the award.

(6) [1]Where the arbitral tribunal cannot reach a majority opinion, the arbitral award shall be rendered in accordance with the presiding arbitrator's opinion. [2]The written opinions of the other arbitrators shall be kept with the file and may be appended to the award. [3]Such written opinions shall not form a part of the award.

(7) [1]Unless the arbitral award is made in accordance with the opinion of the presiding arbitrator or the sole arbitrator and signed by the same, the arbitral award shall be signed by a majority of the arbitrators. [2]An arbitrator who has a dissenting opinion may or may not sign his/her name on the award. [3]An electronic signature of an arbitrator bears the same effect of his/her handwritten signature.

(8) The date on which the award is made shall be the date on which the award comes into legal effect.

(9) The arbitral award is final and binding upon both parties.

(10) [1]The arbitral award shall be delivered to the parties in hard copies. [2]Where the parties agree, or where CIETAC deems it necessary, the arbitral award may be delivered to the parties in an electronic form.

By implementing and supplementing Art. 54 and 57 PRC Arbitration Law[1], Art. 52 **1**
governs the basics of the making of an Arbitral Award and the legal effect of an Arbitral Award.

---

[1] Art. 73, 76 Draft Revised PRC Arbitration Law (2021).

A. A fair and reasonable arbitral award

2 Para. 1 sets forth the foundations:
1. Facts, contract and law,
2. "with reference to international practices" and respecting the principles of "fairness and reasonableness" and
3. "independency and impartiality"[2].

3 Para. 1 not only reaffirms the procedural commitment to fairness as set forth in Art. 35(1) sent. 2 (→ Art. 35 mn. 1). It also requires **fairness and reasonableness** on the level of the award making and writing and thereby on the level of the substantive application of the law (or principles of law, para. 2) and of the application of the contract as the law of the parties.[3] By no means does the rule imply that the Arbitral Tribunal is free to merely decide on the basis of equity – *ex aequo et bono*.[4] Rather, the general reference to fairness may be sensed as a reference to the general **goal of living in universal harmony** (*he wei gui*: 和为贵, → Ch. 1 mn. 3). It may be seen as a general reference to strive for justice by applying the law – which should be a goal for all legal systems.

4 As to the **technique of applying fairness** to the interpretation of a contract, in international arbitration, an Arbitral Tribunal may wish to note or even refer to the bridge built between different approaches to interpretation in Chapter 4 of the **Unidroit Principles of International Commercial Contracts** which embrace general principles of interpreting international commercial contracts (→ mn. 8). Based on an overarching application of the principle of good faith and fair dealing,[5] they invite to interpret a contract according to the common intention of the parties (i.e., if such intention can be established under the facts of the case), or otherwise, if such intention cannot be established, to interpret the contract "according to the meaning that reasonable persons of the same kind as the parties would give to it in the same circumstances."[6] The rules laid down in Chapter 4 of the Unidroit Principles merge the different approaches to interpretation around the globe and are essentially compatible with most legal systems;[7] they thus build a bridge that can be helpful to use by an Arbitral Tribunal when settling an international dispute. Obviously, if a specific domestic law is applicable to the substance of the dispute under a contract pursuant to para. 2, the rules on interpretation of such domestic law have priority. They may sometimes also require interpreting a contract with regard to the general principle of good faith and fair dealing.[8] Other

---

[2] Note the Chinese word "公正" can also refer to "justice".

[3] This formulation has its roots in Art. 1134(1) of the French Civil Code (initial version), unchanged in this regard since 1804, and today placed in Art. 1103 French Civil Code.

[4] See in detail Kniprath, Die Schiedsgerichtsbarkeit der Chinese International Economic and Trade Arbitration Commission (CIETAC), p. 52; Yu/Cao, A Guide to the CIETAC Arbitration Rules and Practice, mn. 11.30.

[5] Art. 1.7 Unidroit Principles, with multiple concrete and more specific rules applying that principle to different contractual scenarios; see, with multiple further references, Brödermann, Unidroit Principles Commentary, Art. 1.7 mn. 4 (p. 92) [Chinese translation of 1st edn = pp. 31–33].

[6] Art. 4.1 (2) Unidroit Principles, whereby Art. 4.3 lists the different criteria to be considered in this context.

[7] Brödermann, Unidroit Principles Commentary, Introduction to Chapter 4, mn. 2 (p. 208) [Chinese translation of 1st edn = Art. 4.1 mn. 2 (p. 113)]; with reference to Vogenauer in Vogenauer, Commentary on the Unidroit Principles of International Commercial Contracts, Art. 4.1 mn. 16.

[8] See e.g. for Germany §§ 133, 157 BGB.

domestic laws may not include detailed rules on the interpretation of contract,[9] let alone international contracts which have been concluded between parties from different cultures, languages and/or legal backgrounds. In these cases, it can be helpful to refer to Chapter 4 of the UNIDROIT Principles to **interpret or supplement the domestic law on contract interpretation**. Such interpretation or supplementation of domestic laws constitutes one of the purposes of the compilation of general principles and rules of international contract law in the UNIDROIT Principles pursuant to their Preamble, para. 6[10] This technique of interpreting or supplementing domestic law by referencing to the UNIDROIT Principles has been often used by international Arbitral Tribunals, including references to Art. 4.1–4.8 UNIDROIT Principles in the context of contract interpretation.[11] For example, Chapter 4 of the UNIDROIT Principles lists in article Art. 4.3 relevant circumstances which an Arbitral Tribunal may wish to consider in its interpretation of an international contract. Where the applicable domestic law is mute on the issue of contract interpretation, the criteria listed in Art. 4.3 of the UNIDROIT Principles may give guidance.[12] In the same vein, and as a further example, Art. 4.7 of the UNIDROIT Principles contains a special rule on interpretation drawn up in two or more languages. This is a scenario which is usually not covered by domestic laws, especially when only one language is the official language in the jurisdiction for which the domestic law is made. Applying the technique of interpreting or supplementing the applicable domestic law in such cases with regard to the multi-lingual circumstances of the case would be consistent with the goal of **fairness and reasonableness** on the level of the award making and writing, as required by para. 1.

B. Private international law (choice of law), general principles

Further proof of the commitment to apply the law is para. 2, inserted in 2015 and 5
modified by the 2024 CIETAC Rules, by which CIETAC has created **private international law rules for arbitrations.** Pursuant to sentence 1, the **parties may choose** a domestic law that shall apply to their contract. Absent such a choice of law clause pursuant to sentence 1, the Arbitral Tribunal will apply pursuant to sentence 2 the applicable substantive law or principles of law.

The reference to **principles of law**, added in 2024, englobes **soft law codifying general** 6
principles. For international (commercial)[13] contracts, general principles have been

---

[9] For example, Chinese contract law does not contain a specific clause on interpretation of contracts in accordance with the principle of good faith and fair dealing, but the general foundation of Chinese contract law on good faith in Art. 6 and 7 of the general part of the Chinese contract law (中华人民共和国民法总则 of March 15, 2017, people's newspaper (人民日报) of March 19, 2017, p. 1, German translation by Klages/Leibküchler/Pißler, Zeitschrift für Chinesisches Recht 2017, 208) requires that any interpretation of a contract under Chinese contract law should give regard to the principle of good faith and fair dealing. See Schubert, Zeitschrift für Chinesisches Recht 2019, 34. German readers may wish to read further Binding/Pißler/Xu, Chinesisches Zivil- und Wirtschaftsrecht, p. 47, mn. 41 et seq.

[10] See, e.g., with further references, Brödermann, UNIDROIT Principles Commentary, Preamble mn. 12–12b (pp. 31–36) [Chinese translation of 1st edn = pp. 14, 18–19).

[11] See Brödermann, UNIDROIT Principles Commentary, Annex to Preamble – UNIDROIT Principles of International Institute for the Unification of Private Law (UNIDROIT) International Commercial Contract Law, mn. 20–23 (pp. 52–55) with detailed references to multiple arbitral awards.

[12] Both state courts and arbitral tribunals are often using the UNDROIT Principles to supplement national law, see the summary of E. Brödermann, UNDROIT Principles Commentary, Annex to Preamble mn. 20–23, 32–33 (pp. 52–55, 60–65).

[13] It follows from the materials of the UNDROIT Principles that they relate also to other contracts, see the summary records of the meeting of the Working Group for the preparation of the UNIDROIT Principles held in Rome from May 27 to 31, 1991 (P.C. Misc. 18), p. 6 (available at https://www.unidroit.org/

compiled by the International Institute for the Unification of Private Law (UNIDROIT) which was set up in 1926 as an auxiliary organ of the League of Nations. Following first international studies of 1970, *inter alia* of the Max-Planck-Institute for Comparative and International Law in Hamburg (Germany), international working groups set up by UNIDROIT with experts from around the globe have compiled and developed between 1980 and 2016 international compromises between the major legal orders. As a whole, these "**UNIDROIT Principles of International Commercial Contracts"**[14] qualify as **general principles of law.**[15] Since 1995, following the first release of the first UNIDROIT Principles in 1994 (which have been essentially supplemented in subsequent editions), **hundreds of arbitral awards and domestic court decisions** in multiple jurisdictions have refered to the UNIDROIT Principles as general principles of law.[16] A CIETAC award of 2020 has even used the general principles of international contract law in the UNIDROIT Principles to manifest the law of Singapore absent sufficient proof of the parties of the chosen Singapore law.[17] The qualification of the UNIDROIT Principles – as a whole – as general principles and rules of law in the field of international contracts follows from five strings of arguments including

1. the wording of the Preamble of the UNIDROIT Principles,
2. the contents of the UNIDROIT Principles embracing the essence of most legal orders,
3. the history of the making of the UNIDROIT Principles,
4. international practice in hundreds of arbitral awards and national court decisions, and
5. an emerging international *opinio iuris.*[18]

7 In their preamble, the UNIDROIT Principles explicitly mention the purpose to be used in case of a contractual reference to general principles of law in a contract (para. 3) or if the parties have not chosen any law to govern their contract (para. 4) which is exactly the scenario covered by para. 2 sent. 2. The United Nations Commission on International Trade Law (UNCITRAL) has also recommended several times, last in 2021[19], to

---

instruments/commercial-contracts/unidroit-principles-2016/preparatory-work/) as referenced by Brödermann, UNIDROIT Principles Commentary, Preamble mn. 2 (p. 26).

[14] See, generally on the UNIDROIT Principles www.unidroit.org (including Official Comments of UNIDROIT and multiple translations such as the Chinese translation of the blackletter rules at https://www.unidroit.org.). See further case law at www.unilex.info (including a Chinese version) and, as an example from literature with multiple further references, Brödermann, UNIDROIT Principles Commentary, including (only in the 2nd edn) an "Annex to Preamble – UNIDROIT Principles as General Principles of International Commercial Contract Law" at pp. 41–73; see further UNCITRAL et al., Tripartite Legal Guide; Vogenauer, Commentary on the UNIDROIT Principles of International Commercial Contracts.

[15] Brödermann, UNIDROIT Principles Commentary, Annex to Preamble – UNIDROIT Principles as General Principles of International Commercial Contract Law, pp. 41–73.

[16] See, (i) by way of example, *Ad hoc, Nurhima Kiram Fornan et al. v Malaysia*, Preliminary Award on Jurisdiction and Applicable Substantive Law of 25 May 2020, at mn. 141, and (ii) with detailed references, Brödermann, UNIDROIT Principles Commentary, Preamble mn. 12–17 (pp. 46–51) and mn. 30 (p. 59–60).

[17] Brödermann, UNIDROIT Principles Commentary, Annex to Preamble – UNIDROIT Principles of International Commercial Contract Law, mn. 20 (p. 52) with reference to Tung/Zhu/Chen, IPBA/Lexology online at https://lexology.com.

[18] For details see Brödermann, UNIDROIT Principles Commentary, in the Annex to Preamble – UNIDORIT Principles as General Principles of International Commercial Contract Law, mn. 1–45 (at pp. 41–70); and *Ad hoc, Nurhima Kiram Fornan et al. v Malaysia*, Preliminary Award on Jurisdiction and Applicable Substantive Law of 25 May 2020, at mn. 154 A.4.

[19] Report of the United Nations Commission on International Trade Law on the Work of its Fifty-fourth Session (28 June – 16 July 2021), Official Records of the General Assembly, Seventy-sixth Session, Supplement No. 17 at "XIII. Endorsement of texts of other organizations: UNIDROIT Principles of International Commercial Contracts 2016", pp. 51–52 at mn. 267–268 as referenced by Brödermann, UNIDROIT Principles Commentary, Annex to Preamble mn. 37 (p. 67).

use the UNIDROIT Principles for their intended purposes. This includes the application of the UNIDROIT Principles as general principles absent an explicit choice of a domestic law by the parties, pursuant to the Preamble to the UNIDROIT Principles (para. 3 and 4 read jointly). In 2022, the Union Internationale des Avocats (UIA) was the first international Bar Organization to officially recommend the UNIDROIT Principles to lawyers worlwide. Therefore, the optional opening to general principles in sentence 2 in the 2024 version is consistent with an international trend and international arbitration practice.

Para. 1 and 2 also cover the scenario that the parties have chosen in their contract the application of the UNIDROIT Principles in a **"choice of the UNIDROIT Principles-clause"** which is combined with a CIETAC arbitration clause. In view of the **cohesion** of the universal, neutral and general UNIDROIT Principles of International Commercial Contracts with both Chinese law and all other legal civil and common law legal orders,[20] it is particularly appropriate – and practice of the author since many years[21] – to use the UNIDROIT Principles for China-related international contracts. Why should a Chinese party accept foreign law? Why should the foreign party accept Chinese law for an international contract? Any domestic law may be excellent, but it can be very expensive for the foreign contract partner to familiarize itself with the foreign law. In the alternative of choosing a neutral domestic law, both parties would incur such costs of research.[22] By agreeing on the UNIDROIT Principles, this can be avoided.[23] From a Chinese perspective, an agreement on the the UNIDROIT Principles can be easily accepted because the UNIDROIT Principles of International Commercial Contracts correlate well with Chinese contract law because the UNIDROIT Principles have served as an **important source of law for the Chinese civil law.**[24] This has been the case since 1999, when China moved away from a "negligence" – and German law – based conception of civil liability to a CISG and UNIDROIT Principles oriented conception of responsibility by spheres whereby each party is responsible for its own sphere.[25] Choosing the UNIDROIT Principles **levels the playing field** for international contracts and furthers the general goal of living in universal harmony (*he wei gui*: 和为贵, → Ch. 1 mn. 3) by treating each other with respect and curtesy. This reflects the modern **Simplified Global Contracting** approach that combines a choice of the UNIDROIT Principles with an arbitration clause.[26] In 2022/2023, a major Chinese-US software acquisition (with connections to 84 jurisdictions) at a volume of 69 billion USD followed this scheme of combining a choice of the UNIDROIT Principles clause with an arbitration clause.[27] 8

Under para. 1 and 2, an Arbitral Tribunal acting under the CIETAC Rules will have to **honor a choice of the UNIDROIT Principles**, in line with the international trend that 9

[20] For details see, with multiple further references, UNCITRAL et al., Tripartite Legal Guide, mn. 326–330 (pp. 72, 73); Brödermann, UNIDROIT Principles Commentary, Introduction mn. 5–8a (pp. 5–8) and Annex to Preamble – UNIDROIT Principles as General Principles of International Commercial Contract Law, mn. 1–51 (pp. 41–73).

[21] For example, for (i) a cooperation agreement between a German and a Chinese law firm (approx. 2004), (ii) a contract between a German planning and consulting company for zoological and theme park architecture and a Chinese theme park and aquarium operator (2020); or (iii) for three inter-company Licensing Agreements between Austrian or German licensors and Chinese licencees (2023).

[22] Discussed, e.g., by Bonell, Unif. Law Rev. 2018, 15 (17).

[23] Discussed, e.g., with further references, by Brödermann, Tulane J Int. Comp. L 2020, 193, (255 and 209).

[24] It has been argued that 47.3 % of the general part of the Chinese contract law was influenced by the UNIDROIT Principles; see Michaels in Vogenauer, Preamble I mn. 164 with reference to Y. Zhang in fn. 546.

[25] See, e.g., Brödermann, UNIDROIT Principles Commentary, Introduction to Chapter 7 mn. 2 and Art. 7.1.1 mn. 2. For Chinese law see Art. 107 of the Contract Law of the People's Republic of China of 1999, as recently confirmed by Art. 176 et seq., in particular Art. 176–177 of the General Provisions of the Civil Code of the People's Republic of China (in force since May 28, 2020), above note 13.

[26] See Brödermann, UNIDROIT Principles Commentary, Introduction mn. 2 (p. 2).

[27] Transaction between Broadcam Inc. (AVGO), a public company with its headquarter in Shenzen, China and US based and owned VMware (thank you to William Turner for this high-level information).

arbitral rules accept the choice of rules of law.[28] Under the CIETAC Rules an arbitral tribunal can honor a "choice of the UNIDROIT Principles-clause" arguably under sentence 2 or sentence 1. To apply sentence 1 on choice of law (which only refers to agreements on the "law" applicable to the merits of their dispute) requires **interpretation** with regard to the context of para. 2 sent. 2. The context of sentence 1 suggests that the reference to "law" ("法(律)"; → Ch. 1 mn. 4) embraces principles of law ("法律规则") as referenced in sentence 2. In the end, this **distinction** does not matter and can be left open in an arbitral award for two reasons:

10 *Firstly*, if an arbitral tribunal acting under the 2024 CIETAC Rules were to decide that a "choice of the UNIDROIT Principles-clause" does not constitute a proper "choice of law" in the context of para. 2 sent. 1, it would then have to apply para. 2 sent. 2 which explicitly permits to apply general principles of law. In view of the explicit choice of the parties to apply the UNIDROIT Principles pursuant to the "choice of the UNIDROIT Principles-clause", the **commitment to fairness and reasonableness**, to be sought for pursuant to para. 1, would require **honoring the choice of the parties**. As a consequence of this interplay between sentence 1 and 2 of para. 2, the arbitral tribunal must thus apply the UNIDROIT Principles because of the parties' choice in the "choice of the UNIDROIT Principles-clause", even if the arbitral tribunal does not qualify such choice as a choice of law in the sense of sentence 1.

11 *Secondly*, overcoming the distinction between law mentioned in sentence 1 ("法(律)") and principles of law mentioned in sentence 2 would be in line with **international practice** to recognize any choice of the UNIDROIT Principles at least as an **incorporation** of the UNIDROIT Principles into a contract. This is the road taken by the European compromise in recital 13 Rome I Regulation. That Regulation contains the private international law for contracts when they are interpreted by a Member State court. In the end, and contrary to the initial proposal of the European Commission, the European legislator only permitted the choice of Member State law. To balance this approach, the Rome I Regulation reminds in its recital 13 the possibility to refer to a "non-State body of law" by way of incorporation, as emphasized in 2021 by a legal guide issued by the United Nations Commission on International Trade Law, the Hague Conference on Private International Law and UNIDROIT.[29] Yet, in view of the interpretation of para. 2 set forth above at "Firstly" (→ mn. 10), under the CIETAC Rules it is not necessary to argue with a mere substantive incorporation of the UNIDROIT Principles into a contract. Rather, it is submitted that a choice of the UNIDROIT Principles must be **directly recognized** by an arbitral tribunal acting under the 2024 CIETAC Rules. This assessment puts the CIETAC Rules in line with international arbitration practice because, under both Art. 28(1) UNCITRAL Model Law on Commercial Arbitration (→ Ch. 1 mn. 16) and under just about all major institutional arbitration rules, a choice of the UNIDROIT Principles will be recognized.[30]

12 With the choice of the CIETAC Rules, the parties also choose the **choice of law rules** in para. 2. They are not part of the Chinese private international "law" which is set out in the 2010 Law of the People's Republic of China on the Laws Applicable to Foreign-related Civil Relations, but Art. 3 of that law does recognize party autonomy and thereby also the indirect determination of the applicable law via para. 2. In an arbitral

---

[28] Brödermann, UNIDROIT Principles Commentary, Preamble mn. 3 (pp. 26–27) with further references, *inter alia* to Art. 35 of the CEAC Arbitration Rules (today Art. 35 of the Arbitration Rules of the Asian European Arbitration Centre). See also, e.g., Art. 21(1) ICC Arbitration Rules.

[29] UNCITRAL et al., Tripartite Legal Guide, mn. 56 (at p. 15) and mn. 340 (p. 75).

[30] See, with further references, Brödermann, UNIDROIT Principles Commentary, Preamble mn. 2 (pp. 26–27) [Chinese translation of 1st edn = Preamble mn. 2 (pp. 15–16)].

pleading or award, one may leave open the rather academic question if para. 2 applies directly as a result of its integration into the party agreement as a part of the CIETAC Rules, or if it is preferable to also cite Art. 3 of the Law of the People's Republic of China on the Laws Applicable to Foreign-related Civil Relations.

It must be observed in this context that, obviously, and in accordance with both Art. 1.4 of the UNIDROIT Principles and the law as referenced in para. 1, an arbitral award applying the UNIDROIT Principles as general principles of law will also have to apply **mandatory law** which requires its application with regard to the facts and circumstances of the case, and irrespective of the choice of law of the parties. The scope of mandatory law will thus usually be limited to **internationally mandatory law**.[31] The reference to mandatory law reminds arbitrators in the making of their award (and the parties when pleading) that **internationally binding law** needs to be respected which cannot be escaped by a choice of law clause. This is also in the interest of enforceability of the arbitral award (Art. V(2)(b) NYC, Art. 291(2) PRC Civil Procedure Law (2024 version). 13

Subject to this obvious limitation by the boundaries of mandatory law (i.e., an inherent limit to the freedom of choosing the applicable law), an arbitral tribunal acting under the 2024 CIETAC arbitration rules, will thus **honor a choice of the UNIDROIT Principles.** 14

III. Contents of the award, minority opinions

In part, **para. 3–4** repeat with Art. 54 PRC Arbitration Law[32]: (i) the **essence of an arbitral award** mentioned in **para. 3 sent. 1** correspond to solid international arbitration practice (when performing *Scrutiny* pursuant to Art. 51, CIETAC watches out that these essentials are met and accepts variations, e.g. with regard to the detail in which the procedure is being reported in the award); (ii) pursuant to **para. 3 sent. 2**, the parties can **agree** that the facts and the reasons are not to be stated in the award; the same applies to a **"Settlement Arbitration Award"** pursuant to Art. 47(6); (iii) according to **para. 4**, CIETAC shall affix its **seal** to the award. 15

In part, **para. 3–4** go beyond Art. 54 PRC Arbitration Law: (i) The authority given to the Arbitral Tribunal in **para. 3 sent. 3** provides an incentive to **fix a deadline** for the performance of the award (→ Art. 55); (ii) as a Claimant or Counter-Claimant, one might **request** that a certain time frame be determined in the award. 16

C. Decision making

While **para. 7 sent. 2** – which correlates with Art. 54 sent. 4 PRC Arbitration Law – leaves it to the discretion of a co-arbitrator who was outvoted (→ **para. 5 sent. 1** and **para. 6**) **to sign the arbitral award**, **para. 5 sent. 2** regulates the fate of a **minority vote**: It can (not: must) be attached to the award as a non-integral part, but it needs to be taken to the file. 17

Para. 6 emphasizes the **strong role of the Presiding Arbitrator** (→ Art. 26 mn. 4): The opinion of the Presiding Arbitrator is decisive if, in the deliberations, there are three opinions in the room (e.g. on the assessment of damages where there may often be three possible answers within a range of reasonable assessment of damages). The 18

[31] See again Brödermann, UNIDROIT Principles Commentary, Art. 1.4 mn. 2–4 (pp. 81–83) [Chinese translation of 1st edn = Art. 1.4 (pp. 25–27)].

[32] Art. 73 Draft Revised PRC Arbitration Law (2021).

Presiding Arbitrator then writes the Arbitral Award alone while the two (different) deviating opinions of the co-arbitrators are taken to the file or are attached as a non-integral part to the arbitral award. It has been (orally) reported that this legal set-up sometimes leads to deliberations in which the opinion of the co-arbitrators is not given great importance. On the other hand, in an internationally composed arbitration, a strong and experienced presiding arbitrator will be inclined to integrate the co-arbitrators and to lead them to a unanimous decision, in which, at the most, in some parts of the award there may be a reference that an issue was decided "by the majority of the Arbitral Tribunal" (which may even include sometimes one and other times the other arbitrator). This approach is likely to bring about awards which are better accepted by the parties. From a German perspective, it may be noted that, since 2018, the provision in Art. 14.2 sent. 2 of the German DIS Rules now contains a rule which is similar to para. 6 (while traditionally it used to be in Germany that the Arbitral Tribunal had to thrive to come to a majority opinion). A rare exception is the case in which the two co-arbitrators unite their positions against the Presiding Arbitrator (in an internationally composed arbitration even that may happen).

19 **Para. 7** regulates the **written form** and correlates with Art. 54 sent. 3 PRC Arbitration Law (→ above no. 6). Through an addition of 2024, electronic signatures of an award have become possible (para. 7 **sent. 3**). A dissenting arbitrator is not obliged to sign the award (**sent. 2**). In order to enhance the impact of arbitral awards as an instrument of justice equating a court decision, it is however advisable, at least for international or foreign-related CIETAC arbitrations, that all arbitrators sign the award and rather indicate otherwise, that a given issue was decided by a majority.

D. Finalisation, issuance, effect and service of the award

20 Pursuant to **para. 8**, the Arbitral Award becomes **binding with its rendering**. Pursuant to **para. 9**, this implies a **"final"** and **binding** relationship between the parties and an interdiction to request anywhere a substantive revision (other than a correction of obvious errors under Art. 56).

21 Pursuant to **para. 10 sent. 1**, the award will be issued in hard copies. Under **sentence 2**, supplemented with the 2024 version of the CIETAC Rules, a **digital service** to the parties in electronic form is possible upon agreement of the parties or if deemed necessary by CIETAC. Especially in long distance international arbitrations, such electronic service may sometimes be the best option (e.g., to reach a party in remote areas).

As counsel, it may be sensitive to consider the formal requirements of the law in jurisdictions where enforcement may be sought and apply for a non-digital service if these jurisdictions do not recognize a digital award.

Article 53
Partial Award

(1) [1]Where the arbitral tribunal considers it necessary, or where a party so requests and the arbitral tribunal agrees, the arbitral tribunal may first render a partial award on any part of the claim before rendering the final award. [2]A partial award is final and binding upon both parties.

(2) Failure of either party to perform a partial award shall neither affect the arbitral proceedings nor prevent the arbitral tribunal from making the final award.

1 In addition to the conciliation statement pursuant to Art. 47(5), there are various types of arbitral awards to settle the proceedings; i.e., the interim award (new Art. 49) and partial award and an award despite the absence of a party (Art. 39(2)). A **partial award and a default award** are binding upon the parties; however, that seems disputed with regard to interim awards (→Art. 49 mn. 6), and there is no appeal against the award (however, see the rules to set aside arbitral awards, Art. 58 PRC Arbitration Law for national awards, Art. 70 PRC Arbitration Law for arbitration awards containing a foreign element). The application **to set aside the award shall be filed within a deadline of six months** after the arbitration award has been received (Art. 59 PRC Arbitration Law).

2 **Partial awards**, however, are binding and enforceable. They are rendered when rights of the parties are to be protected or if it is expected that the main proceedings could be delayed or settled. Usually, partial awards are used to determine the effectiveness of a contract, the applicable law and the limitation period, whether there is a liability on the merits, or in complicated and protracted proceedings, e.g., if it is intended to separate the liability issue from the issue of damages, or if several claim items were connected that can be dealt with individually or that can be separated again.

Article 54
Scrutiny of Draft Award

The arbitral tribunal shall submit its draft award to CIETAC for scrutiny before signing the award. CIETAC may bring to the attention of the arbitral tribunal issues addressed in the award on the condition that the arbitral tribunal's independence in rendering the award is not affected.

1 The Arbitral Tribunal shall submit the arbitral award to the arbitration commission for review before it is **signed** ("scrutiny"). The vague wording of the review is not intended to affect the independent decision of the arbitrators (comparable to the regulation in ICC proceedings) – according to the explicit wording of the statutory regulation – but it raises questions about the independence of the Arbitral Tribunal. In practice, the review is carried out by a special team at CIETAC. The "CIETAC case manager" (→ Art. 13 mn. 6) merely ensures that the review is carried out promptly. Usually, only formal corrections are required and the independence of the arbitral tribunal will not be affected.

Article 55
Allocation of Fees

(1) The arbitral tribunal has the power to determine in the arbitral award the arbitration fees and other expenses to be paid by the parties to CIETAC.

(2) [1]The arbitral tribunal has the power to decide in the arbitral award, having regard to the circumstances of the case, that the losing party shall compensate the winning party for the expenses reasonably incurred by it in pursuing the case. [2]In deciding whether or not the winning party's expenses incurred in pursuing the case are reasonable, the arbitral tribunal shall take into consideration various factors

such as the outcome and complexity of the case, the workload of the winning party and/or its representative(s), the amount in dispute, etc.

1 Arbitration costs have to be paid by the Claimant (and in the case of a counterclaim by the Respondent) at the start of the arbitration proceedings pursuant to the table of fees of the court of arbitration. The **fees** vary depending on the type of competence, whether it is a domestic or foreign/Hong Kong procedure (→ Art. 3 mn. 3 et seq.). They are based on the amount in dispute and are supposed to cover the **costs for the arbitrators** as well as the **administrative costs** of the arbitration commission.

2 There is further a **registration fee** of RMB 10,000 for each request for arbitration for international or foreign-related disputes (Art. 3(2) no. 1) and for disputes related to the Hong Kong Special Administrative Region, the Macao Special Administrative Region and the Taiwan region (Art. 3(2) no. 2). The registration fee for domestic disputes (Art. 3(2) no. 3) however is calculated according to the amount in dispute (see Fee Schedule II).

3 **Additional fees** may be levied by the arbitration commission, e. g., costs for experts or reviewers appointed by the court, or e. g., additional costs arising due to the participation of a foreign arbitrator.

4 As a matter of principle, **the losing party has to bear the costs**. However, the issue whether the losing party also has to bear the costs for the legal defense of the winning party is open and left to the decision of the Arbitral Tribunal. Previously (until 2005), the losing party had to bear 10 % of the amount of the claim awarded to the successful party, now the costs are only limited to "reasonable" expenses. Usually, if a party wins the case, it can assume that it will receive a full refund of adequate legal costs incurred.

Article 56
Correction of Award

(1) Within a reasonable time after the award is made, the arbitral tribunal may, on its own initiative, make corrections in writing of any clerical, typographical or calculation errors, or any errors of a similar nature, or omissions contained in the award.

(2) [1]Within thirty (30) days from its receipt of the arbitral award, either party may request the arbitral tribunal in writing for a correction of any clerical, typographical or calculation errors, or any errors of a similar nature, or omissions contained in the award. [2]If such an error does exist in the award, the arbitral tribunal shall make the correction in writing within thirty (30) days of its receipt of the written request for the correction.

(3) The above written correction shall form a part of the arbitral award and shall be subject to the provisions in Paragraphs 4 to 10 of Article 52 of these Rules.

1 The arbitrators are allowed to **correct** the award after it has been rendered. However, such corrections are limited to calculation errors, clerical errors or similar errors or if – in practice – the award has not been worded sufficiently clearly. Art. 56 now includes also omissions, which were previously covered under Art. 54 of the 2015 version (Additional award); however, they are **restricted to any omission other than "omissions of decisions on claim and counterclaim"** (which are now dealt with in Art. 57).

2 The parties are also entitled to file respective applications (Art. 56 sent. 2 PRC Arbitration Law).

Article 57
Additional Award

(1) Where any claim or counterclaim which should have been decided by the arbitral tribunal was omitted from the arbitral award, the arbitral tribunal may, on its own initiative, make an additional award within a reasonable time after the award is made.

(2) [1]Either party may, within thirty (30) days from its receipt of the arbitral award, request the arbitral tribunal in writing for an additional award on any claim or counterclaim which was advanced in the arbitral proceedings but was omitted from the award. [2]If such an omission does exist, the arbitral tribunal shall make an additional award within thirty (30) days of its receipt of the written request.

(3) Such additional award shall form a part of the arbitral award and shall be subject to the provisions in Paragraphs 4 to 10 of Article 52 of these Rules.

The revised Art. 57 now deals with omissions but is **now limited to the important issues of "omission of claim and counterclaim" only** (the old Art. 54 previously covered all kinds of "omissions"). If the decision on a claim or counterclaim issue has been omitted in the arbitral award, it is also possible that a party applies for an additional award within the 30-day deadline. This application will most likely be granted if there is actually a decision on any claim or counterclaim missing. A correction *ex officio* is also possible. The additional award and also a correction will then become an integral part of the original award. 1

Article 58
Performance of Award

(1) [1]The parties shall perform the arbitral award within the time period specified in the award. [2]If no time period is specified in the award, the parties shall perform the award immediately.

(2) Where one party fails to perform the award, the other party may apply to a competent court for enforcement of the award in accordance with the law.

A compulsory enforcement of a CIETAC arbitral award within Mainland China, whether it deals with a foreign-related case or a purely domestic case, can only be carried out by a People's Court in Mainland China. In principle according to Art. 2(1) of the "Provisions of the Supreme People's Court on Several Issues concerning the Handling of Cases regarding Enforcement of Arbitral Awards" the Intermediate People's Court, in whose district the respondent has his domicile or his property is located, is competent for decision of the compulsory enforcement.[33] In special cases the Intermediate People's Court can – with the approval of the responsible High People's Court – also designate a Primary People's Court to make the decision. 1

According to Art. 77(2) the arbitral award of an arbitration which is administered by the CIETAC Hong Kong Arbitration Center, shall be seen as a Hong Kong award. For the compulsory enforcement of such an arbitral award, an application for its recognition 2

---

[33] English version available: http://www.lawinfochina.com, interpreted also in Jiang, Understanding and application of the provisions of the new Civil Procedure Law, p. 1365.

is required. The Intermediate People's Court, in whose district the respondent has his domicile or his property is located is responsible for the decision of the recognition and enforcement is award.[34]

3 There were **reports on problems with the enforcement of arbitral awards in previous years, however the situation has improved**. In accordance with Art. 2 and 3 of the "Relevant Provisions on Issues concerning Applications for Verification of Arbitration Cases under Judicial Review" every decision of non-enforcement of an arbitral award, whether it is a foreign or a domestic arbitral award or an arbitral award from Hong Kong, Macau or Taiwan, must be submitted to and examined by the responsible High People's Court and the Supreme People's Court. Only with the approval of these courts an application for the enforcement can be rejected. Through this mechanism the Supreme People's Court is effectively able to scrutinize and carefully evaluate the enforceability of any arbitral awards to be enforced in Maninand China.[35]

4 To apply for a **compulsory enforcement of an CIETAC arbitral award**, only **an application and the arbitral award together with its Chinese translation shall be submitted** in accordance with Art. 525 and 538 of the Civil Procedure Law.[36] In most cases the submission of the arbitration agreement will also be required, as provided for in Art. 18 no. 2 and Art. 19 Provisions of the Supreme People's Court on Several Issues Concerning the Enforcement Work of the People's Courts (for Trial Implementation)[37] and in no. 3 and the second sentence of no. 4 of the "Arrangements on the Mutual Enforcement of Arbitral Awards between the Mainland and the Hong Kong Special Administrative Region".

5 Since every decision of a rejection of the enforcement might eventually examined by the Supreme People's Court itself, it is not surprising that many local People's courts pay special attention to this issue, which may also be the reason for the request of additional documents in certain cases.

6 Although the PRC has not yet officially recognized *ad hoc* arbitration in Mainland China (see Art. 18 PRC Arbitration Law), this does not prevent the enforcement of an award of a non-domestic *ad hoc* arbitration award in accordance with the New York Convention.[38] Likewise, an *ad hoc* arbitration award from Hong Kong, Taiwan or Macau is enforceable in Mainland China.The same applies to an award of a domestic *ad hoc* arbitration, which has been allowed to carry out in the "Pilot Free Trade Zones" since 2016.[39]

7 After a successful recognition the enforcement is the next and in most cases the crucial step. For **compulsory enforcement** between Mainland China and Hong Kong

---

[34] No. 2, Arrangements on the Mutual Enforcement of Arbitral Awards between the Mainland and the Hong Kong Special Administrative Region; no. 3, Supplemental Arrangement Concerning Mutual Enforcement of Arbitral Awards between the Mainland and the Hong Kong Special Administrative Region.

[35] Art. 2 and Art. 3 of the Relevant Provisions on Issues concerning Applications for Verification of Arbitration Cases under Judicial Review 2021 [最高人民法院关于仲裁司法审查案件报核问题的有关规定 2021] in English under Pkulaw.com [CLI Code] CLI.3.5112815(EN).

[36] Office of Leading Small Group of the Supreme People's Court on the work of implementation and enforcement of the Civil Code, Understanding and application of the provisions of the new Interpretation of the Civil Procedure Law, pp. 1164, 1180–1181.

[37] Art. 18 no. 2, Art. 19 Provisions of the Supreme People's Court on Several Issues Concerning the Enforcement Work of the People's Courts (for Trial Implementation); English version available under Pkulaw.com [CLI Code] CLI.3.349750(EN).

[38] See Guiding Case No. 200 of the Supreme People's Court: Svensk Honungsforadling AB's Application for Recognition and Enforcement of a Foreign Arbitral Award.

[39] Opinions of the Supreme People's Court on Providing Judicial Guarantee for the Building of Pilot Free Trade Zones, No. 34 [2016] of the Supreme People's Court.

the application for compulsory enforcement both in Mainland China and Hong Kong is regulated in Art. 2(3) of the "Supplemental Arrangement concerning mutual Enforcement of Arbitral Awards between the Mainland and the Hong Kong".[40]

Unless the applicant had been able to **freeze property** through preservation measures **8**
in advance the success of a compulsory enforcement depends very much on whether the respondent has enough property or assets in Mainland China.[41]

It is not unusual that many respondents attempt to move or hide their assets after **9**
they have lost an arbitration procedure. In such cases, a complex "tracing of assets" in China and abroad may become necessary. Since Chinese debtors also increasingly tend to have assets abroad, there are sometimes interesting enforcement options (→ Ch. 3 mn.3).

---

[40] Art. 2(3) of the Arrangement is amended as: "If the party against whom the application is filed is domiciled or has property in both the Mainland and the HKSAR which may be subject to enforcement, the applicant may file applications for enforcement with the courts of the two places respectively. The courts of the two places shall, at the request of the court of the other place, provide information on its status of the enforcement of the arbitral award. The total amount to be recovered from enforcing the arbitral award in the courts of the two places must not exceed the amount determined in the arbitral award." See: https://www.doj.gov.hk/en/mainland_and_macao/pdf/supplemental_arrangementr_e.pdf.

[41] See: Guiding Case No. 37 of the Supreme People's Court: *Shanghai Jwell Machinery Co., Ltd. v. Retech Aktiengesellschaft.*

Chapter IV
Summary Procedure

Article 59
Application

(1) The Summary Procedure shall apply to any case where the amount in dispute does not exceed RMB 5,000,000 unless otherwise agreed by the parties; or where the amount in dispute exceeds RMB 5,000,000, yet one party applies for arbitration under the Summary Procedure and the other party agrees in writing; or where both parties have agreed to apply the Summary Procedure.

(2) Where there is no monetary claim or the amount in dispute is not clear, CIETAC shall determine whether or not to apply the Summary Procedure after full consideration of relevant factors, including but not limited to the complexity of the case and the interests involved.

1 Disputes with an amount in dispute of up to RMB 5,000,000 will be dealt with in summary proceedings and decided by one single arbitrator unless otherwise agreed by the parties and larger ones only if the parties expressly agree to do so. The award shall be rendered within three months after the Arbitral Tribunal has been constituted (Art. 62(1)). Also in these cases, experience has shown that extensions of the deadline have become more frequent.

Article 60
Acceptance of a Case

Where the Arbitration Court, after examination of the Claimant's Request for Arbitration and its attachments upon receipt, finds that the Request meets the requirements specified in Article 12 of these Rules and that the Summary Procedure shall apply, it shall send a Notice of Arbitration to both parties.

1 The newly worded Art. 60 clarifies that after examination of the formal requirements of the Request for Arbitration (Art. 12) and also the requirements of Art. 59 (Summary Procedure) are met, then the Arbitration Court will send the Notice of Arbitration to both parties. The regulations of Art. 13 with regard to the additional formalities respectively apply (Art. 67).

Article 61
Formation of the Arbitral Tribunal

Unless otherwise agreed by the parties, a sole-arbitrator tribunal shall be formed in accordance with Article 28 of these Rules to hear a case under the Summary Procedure.

1 Since the limit has now been increased significantly (to RMB 5,000,000), it is possible to enter into a deviating agreement in the arbitration clause also for lower amounts in dispute.

Article 62
Defense and Counterclaim

(1) The Respondent shall submit its Statement of Defense, evidence and other supporting documents within twenty (20) days of its receipt of the Notice of Arbitration. Counterclaim, if any, shall also be filed with evidence and supporting documents within such time period.

(2) The Claimant shall file its Statement of Defense to the Respondent's counterclaim within twenty (20) days of its receipt of the Notice of Acceptance of the Counterclaim.

(3) [1]If a party has justified reasons to request an extension of the time period, the arbitral tribunal shall decide whether to grant such extension. [2]Where the arbitral tribunal has not yet been formed, such decision shall be made by the Arbitration Court.

Under the newly worded Art. 62 (previously Art. 59) the 20-day period now only starts once the Claimant has received the "**Notice of Acceptance of the Counterclaim**" (while previously the deadline started already at the time he received the Counterclaim and its attachments). Thus, first an examination of the Arbitration Court takes place, probably in most cases whether upon the submission of the counterclaim the conditions for a Summary Procedure are still applicable. 1

In comparison to the general proceeding rules, where the response time to a counterclaim is 30 days (45 days), (Art. 16), the deadlines of 20 days in each case are significantly shorter and difficult to meet, especially in proceedings containing a foreign element. Consequently, there are often applications for extensions of time, which are usually granted when there is a foreign element or in other justified cases. 2

Article 63
Conduct of Hearing

[1]The arbitral tribunal may examine the case in the manner it considers appropriate. [2]The arbitral tribunal may decide whether to examine the case solely on the basis of the written materials and evidence submitted by the parties or to hold an oral hearing after hearing from the parties of their opinions.

Even if this is not foreseen as a rule, there is often a – albeit short (1–2 days) – **oral hearing**. As with other arbitration institutions during COVID-19, arbitration hearings have increasingly taken place **online**. CIETAC has issued special rules for online hearings.[1] Further, since January 1, 2019, a CIETAC online case filing system has been put into use to improve the efficiency of the case filing procedures. On January 28, 2020, CIETAC published the "Urgent Notice on Work Arrangements during the Prevention 1

[1] CIETAC Guidelines on Proceeding with Arbitration Actively and Properly during the COVID-19 Pandemic, issued on April 28, 2020; CIETAC Guidelines on Proceeding with Arbitration Actively and Properly during the COVID-19 Pandemic issued on 28 April 2020 (中国国际经济贸易仲裁委员会关于新冠肺炎疫情期间积极稳妥推进仲裁程序指引（试行）), available at: http://www.cietac.org.

and Control of the COVID-19", encouraging the parties to file their arbitration applications through its online case filing system.

2 In principle, the arbitral tribunal can decide to hold online hearings, even if one party opposes. However, in practice online hearings have not taken place, if one party opposes. There is in particular a decision by the Supreme Court of the PRC stating that an **online hearing can not be held if one party does not agree to such hearings**. Irrespective of COVID-19, a considerable number of hearings will be conducted online in the future and CIETAC is gearing up to ensure a secure and reliable platform for such online hearings. There remain obstacles for foreign related arbitrations as sometimes CIETAC is not as "international" as it claims, as some features are offered only in Chinese.

Article 64
[Trial of] Oral Hearing

(1) [1]For a case examined by way of an oral hearing, after the arbitral tribunal has fixed a date for the first oral hearing, the parties shall be notified of the date at least fifteen (15) days in advance of the oral hearing. [2]A party having justified reasons may request a postponement of the oral hearing. [3]However, the party shall communicate such request in writing to the arbitral tribunal within three (3) days of its receipt of the notice of the oral hearing. [4]The arbitral tribunal shall decide whether or not to postpone the oral hearing.

(2) If a party has justified reasons for failure to submit a request for a postponement of the oral hearing in accordance with the preceding Paragraph 1, the arbitral tribunal shall decide whether to accept such a request.

(3) A notice of a subsequent oral hearing, a notice of a postponed oral hearing, as well as a request for postponement of such oral hearing, shall not be subject to the time periods specified in the preceding Paragraph 1.

1 In this case, the **deadlines** are also shortened in comparison to the general proceedings (notice of the oral hearing 20 days in advance; extension of time to be applied for within 5 days) and are also often extended in proceedings containing a foreign element.

Article 65
Time Period for Rendering Award

(1) The arbitral tribunal shall render an arbitral award within three (3) months from the date on which the arbitral tribunal is formed.

(2) Upon the request of the arbitral tribunal, the President of the Arbitration Court may extend the time period if he/she considers it truly necessary and the reasons for the extension truly justified.

(3) Any suspension period shall be excluded when calculating the time period in the preceding Paragraph 1.

1 The deadline (para. 1) is reduced from six to three months in comparison to the general proceedings. However, arbitration proceedings with a low amount in dispute are also often complex, so that in practice this deadline is often extended, sometimes several times.

Article 66
Change of Procedure

[1]The Summary Procedure shall not be affected by any amendment to the claim or by the filing of a counterclaim. [2]Where the amount in dispute of the amended claim or that of the counterclaim exceeds RMB 5,000,000, the Summary Procedure shall continue to apply unless the parties agree or the arbitral tribunal decides that a change to the general procedure is necessary.

There is the option here to change the general procedure and with that to also have 1 the opportunity that the procedure is continued before a tribunal consisting of three arbitrators. It is necessary in this case to carefully weigh all aspects; often, the change fails because the party who expects to stand a better chance with one single arbitrator refuses to give its consent.

Article 67
Context Reference

The relevant provisions in the other Chapters of these Rules shall apply to matters not covered in this Chapter.

In order avoid repetition, reference is made to the remaining provisions of the Rules 1 of Arbitration; this is appropriate.

Chapter V
Special Provisions for Domestic Arbitration

While the Rules of Arbitration also contain rules on national arbitration proceedings, the majority of national arbitration proceedings are dealt with before the more than 200 national courts of arbitration. The Beijing Arbitration Commission and the Shanghai Arbitration Commission are of particular importance in this regard. However, as national arbitration cases, disputes between foreign-invested companies (that are usually legal persons under Chinese law) and merely national companies are significant. In this case, the foreign investor prefers the more international platform of CIETAC.

Article 68
Application

(1) The provisions of this Chapter shall apply to domestic arbitration cases.

(2) The provisions of the Summary Procedure in Chapter IV shall apply if a domestic arbitration case falls within the scope of Article 59 of these Rules.

1 According to para. 1, Art. 69–75 shall apply to domestic cases. **Domestic arbitration cases** are disputes between Chinese natural and legal persons. The Arbitration Rules themselves provide no definition of what constitutes "a domestic case". Therefore, the question, whether a case is domestic or not, is to be determined according to the Art. 1 of the "Interpretations of the Supreme People's Court on Several Issues Concerning Application of the Law of Law for Foreign-Related Civil Relationships (I)" and Art. 520 of the "Interpretation of the Supreme People's Court on the Application of the Civil Procedure Law":

Article 1[1]

Where a civil relationship falls under any of the following circumstances, the people's court may determine it as foreign-related civil relationship:

1. **where either party or both parties are foreign citizens, foreign legal persons or other organizations or stateless persons;**
2. **where the habitual residence of either party or both parties is located outside the territory of the People's Republic of China;**
3. **where the subject matter is outside the territory of the People's Republic of China;**
4. **where the legal fact that leads to establishment, change or termination of civil relationship happens outside the territory of the People's Republic of China; or**
5. **other circumstances under which the civil relationship may be determined as foreign-related civil relationship.**

[1] Source: https://shlx.pkulaw.com [CLI Code] CLI.3.349805(EN).

Article 520[2]

The people's court can determine a civil case as one involving foreigners or foreign affairs in any of the following situations:

i. One or both parties concerned are foreigners, stateless persons, foreign enterprises or organizations;
ii. The habitual residence of one or both parties concerned is outside the territory of the People's Republic of China;
iii. The subject matter is outside the territory of the People's Republic of China;
iv. The legal facts incurring, modifying or eliminating the civil relationship occur outside the territory of the People's Republic of China;
v. Other situations can be recognized as a civil case involving foreigners or foreign affairs.

According to these rules, a case can basically be regarded as **non-domestic**, when the subjects, the objects, the content of the civil relationships in question or the habitual residence of either party or both parties contain foreign-related elements. Other than that, according to the general clause of Article 1 no. 5 a case can also be regarded as non-domestic, if there are other justifying circumstances.[3] 2

Thus, an arbitration case will be considered domestic, if none of the conditions quoted in either of Art. 1 above or Art. 520 above is fulfilled. 3

Whether a case is identified as "foreign-related" or "domestic", **not only has an impact on the application of the arbitral procedures,** but also determines the criteria for the judicial review of the enforceability of its award. An arbitral award of a domestic case cannot be enforced, when one of the seven conditions in Art. 248 Civil Procedure Law PRC is fulfilled. On the other hand, an arbitral award of a foreign-related case will be declared as "unenforceable" only due to the five reasons which are listed in Art. 291 Civil Procedure Law PRC (→ Ch. 3 mn. 28). 4

Further an **enterprise, which is registered or has its domicile in Mainland China**, is in accordance with Art. 2(3) and Art. 31 Foreign Investment Law of the PRC[4] also **a Chinese legal person or a Chinese partnership, even if it is wholly owned by foreign shareholders/partners**. Therefore, an arbitration case between another domestic party and such an enterprise will also be considered a domestic case. 5

Chinese law does not view Hong Kong SAR, Macao SAR and Taiwan as foreign countries. Therefore, the provisions of foreign-related cases are not appliable. Instead, **China defines itself as a country with multi-legal regions**[5] **and applies rules of** 6

---

[2] Source: https://shlx.pkulaw.com/en_law/12e67f26d4b80606bdfb.html, [CLI Code] CLI.3.349767(EN).

[3] Leading Small Group of the Supreme People's Court to work on the implementation and enforcement of the Civil code, Encyclopedia of the application of the Civil Code of China, Vol. I, p. 11; Office of Leading Small Group of the Supreme People's court to the work of implement and enforce of Civil code, Understanding and application of the provisions of the new Interpretation of the Civil Procedure Law, p. 1159.

[4] Article 2(3): For the purpose of the Law, a foreign-funded enterprise refers to an enterprise that is incorporated under the Chinese laws within the territory of China and is wholly or partly invested by a foreign investor.
Article 31: The organization form, institutional framework and standard of conduct of a foreign-funded enterprise shall be subject to the provisions of the Company Law of the People's Republic of China, the Partnership Law of the People's Republic of China, and other laws. Source: https://en.ndrc.gov.cn/policies/202105/t20210527_1281403.html.

[5] Leading Small Group of the Supreme People's Court to work on the implementation and enforcement of the Civil Code, Encyclopedia of the application of the Civil Code of China, Vol. I, p. 57.

interregional conflict law, whose content makes reference to the rules for foreign-related cases. For example, with regard to the application of procedural law, according to Art. 549 of the "Interpretation of the Supreme People's Court on the Application of the Civil Procedure Law" a court, which deals with a case related to these three regions, can refer to the special provisions for civil proceedings involving foreigners or foreign affairs.[6]

7 From the perspective of substantive law, Art. 17 of the Interpretations of the Supreme People's Court on Several Issues Concerning Application of the Law of Law for Foreign-Related Civil Relationships (I)[7] and Art. 1 of the Provisions of the Supreme People's Court on the Application of Law in the Trial of Taiwan-Related Civil and Commercial Cases[8] stipulate that the **rules of Private International Law can be used as reference**[参照] when dealing with the parties or case related to these three regions. Thus, due to those special rules of the interregional conflict law, disputes with parties from Taiwan, Hong Kong SAR and Macau SAR are not considered as domestic cases under Art. 68(1).

8 According to Art. 68(2) the provisions of Chapter IV (Summary Procedure) shall apply if the **amount in dispute** is below RMB 5,000,000 and the parties have not agreed otherwise concerning the procedures.

9 Since the procedures for domestic cases contain mostly the same rules, e.g., deadlines for submission of defense and counterclaim and the notice of oral hearing under a summary procedure and under a procedure for domestic cases do not have any substantive difference, except of course for the number of arbitrators. While summary procedures shall – as a general rule – be handled according to Art. 61 and Art. 28 by one arbitrator, in procedures for domestic cases, where the amount in dispute is more than RMB 5,000,000 a tribunal composed of three arbitrators shall be formed according to Art. 70 and Art. 25(2), unless the parties have agreed otherwise.

Article 69
Acceptance of a Case

Where the Arbitration Court, after examination of the Claimant's Request for Arbitration and its attachments upon receipt, finds that the Request meets the requirements specified in Article 12 of these Rules and that the Special Provisions for Domestic Arbitration shall apply, it shall send a Notice of Arbitration to both parties.

---

[6] Article 549: Where a people's court tries a civil lawsuit involving Hong Kong SAR, Macao SAR and Taiwan China, the special provisions of the procedure for civil proceedings involving foreigners or foreign affairs shall be referred to and applicable. See also Office of the Leading Small Group of the Supreme People's Court to the work on the implementation and enforcement of the Civil Code, Understanding and application of the provisions of the new Interpretation of the Civil Procedure Law, p. 1203.

[7] Article 17: Issues concerning application of law in connection with civil relationships involving the Hong Kong Special Administration Region and the Macau Special Administration Region are subject to these Interpretations by analogy.

[8] Article 1: The people's courts shall apply the relevant provisions of the law and judicial interpretations, when handling civil and commercial cases involving Taiwan. According to the rules for selecting applicable laws in laws and judicial interpretations, if it is determined that the civil laws of Taiwan are applicable, the People's Court shall apply. Source: https://shlx.pkulaw.com/en_law/a153992a8d7f290cbdfb.html, [CLI Code] CLI.3.143267(EN).

Article 70
Formation of the Arbitral Tribunal

The arbitral tribunal shall be formed in accordance with the provisions of Articles 25, 26, 27, 28, 29 and 30 of these Rules.

In contrast to the proceedings containing a foreign element, the selection criteria pursuant to Art. 30 (applicable law, language and nationality of the parties) regularly do not play a role. In particular, there are hardly any circumstances under which Chinese law does not apply. 1

Article 71
Defense and Counterclaim

(1) [1]Within twenty (20) days from the date of its receipt of the Notice of Arbitration, the Respondent shall submit its Statement of Defense, evidence and other supporting documents. [2]Counterclaim, if any, shall also be filed with evidence and other supporting documents within the time period.

(2) The Claimant shall file its Statement of Defense to the Respondent's counterclaim within twenty (20) days from the date of its receipt of the Notice of Acceptance of the Counterclaim.

(3) [1]If a party has justified reasons to request an extension of the time period, the arbitral tribunal shall decide whether to grant such extension. [2]Where the arbitral tribunal has not yet been formed, such decision shall be made by the Arbitration Court.

In this case, the deadlines are also significantly reduced from 45 to 20 days in comparison to the general procedure which, however, is acceptable due to the fact that the parties are usually based in China. 1

Article 72
[Trial of] Oral Hearing

(1) [1]For a case examined by way of an oral hearing, after the arbitral tribunal has fixed a date for the first oral hearing, the parties shall be notified of the date at least fifteen (15) days in advance of the oral hearing. [2]A party having justified reason may request a postponement of the oral hearing. [3]However, the party shall communicate such request in writing to the arbitral tribunal within three (3) days of its receipt of the notice of the oral hearing. [4]The arbitral tribunal shall decide whether or not to postpone the oral hearing.

(2) If a party has justified reasons for failure to submit a request for a postponement of the oral hearing in accordance with the preceding Paragraph 1, the arbitral tribunal shall decide whether to accept such a request.

(3) A notice of a subsequent oral hearing, a notice of a postponed oral hearing, as well as a request for postponement of such oral hearing, shall not be subject to the time periods specified in the preceding Paragraph 1.

Article 73
Record of Oral Hearing

(1) [1]The arbitral tribunal shall make a written record of the oral hearing. [2]Any party or participant in the arbitration may apply for a correction upon finding any omission or mistake in the record regarding its own statements. [3]If the application is refused by the arbitral tribunal, it shall nevertheless be recorded and kept with the file.

(2) The written record shall be signed or sealed by the arbitrator(s), the recorder, the parties, and any other participant in the arbitration.

1 In the past, it was often difficult for the parties to obtain a copy of the written record. However, this practice seems to have improved, so that the parties may now obtain a copy.

Article 74
Time Period for Rendering Award

(1) The arbitral tribunal shall render an arbitral award within four (4) months from the date on which the arbitral tribunal is formed.

(2) Upon the request of the arbitral tribunal, the President of the Arbitration Court may extend the time period if he/she considers it truly necessary and the reasons for the extension truly justified.

(3) Any suspension period shall be excluded when calculating the time period in the preceding Paragraph 1.

1 **Extensions** are supposedly common also in national procedures.

Article 75
Context Reference

The relevant provisions in the other Chapters of these Rules, with the exception of Chapter VI, shall apply to matters not covered in this Chapter.

Chapter VI
Special Provisions for Hong Kong Arbitration

The establishment of the CIETAC Arbitration Center in Hong Kong takes account of the increased importance of Hong Kong as a place of arbitration between Chinese and international parties. Moreover, the establishment is supposed to highlight the internationality of CIETAC.[1] With its rules of arbitration, CIETAC constitutes an alternative to the Hong Kong International Arbitration Center (HKIAC).

Article 76
Application

(1) [1]CIETAC has established the CIETAC Hong Kong Arbitration Center in the Hong Kong Special Administrative Region. [2]The provisions of this Chapter shall apply to arbitration cases accepted and administered by the CIETAC Hong Kong Arbitration Center.

(2) Where the parties have agreed to submit their disputes to the CIETAC Hong Kong Arbitration Center for arbitration or to CIETAC for arbitration in Hong Kong, the CIETAC Hong Kong Arbitration Center shall accept the arbitration application and administer the case.

Article 77
Place of Arbitration and Law Applicable to the Arbitral Proceedings

Unless otherwise agreed by the parties, for an arbitration administered by the CIETAC Hong Kong Arbitration Center, the place of arbitration shall be Hong Kong, the law applicable to the arbitral proceedings shall be the arbitration law of Hong Kong, and the arbitral award shall be a Hong Kong award.

Art. 77 contains important clarifications, in particular the applicability of the 1 "Arbitration Ordinance" and the fact that the arbitral award applies as a Hong Kong award. As a consequence, enforcement depends on the particular enforcement arrangements between Mainland China and the Hong Kong SAR ("Arrangement concerning Mutual Enforcement of Arbitral Awards Between the Mainland and the Hong Kong Special Administrative Region"), which was signed on June 1, 1999, and entered into force in Mainland China on February 1, 2000. These provisions emphasize the openness of CIETAC and the preparedness to take over international arbitration practice from Hong Kong.[2]

[1] Annual report on International Commercial Arbitration in China (2014), p. 45.
[2] Annual report on International Commercial Arbitration in China (2014), p. 45–46.

Article 78
Decision on Jurisdiction

[1]Any objection to an arbitration agreement and/or the jurisdiction over an arbitration case shall be raised in writing no later than the submission of the first substantive defense. [2]The arbitral tribunal has the power to determine the existence and validity of the arbitration agreement and its jurisdiction over the arbitration case.

1 Sentence 2 expressly confers the Arbitral Tribunal the "competence – competence". It is important, however, to also pay attention to the provisions in Art. 6(4), since if any law applicable to to the arbitral proceedings provides otherwise, such provision shall prevail.

Article 79
Nomination or Appointment of Arbitrator

[1]The CIETAC Panel of Arbitrators in effect shall be recommended in arbitration cases administered by the CIETAC Hong Kong Arbitration Center. [2]The parties may nominate arbitrators from outside the CIETAC's Panel of Arbitrators. 3An arbitrator so nominated shall be subject to the confirmation of the Chairman of CIETAC.

1 On this issue, it was apparently not possible to fully abandon the principle of the panel of arbitrators which also applies in CIETAC in mainland China. In the case of a dispute, the parties will rarely agree on arbitrators outside of the panel. The confirmation does not only seem to be a formality; there are cases where such confirmation was refused.

Article 80
Interim Measures and Emergency Relief

(1) Unless otherwise agreed by the parties, the arbitral tribunal has the power to order appropriate interim measures at the request of a party.

(2) Where the arbitral tribunal has not yet been formed, a party may apply for emergency relief pursuant to the CIETAC Emergency Arbitrator Procedures (Appendix III).

1 The issue of interim measures is also dealt with to a certain extent above in the commentary to Art. 49 (→ Art. 49 mn. 3 et seq.); however certain special aspects apply in the context of CIETAC Hong Kong arbitration cases.

2 On October 1, 2019, the "Arrangement Concerning Mutual Assistance in Court-ordered Interim Measures in Aid of Arbitral Proceedings by the Courts of the Mainland and of the Hong Kong SAR" (hereinafter referred to as "Arrangement") entered into force.

With regard to an arbitration case in Hong Kong, according to Art. 3 and Art. 1 Arrangement a party of an arbitration in Hong Kong can apply for **Interim Measures in Mainland China**, including a property preservation, evidence preservation and conduct preservation at the Intermediate People's Court, in whose district the respondent has his domicile or in whose district the property of respondent or the evidence is situated. 3

According to Art. 2 Arrangement an **arbitration in Hong Kong** means an arbitral proceeding that takes place in the HKSAR and is administered by a listed arbitral institution. CIETAC HK is one of the listed arbitral institutions.[3] Therefore, an interim measure in accordance with Art. 80 is not only enforceable in Hong Kong SAR but also in Mainland China, although it is not a "final decision". From October 1, 2019 to October 22, 2021, the People's Courts in Mainland China handled 54 cases of assistance in Interim Measures of Arbitral Proceedings in HKSAR, among which were 51 applications for property preservation with a total value of USD 2.3 billion, 2 applications for evidence preservation and 1 application for conduct preservation.[4] According to a report of another listed arbitral institution (i.e., HKIAC), HKIAC handled up to 86 applications for interim measures from 2019 to 2022[5]. In the year 2021 it handled 25 applications with a value of RMB 3.5 billion[6] and in 2022 26 applications with a total value of RMB 7.6 billion[7]. 4

On the other hand, with regard to an arbitration case in Mainland China, according to Art. 6 Arrangement a party to an arbitration administered by a Mainland arbitral institution can also apply for Interim Measures in Hong Kong SAR before the High Court of the HKSAR. "**Mainland arbitral institutions"** refer to all arbitral institutions in Mainland China, which includes also CIETAC and all its sub-commissions in mainland China. An interim measure, which is decided by them in accordance with Art. 23, is enforceable in Hong Kong. 5

It is likely that this option will more often be used in the future. As a result of this legislative change, the interim measures are now enforceable both in Hong Kong and in Mainland China. It provides the foreign parties with a possible method to take hold of the **assets** of the Chinese party at an earlier stage (→ Ch. 3 mn. 2, 38). 6

Article 81
Seal on Award

The seal of the CIETAC Hong Kong Arbitration Center shall be affixed to the arbitral award.

In addition to the signatures, the arbitral award of course also contains a "classic" seal. 1

---

[3] Until the end of 2023 there were other five listed arbitral institutions besides CIETAC HK, such as HKIAC, ICC(ASIA-Office), HKMAG, SCIA(HK) and Ebram; see https://www.doj.gov.hk/sc/community_engagement/announcements/pdf/Interim_Measures_Arrangement_Contact_Details_of_Arbitral_Institutions_sc.pdf (last visited December 28, 2023).

[4] The Fourth Senate for civil proceedings of the Supreme People's Court, The annual report of the Supreme People's court about the judicial examination of commercial arbitrations 2020, p. 16.

[5] https://www.hkiac.org/zh-hans/news/hkiac-releases-statistics-2022.

[6] https://www.hkiac.org/zh-hans/about-us/statistics.

[7] https://www.hkiac.org/zh-hans/about-us/statistics.

Article 82
Arbitration Fees

The CIETAC Arbitration Fee Schedule III (Appendix II) shall apply to the arbitration cases accepted and administered in accordance with this Chapter.

Article 83
Context Reference

The relevant provisions in the other Chapters of these Rules, with the exception of Chapter V, shall apply to matters not covered in this Chapter.

Chapter VII
Supplementary Provisions

Article 84
Language

(1) Where the parties have agreed on the language of arbitration, their agreement shall prevail.

(2) [1]In the absence of such agreement, the language of arbitration shall be Chinese. [2]CIETAC may also designate one or more language(s) as the language(s) of arbitration after taking into proper consideration of all the circumstances of the case including the language(s) of the contract. [3]The arbitral tribunal, after it is formed, may redesignate the language(s) to be used in the proceedings having regard to the circumstances of the case.

(3) If a party or its representative(s) or witness(es) requires interpretation at an oral hearing, an interpreter may be provided either by the Arbitration Court or by the party.

(4) The arbitral tribunal or the Arbitration Court may, if it considers it necessary, require the parties to submit a corresponding translation of their documents and evidence into Chinese or other languages.

Para. 1 entitles the parties to choose the language that shall be used in the arbitral proceedings. 1

The choice of the language should not be underestimated and should be one of the important considerations when drafting an arbitration clause for CIETAC arbitration with foreign parties, who wish to have another language than Chinese in case of arbitration.

The choice of language not only determines the costs and fees of translation, which do arise due to necessity to translate of documents and the interpretation during oral hearing, but it also impacts on the **schedule and efficiency** of the arbitration procedure. 2

Moreover, the language is especially of importance due to the CIETAC system which (usually) only allows arbitrators chosen from the **current list of arbitrators**.[1] For example, there were only 37 German-speaking candidates and 18 Russian-speaking candidates on the CIETAC list of arbitrators for 2021.[2] If the parties select one of these languages as the language of the proceedings, then the number of available candidates will therefore be considerably less than if the arbitration language would be English. 3

On the other hand, if the parties do not reach an agreement on the language of the proceeding, **Chinese** is as a general rule the **default language** as stated in para. 2. Previously, this default was strictly applied and was often a surprise for foreign parties when they entered into arbitration proceedings with a Chinese business partner. Obviously, the Chinese party would hardly relinquish his assumed "advantage" to 4

---

[1] The author is aware of several CIETAC arbitration cases where one of the parties applied for the appointment of an arbitrator outside the CIETAC arbitrator list. The application was rejected in all of these cases.

[2] http://www.cietac.org/Uploads/202310/Panel of Arbitrators.pdf.

communicate in its own language. Such a situation would then mean in the past that mostly Chinese arbitrators would be appointed by CIETAC/nominated by the parties, since the number of foreign arbitrators able to handle Chinese language arbitration is still very limited. However, the amended para. 2 now gives CIETAC the power to redesignate the arbitration language if it considers this appropriate and further – after the establishment of the arbitration tribunal – the arbitral tribunal has also the power to decide on the language(s) of the arbitration. This, at least give a respective foreign party the chance to apply for a change of the language if Chinese is the default language. How this is handled in the future by CIETAC remains to be seen.

5 If **no arbitration language** has been chosen, many factors will determine which language will eventually be used in CIETAC arbitration proceedings. In the first place, it depends on which **document and evidence** would eventually be submitted to the arbitral tribunal. For instance, if a contract and all other evidence in question are only in Chinese, it would be uneconomic and inconvenient to translate all these documents into another language. Otherwise, if a contract is bi-lingual and the contract itself provides for equality of the English and the Chinese language versions (such a provision is not uncommon in contracts with Chinese contract partners.), then it might indeed offer a certain chance under the para. 2 to have arbitration (also) in English.

6 The second relevant element on the decision of the language of the proceedings is the possible **language advantage**, which should not be underestimated in any phase of the proceeding. When the language of the proceeding is the mother tongue of a party or his representative, he can present his arguments and respond to the questions or counter-arguments more efficiently. Then he may be able to have a greater impact on the direction of the of the procedure. Such circumstances could however violate the principle of the equality in accordance with Art. 52(1).

7 Once a certain language has been chosen by the parties or determined by the CIETAC as the language of the proceeding, it has to be ensured at the phase of the choice of the arbitrators that they are proficient in this language. Usually, if the arbitration language is English and two English speaking arbitrators are chosen, the presiding arbitrator chosen by CIETAC (which will probably remain the standard case) will appoint a well-versed English speaking presiding arbitrator.

8 Neither Art. 84 nor other CIETAC rules determine a fixed method in selecting the **interpreters**. The parties can according to para. 3 either bring an interpreter which is chosen by himself or require CIETAC to provide an interpreter.

It is highly recommended for a party to rely on his own interpreters to ensure the quality of the translation; this is particularly true for languages other than English and Chinese.

9 Although Artificial Intelligence (AI) might at some point in the foreseeable future replace humans in translation,[3] there is no sufficient indicator that a personal translation can and will be replaced by a machine translation very soon. However, no matter whether (charged) AI translation or translations by humans, the parties have always to bear the costs and fees of translation and interpreters according to Art. 85(1) and (4).

[3] Habash, 'How is Artificial Intelligence Changing the Translation Services Industry?' https://www.getblend.com/blog/artificial-intelligence-changing-the-translation-services-industry/.

Article 85
Arbitration fees and costs

(1) [1]Apart from the arbitration fees charged in accordance with its Arbitration Fee Schedule, CIETAC may charge the parties for any other additional and reasonable actual costs, including but not limited to arbitrators' special remuneration, their travel and accommodation expenses incurred in dealing with the case, engagement fees of stenographers, as well as the costs and expenses of experts, appraisers or interpreters appointed by the arbitral tribunal.

[2]The special remuneration of an arbitrator may be based on an hourly rate, if agreed by the parties or proposed by the arbitrator with the consent of the Arbitration Court after consulting the parties concerned and may be determined with reference to the standards set forth in Article III, Paragraph B Arbitrator's Fees and Expenses (Based on an Hourly Rate) of the CIETAC Arbitration Fee Schedule III (Appendix II).

(2) Where a party has nominated an arbitrator but fails to advance a deposit for such actual costs as the special remuneration, travel and accommodation expenses of the nominated arbitrator within the time period specified by CIETAC, the party shall be deemed not to have nominated the arbitrator.

(3) [1]Where the parties have agreed to hold an oral hearing at a place other than the domicile of CIETAC or its relevant sub-commission/arbitration center, they shall advance a deposit for the actual costs such as travel and accommodation expenses incurred thereby. [2]In the event that the parties fail to do so within the time period specified by CIETAC, the oral hearing shall be held at the domicile of CIETAC or its relevant sub-commission/arbitration center.

(4) Where the parties have agreed to use two or more than two languages as the languages of arbitration, or where the parties have agreed on a three-arbitrator tribunal in a case where the Summary Procedure shall apply in accordance with Article 59 of these Rules, CIETAC may charge the parties for any additional and reasonable costs.

(5) [1]When providing ad hoc arbitration service to the parties in accordance with Paragraph 7 of Article 2 of these Rules, CIETAC may, taking into account of the request of the parties and the circumstances of the case, and after consulting with the parties, decide to charge the parties relevant arbitration fees and notify the parties to pay within a specified time period. [2]Where the parties fail to pay or pay in full, CIETAC may suspend its ad hoc arbitration service in whole or in part, and the relevant service request of the parties may be deemed to have been withdrawn.

Para. 1 and 4 entitles CIETAC to charge the parties for other additional and reasonable costs, which arise during the proceedings, such as the special remunerations for arbitrators, the travel and accommodation expenses of arbitrators and the costs for interpreters and additional arbitrators. 1

The newly revised second sentence of para. 1 allows all arbitrators of a CIETAC proceeding in Mainland China to charge a **special remuneration** based on an hourly rate with the consent of the parties, which was originally just designed for the proceedings in Hong Kong and in recent years has also become the practice of CIETAC proceedings in Mainland China as an alternative for foreign arbitrators other than a fixed remunerations based on the amount of dispute. 2

3 According to para. 2 after an arbitrator has been nominated by a party, CIETAC can set a **period** for this party to pay in above mentioned costs in advance. If this party has not paid these costs within this period, it would be deemed that the arbitrator has not been nominated. It is not uncommon in practice that the appointment of an arbitrator becomes invalid because the parties do not pay their costs on time.

4 If the parties have selected a place other than where the CIETAC or its sub-commissions are located as the **place of hearing**, they have to pay the extra costs arising due to travel and accommodation expenses of arbitrators between these two places. Otherwise, the oral hearing will take place in accordance with para. 3 at the seat of CIETAC or its sub-commissions.

5 The new para. 5 deals with service fees for an ***ad hoc* arbitration** in accordance with Art. 2(7). Although according to Art. 18 PRC Arbitration Law the PRC has not yet officially recognized *ad hoc* arbitration, such proceedings have been already allowed to carry out in the "Pilot Free Trade Zones" since 2016.[4]

Article 86
Limitation of Liability

CIETAC, its staff members, the arbitrators, the emergency arbitrators and relevant persons engaged by the arbitral tribunal, shall not bear any civil liability to any person for any act, including any negligence, action or omission, in connection with any arbitration under these Rules, and shall not bear any obligation to testify, unless otherwise provided in the law applicable to the arbitration.

1 Art. 86 exempts arbitrators, staff of the arbitral tribunal and CIETAC staff from liability for the arbitration and the duty of testifying.

2 The **scope** of the exemption is wide. It covers all kinds of **negligence** in connection with the arbitration, whether in form of an **act or omission**. Furthermore, the arbitrators, staff of the arbitral tribunal and CIETAC staff are granted the privilege to refuse to testify against a party of the arbitration.

3 Based on the traditions in **civil law**, the arbitration is regarded as a civil contract. "It is the agreement to arbitrate that alone gives the arbitrators the authority to make the award. They, in turn, in resolving the dispute, are acting as the agents or 'mandataires' of the parties."[5]. Thus, just like in case of other contracts, he, who fails to fulfil his duties from the contract, has also to bear the liability. In accordance with this concept of breach of contract, an arbitrator would thus in principle be liable to the damage and loss of parties if he fails to fulfil his duty as an impartial, independent and competent "judge", which therefore has been chosen and paid by the parties.[6] Besides, "there is no concept of an absolute immunity of the judiciary for judicial acts in civil law jurisdictions."[7] Thus, the root of such an exemption from liability cannot be found in the civil law doctrine.

4 However, under **common law principles**, immunity is long established. Based on the long-established tradition of judicial immunity in England,[8] it is regarded as the ground

---

[4] See Opinions of the Supreme People's Court on Providing Judicial Guarantee for the Building of Pilot Free Trade Zones.

[5] Samuel, Jurisdictional problems in international commercial arbitration, p. 34.

[6] Zhan, Commentary to the Liability of Arbitrators in Hong Kong and Mainland China, pp. 31–37.

[7] Hausmaniger, Journal of International Arbitration 1990, 13.

[8] Yu/Shore, International and Comparative Law Quarterly 2003, 935–967.

of public policy that "neither party, witness, counsel, jury, nor judge, can be put to answer civilly or criminally for words spoken in office"[9]. On this ground, arbitral immunity was upheld through a series of decisions of the House of Lords.[10] "[S]ince arbitrators are in much the same position as judges, in that they carry out more or less the same functions, the law has for generations recognized that public policy requires that they too shall be accorded the immunity", because "with such immunity arbitrators would [not] be harassed by actions which would have very little chance of success". Furthermore, it may also be taken into account that "an arbitrator might be influenced by the thought that he was more likely to be sued if his decision went one way than if it went the other way, or that in some way the immunity put him in a more independent position to reach the decision which he thought right"[11]. Such an immunity could prevent an arbitrator from being liable for his activities during the course of the arbitration[12] and is generally considered to be the **basic precondition for an impartial arbitrator**: "an immunity is necessary to enable that third party properly to perform an impartial decision-making function. Furthermore, unless a degree of immunity is afforded, the finality of the arbitral process could well be undermined."[13] The same view is also shared in the United States.[14] Obviously, the newly added Art. 86 follows at this point the view of common law, which regards it as essential and important for the sake of the fairness and impartiality of the arbitrations to exempt the arbitrators and other staff members of the arbitration institution from a possible liability.

However, the immunity provided in Art. 86 may be **limited**, when the law applicable **5**
to the arbitration provides otherwise.

This may particularly true if the **law of Mainland China** applies to the case since **6**
according to Art. 38 PRC Arbitration Law an arbitrator shall be investigated for legal responsibilities, if he has secretly met with a party or the agent of a party, or accepted lavish dinner and gift offered by a party or the agent of a party, or asked for or accepted bribes, played favoritism and committed irregularities while conducting arbitration of the case, or conducted arbitration by twisting the law. The legal responsibilities here refer mainly to civil liabilities, either in form of refunding the arbitration fees or in form of compensation of the loss.[15] Generally speaking, an arbitrator shall thus liable for an intentional wrongful act or omission.

Furthermore, if the arbitration commission is also responsible for those wrong acts of **7**
arbitrators, it may have pay **compensation** in an appropriate sum.[16]

If the laws of **Hong Kong** apply, then a liability of the Arbitral tribunal is governed **8**
by Art. 104 Arbitration Ordinance and a liability of the Appointors and administrators in accordance with Art. 105 Arbitration Ordinance, which make them liable in case of an intentional wrongful act or omission.

---

[9] Lopes LJ in *Royal Aquarium and Summer and Winter Garden Society v Parkinson* [1892] 1 QB 431, 451.

[10] See *Sutcliffe v Thackrah* [1974] AC 727; *Arenson v Casson Beckman Rutley & Co.* [1977] AC 405.

[11] [1974] AC 727, 757.

[12] Huang, International Private Law and International Commercial Arbitration, p. 108.

[13] Department Advisory Committee on Arbitration Law, Report on the Arbitration Bill, p. 296.

[14] In *Corey v New York Stock Exchange* 691 F 2d 1205, at 1211, the court has statement "Extension of arbitral immunity to encompass boards which sponsor arbitration is a natural and necessary product of the policies underlying arbitral immunity; otherwise the immunity extended to arbitrators is illusionary. It would be of little value to the whole arbitral procedure to merely shift the liability to the sponsoring association".

[15] Tang/Sun, The new Interpretation of Arbitration Law, pp. 362–363.

[16] Tang/Sun, The new Interpretation of Arbitration Law, p. 363.

Article 87
Interpretation

(1) The headings of the articles in these Rules shall not be construed as interpretations of the contents of the provisions contained therein.
(2) These Rules shall be interpreted by CIETAC.

Article 88
Coming into Force

[1]These Rules shall be effective as of January 1, 2024. [2]For cases administered by CIETAC or its sub-commissions/arbitration centers before these Rules come into force, the Arbitration Rules effective at the time of acceptance shall apply, or where both parties agree, these Rules shall apply.

1 As a general rule, one can assume that the parties will not change the rules of arbitration applicable at the time when the dispute arises. These new rules of arbitration will apply in existing cases only under exceptional instances.

Appendix I
Directory of China International Economic and Trade Arbitration Commission and its Sub-commissions/Arbitration Centers

China International Economic and Trade Arbitration Commission (CIETAC)
6/F, CCOIC Building, No.2 Huapichang Hutong,
Xicheng District, Beijing, 10035, P.R. China
Tel: +86 10 82217788
Fax: +86 10 82217766/64643500
Email: info@cietac.org
Website: http://www.cietac.org

CIETAC South China Sub-Commission
12F, Tower 2, Kerry Plaza, 1 Zhong Xin Si Road, Futian District, Shenzhen 518046, Guangdong Province, P.R.China
Tel: +86 755 88286848
Fax: +86 755 88286861
Email: infosz@cietac.org
Website: http://www.cietac-sc.org

CIETAC Shanghai Sub-Commission
16F, Century Link Tower 1, No. 1198 Century Avenue, Pudong New Area, Shanghai 200122, P.R. China
Tel: +86 21 60137688
Fax: +86 21 60137689
EMail: infosh@cietac.org
Website: http://www.cietacshanghai.org

CIETAC Tianjin Sub-commission (Tianjin International Economic and Financial Arbitration Center)
1803/1804, 18F, Wanhai Building, Tianjin Wanda Center, the Intersection of Six Weft Road and No.8 Dazhigu Road, Hedong District, Tianjin 300170, P.R. China
Tel: +86 22 66285688
Fax: +86 22 66285678
Email: tianjin@cietac.org
Website: http://www.cietac-tj.org

CIETAC Southwest Sub-Commission
Rm 15-5 & 15-6, 15F, NO.1 Lifan Center, Juxianyan Plaza, Jiangbeizui, Chongqing, 400024, P.R. China
Tel: +86 23 67860011
Fax: +86 23 67860022
Email: cietac-sw@cietac.org
Website: http://www.cietacsw.org.cn

CIETAC Hong Kong Arbitration Center
Room 503, 5/F, West Wing, Justice Place, 11 Ice House Street, Central, Hong Kong
Tel: +852 25298066
Fax: +852 25298266
Email: hk@cietac.org
Website: http://www.cietachk.org.cn

CIETAC Zhejiang Sub-Commission
10/F, Building A, Second light Industry Building, Yan'an Road, Hangzhou City 310006, Zhejiang Province, P.R. China
Tel: +86 571 28169009
Fax: +86 571 28169010
Email: zj@cietac.org
Website: http://www.cietac-zj.org

CIETAC Hubei Sub-Commission
11/F, Building B, Hubei Technology Innovation Towers, No. 34 Xiaohongshan East Road, Wuchang District, Wuhan 430070, Hubei Province, P.R. China
Tel: +86 27 87639292
Fax: +86 27 87639269
Email: hb@cietac.org
Website: http://www.cietac-hb.org

CIETAC Fujian Sub-Commission (Fujian FTZ Arbitration Center)
Rm 1602, 16F, Sunshine City Times Square, 357 Xiangban Street, Northern Minjiang CBD, Taijiang District, Fuzhou 350002, Fujian Province, P.R. China
Tel: +86 591 87600275
Fax: +86 591 87600330
Email: cietac-fj@cietac.org
Website: http://www.cietac-fj.org

CIETAC Jiangsu Arbitration Center
31/F, Deji Mansion, No.188 Changjiang Road, Xuanwu District, Nanjing 210018, Jiangsu Province, P.R. China
Tel: +86 25 69515388
Fax: +86 25 69515390
Email: js@cietac.org
Website: http://www.cietacjs.org.cn

CIETAC Silk Road Arbitration Center
22/F, Building 5, Digital China Industrial Park, No. 20 Zhangba Fourth Road, Xi'an Hi-Tech Zone, Xi'an 710075, Shaanxi Province, P. R. China
Tel: +86 29 81119935
Fax: +86 29 81118163
Email: infosr@cietac.org
Website: http://www.cietac.org

CIETAC Sichuan Sub-Commission (Chengdu International Arbitration Center)
12/F, Center for China-Europe Cooperation (CCEC), No.1577 Tianfu Avenue Middle, High-Tech Zone, Chengdu 610041, Sichuan Province, P. R. China
Tel: +86 28 83180751
Fax: +86 28 83199659
Email: sichuan@cietac.org

CIETAC Shandong Sub-Commission
Rm 301, 304, 3/F, Yinfeng Fortune Plaza B, No.1 Long'ao West Road, Jinan 250102, Shandong Province, P.R. China
Tel: +86 531 81283380
Fax: +86 531 81283390
Email: sdinfo@cietac.org
Website: http://www.cietacsd.org.cn

CIETAC European Arbitration Centre
Mariahilfer Straße 47, 1060 Vienna, Austria
Tel: +43 (1) 310 3110
Fax: +43 (1) 310 3110 01

Email: infoeu@cietac.org
Website: https://www.cietac-eu.org

CIETAC North American Arbitration Center
Email: infous@cietac.org

CIETAC Hainan Arbitration Center
Room 1306, 13F, Windows to Global Trade Building, 15A Guoxing Avenue, Meilan District, Haikou 570100, Hainan Province, P.R. China
Tel: +86 898 3638 8800/3638 8877
Fax: +86 898 3638 8877
Email: hn@cietac.org
Website: http://www.cietac.org

CIETAC Xiong'an Sub-Commission
Comprehensive Management Service Center, Xiong'an Pilot Free Trade Zone, Hebei Province, P.R. China (under construction)
Tel: +86 10 82217788
Email: infoxa@cietac.org

Appendix II
China International Economic and Trade Arbitration Commission Arbitration Fee Schedules

Overview

CIETAC operates with different Fee Schedules for foreign related arbitration (including arbitration related to Hong Kong SAR, Macao SAR and Taiwan region), for domestic arbitration and for arbitration administered by CIETAC in Hong Kong, listed below as schedules I, II and III respectively.

For **foreign-related arbitration**, CIETAC charges a progressive Arbitration Fee and a standard Registration Fee of RMB 10,000. However, there is for arbitrations in Mainland China no specific fee schedule for the remuneration of arbitrators. Hence, in such cases, in particular with foreign arbitrators but sometimes also with experienced Chinese arbitrators the fee has to be agreed upon (also described as "special remuneration"). One of the reasons for this special remuneration is that otherwise CIETAC would not be able to attract foreign, international experienced arbitrators as the "standard fees" of CIETAC in such cases do not match international remuneration levels. This is sometimes not clear to parties which have no or little experience with arbitration at CIETAC. Often, the case managers encourage the foreign arbitrators to use the CIETAC Hong Kong Arbitrators Fee Table as reference or to apply him straightforward.

It is recommendable, due to such situation, to create in the future a more transparent, internationally acceptable remuneration system for arbitrators in foreign-related cases.

In **domestic arbitration**, CIETAC charges a progressive fee as registration fee and for the handling of the case a separate handling fee. Unless arbitrators in domestic cases charge a separate "special remuneration" (which does happen sometimes), the arbitrators will be remunerated using (part of) the amount of the handling fee. Thus, in most domestic arbitration cases the registration fee and handling fee will cover all costs with CIETAC.

CIETAC Hong Kong applies its own fee schedules (also including a fee table for arbitrators). This was necessary as CIETAC Hong Kong competes with HKIAC (which has also similar fee schedules but with higher fees) and thus has to stay competitive.

China International Economic and Trade Arbitration Commission Arbitration Fee Schedule I

(This fee schedule applies to arbitration cases accepted under Item (a) and (b), Paragraph 2 of Article 3 of the Arbitration Rules)

Amount in Dispute (RMB)	Arbitration Fee (RMB)
Up to 1,000,000	4 % of the amount, minimum 10,000
From 1,000,001 to 2,000,000	40,000+3.5 % of the amount over 1,000,000
From 2,000,001 to 5,000,000	75,000+2.5 % of the amount over 2,000,000
From 5,000,001 to 10,000,000	150,000+1.5 % of the amount over 5,000,000
From 10,000,001 to 100,000,000	225,000+1 % of the amount over 10,000,000
From 100,000,001 to 300,000,000	1,125,000+0.65 % of the amount over 100,000,000

Amount in Dispute (RMB)	Arbitration Fee (RMB)
From 300,000,001 to 1,000,000,000	2,425,000+0.60 % of the amount over 300,000,000
From 1,000,000,001 to 2,000,000,000	6,625,000+0.45 % of the amount over 1,000,000,000
Over 2,000,000,001	11,125,000+0.4 % of the amount over 2,000,000,000, and the arbitration fee will be capped for the amount over 3,000,000,000

When a case is accepted, an additional amount of RMB 10,000 shall be charged as the registration fee, which shall include the expenses for examining the application for arbitration, initiating the arbitral proceedings, computerizing management and filing documents.

The amount in dispute referred to in this Schedule shall be based on the sum of money claimed by the Claimant. If the amount claimed is different from the actual amount in dispute, the actual amount in dispute shall be the basis for calculation.

Where the amount in dispute is not ascertained at the time of applying for arbitration, or where special circumstances exist, the amount of the arbitration fee shall be determined by CIETAC.

Where the arbitration fee is to be charged in a foreign currency, the amount in the foreign currency shall be equivalent to the corresponding amount in RMB as specified in this Schedule.

Apart from charging the arbitration fee according to this Schedule, CIETAC may also collect other additional and reasonable actual expenses pursuant to the relevant provisions of the Arbitration Rules.

Arbitration Fee Schedule II

(This fee schedule applies to arbitration cases accepted under Item (c), Paragraph 2 of Article 3 of the Arbitration Rules)

I. Registration fee

Amount in Dispute (RMB)	Registration Fee (RMB)
Up to 100,000	4 % of the amount, minimum 100
From 100,001 to 500,000	4,000+2 % of the amount over 100,000
From 500,001 to 1,000,000	12,000+1 % of the amount over 500,000
From 1,000,001 to 50,000,000	17,000+0.5 % of the amount over 1,000,000
From 50,000,001 to 300,000,000	262,000+0.48 % of the amount over 50,000,000
From 300,000,001 to 1,000,000,000	1,462,000+0.46 % of the amount over 300,000,000
From 1,000,000,001 to 2,000,000,000	4,682,000+0.42 % of the amount over 1,000,000,000
Over 2,000,000,001	8,882,000+0.4 % of the amount over 2,000,000,000, and the registration fee will be capped for the amount over 3,000,000,000

II. Handling fee

Amount in Dispute (RMB)	Handling Fee (RMB)
Up to 200,000	Minimum 6,000
From 200,001 to 5000,000	6,000+2% of the amount over 200,000
From 500,001 to 1,000,000	12,000+1.5% of the amount over 500,000
From 1,000,001 to 5,000,000	19,500+0.45% of the amount over 1,000,000
From 5,000,001 to 20,000,000	37,500+0.3% of the amount over 5,000,000
From 20,000,001 to 100,000,000	82,500+0.2% of the amount over 20,000,000
From 100,000,001 to 1,000,000,000	242,500+0.1% of the amount over 100,000,000
Over 1,000,000,001	1,142,500+0.03% of the amount over 1,000,000,000, and the handling fee will be capped for the amount over 3,000,000,000

The amount in dispute referred to in this Schedule shall be based on the sum of money claimed by the Claimant. If the amount claimed is different from the actual amount in dispute, the actual amount in dispute shall be the basis for calculation.

Where the amount in dispute is not ascertained at the time of applying for arbitration, or where special circumstances exist, the amount of the arbitration fee deposit shall be determined by CIETAC in consideration of the specific rights and interests involved in the dispute.

Apart from charging the arbitration fee according to this Schedule, CIETAC may also collect other additional and reasonable actual expenses pursuant to the relevant provisions of the Arbitration Rules.

Arbitration Fee Schedule III

(This fee schedule applies to arbitration cases administered by the CIETAC Hong Kong Arbitration Center under Chapter VI of the Arbitration Rules)

I. Registration fee

When submitting a Request for Arbitration to the CIETAC Hong Kong Arbitration Center, the Claimant shall pay a registration fee of HKD 8,000, which shall include the expenses for examining the application for arbitration, initiating the arbitral proceedings, computerizing management, filing documents and labor costs. The registration fee is not refundable.

II. Administrative fee

1. Administrative fee table

Amount in Dispute (HKD)	Administrative Fee (HKD)
Up to 500,000	25,000
From 500,001 to 1,000,000	25,000+2 % of the amount over 500,000
From 1,000,001 to 5,000,000	35,000+1.6 % of the amount over 1,000,000
From 5,000,001 to 10,000,000	99,000+0.8 % of the amount over 5,000,000
From 10,000,001 to 20,000,000	139,000+0.5 % of the amount over 10,000,000
From 20,000,001 to 40,000,000	189,000+0.2 % of the amount over 20,000,000
From 40,000,001 to 80,000,000	229,000+0.15 % of the amount over 40,000,000
From 80,000,001 to 400,000,000	289,000+0.05 % of the amount over 80,000,000
From 400,000,001 to 1,000,000,000	449,000+0.02 % of the amount over 400,000,000
Over 1,000,000,001	569,000+0.005 % of the amount over 1,000,000,000, maximum 600,000

The administrative fee includes the remuneration of the case manager and the costs of using oral hearing rooms of CIETAC and/or its sub-commissions/arbitration centers.

Claims and counterclaims are aggregated for the determination of the amount in dispute. Where the amount in dispute is not ascertained at the time of applying for arbitration, or where special circumstances exist, the amount of the administrative fee shall be determined by CIETAC taking into account the circumstances of the case.

Apart from charging the administrative fee according to this Table, the CIETAC Hong Kong Arbitration Center may also collect other additional and reasonable actual expenses pursuant to the relevant provisions of the Arbitration Rules, including but not limited to translation fees, written record fees, and the costs of using oral hearing rooms other than those of CIETAC and/or its sub-commissions/arbitration centers.

Where the registration fee and the administrative fee are to be charged in a currency other than HKD, the CIETAC Hong Kong Arbitration Center shall charge an amount of the foreign currency equivalent to the corresponding amount in HKD as specified in this Table.

III. Arbitrator's fees and expenses

A. Arbitrator's fees and expenses (based on the amount in dispute)

1. Arbitrator's fees table

Amount in Dispute	Arbitrator's Fee (HKD, per arbitrator)	
(HKD)	Minimum	Maximum
Up to 500,000	15,000	60,000
From 500,001 to 1,000,000	15,000+2.30 % of the amount over 500,000	60,000+8.50 % of the amount over 500,000
From 1,000,001 to 5,000,000	26,500+0.80 % of the amount over 1,000,000	102,500+4.3 % of the amount over 1,000,000
From 5,000,001 to 10,000,000	58,500+0.60 % of the amount over 5,000,000	274,500+2.30 % of the amount over 5,000,000
From 10,000,001 to 20,000,000	88,500+0.35 % of the amount over 10,000,000	389,500+1.00 % of the amount over 10,000,000
From 20,000,001 to 40,000,000	123,500+0.20 % of the amount over 20,000,000	489,500+0.65 % of the amount over 20,000,000
From 40,000,001 to 80,000,000	163,500+0.07 % of the amount over 40,000,000	619,500+0.35 % of the amount over 40,000,000
From 80,000,001 to 200,000,000	191,500+0.05 % of the amount over 80,000,000	759,500+0.25 % of the amount over 80,000,000
From 200,000,001 to 400,000,000	251,500+0.03 % of the amount over 200,000,000	1,059,500+0.15 % of the amount over 200,000,000
From 400,000,001 to 600,000,000	311,500+0.02 % of the amount over 400,000,000	1,359,500+0.12 % of the amount over 400,000,000
From 600,000,001 to 750,000,000	351,500+0.01 % of the amount over 600,000,000	1,599,500+0.10 % of the amount over 600,000,000
Over 750,000,001	366,500+0.008 % of the amount over 750,000,000	1,749,500+0.06 % of the amount over 750,000,000

Unless otherwise stipulated in this Schedule, the arbitrator's fees shall be determined by CIETAC in accordance with the above Table taking into account the circumstances of the case. The arbitrator's expenses shall include all reasonable actual expenses incurred from the arbitrator's arbitration activities.

The arbitrator's fees may exceed the corresponding maximum amount listed in the Table provided that the parties so agree in writing or CIETAC so determines under exceptional circumstances.

The parties shall advance the payment of the arbitrator's fees and expenses determined by CIETAC to the CIETAC Hong Kong Arbitration Center. Subject to the approval of the CIETAC Hong Kong Arbitration Center, the parties may pay the arbitrator's fees and expenses in installments. The parties shall be jointly and severally liable for the payment of the arbitrator's fees and expenses.

Claims and counterclaims are aggregated for the determination of the amount in dispute. Where the amount in dispute is not ascertainable, or where special circumstances exist, the amount of the arbitrator's fees shall be determined by CIETAC taking into account the circumstances of the case.

B. Arbitrator's fees and expenses (based on an hourly rate)

Where the parties have agreed in writing that the arbitrator's fees and expenses are to be based on an hourly rate, their agreement shall prevail. The arbitrator is entitled to fees based on an hourly rate for all the reasonable efforts devoted in the arbitration. The arbitrator's expenses shall include all reasonable actual expenses incurred from the arbitrator's arbitration activities.

Where a party applies for the Emergency Arbitrator Procedures, the emergency arbitrator's fees shall be based on an hourly rate.

The hourly rate for each co-arbitrator shall be the rate agreed upon by that co-arbitrator and the nominating party. The hourly rate for a sole or presiding arbitrator shall be the rate agreed upon by that arbitrator and both parties. Where the hourly rate cannot be agreed upon, or the arbitrator is appointed by the Chairman of CIETAC, the hourly rate of the arbitrator shall be determined by CIETAC. The hourly rate for the emergency arbitrator shall be determined by CIETAC.

An agreed or determined hourly rate shall not exceed the maximum rate fixed by CIETAC as provided on the CIETAC website on the date of the submission of the Request for Arbitration. The arbitrator's fees may exceed the fixed maximum rate provided that the parties so agree in writing or CIETAC so determines under exceptional circumstances.

The parties shall advance the payment of the arbitrator's fees and expenses to the CIETAC Hong Kong Arbitration Center, which amount shall be fixed by the latter. The parties shall be jointly and severally liable for the payment of the arbitrator's fees and expenses.

C. Miscellaneous

In accordance with the decision of the arbitral tribunal, the CIETAC Hong Kong Arbitration Center shall have a lien over the award rendered by the tribunal so as to secure the payment of the outstanding fees for the arbitrators and all the expenses due. After all such fees and expenses have been paid in full jointly or by one of the parties, the CIETAC Hong Kong Arbitration Center shall release such award to the parties according to the decision of the arbitral tribunal.

Where the arbitrator's fees and expenses are to be charged in a currency other than HKD, the CIETAC Hong Kong Arbitration Center shall charge an amount of the foreign currency equivalent to the corresponding amount in HKD as specified in this Schedule.

Appendix III
China International Economic and Trade Arbitration Commission Emergency Arbitrator Procedures

Overview: the evolving system of emergency arbitration in China

The Emergency Arbitrator Rules are currently still of limited relevance in China as under the current legal system for arbitration, where PRC law is applicable only courts in China are permitted to issue emergency decisions which are enforceable in the PRC.

However, there have been a couple of Emergency Arbitration cases been reported from China. The first one in China was accepted in the end of 2017 with BAC.

In 2019 two decisions on interim measures, one by the emergency arbitrator and the other by the arbitral tribunal, involving the Kyrgyz Republic and Hong Kong respectively, which was the first time that BAC had issued an interim measure applicable outside Hong Kong.[1] Another emergency arbitrator case was handled with the Shanghai Arbitration Commission in 2019.[2]

The 2020 Annual Report of BAC/BAIC lists also two decisions on interim measures, including one case in which the emergency arbitrator procedures were applied and the application was ultimately rejected, which was also the first case of BAC/BIAC in which an emergency arbitrator rejected an application for an interim measure.[3] In the other case in which the arbitral tribunal issued a decision on an interim measures after organizing online hearings with parties located in different countries, and it was the first time that BAC issued a decision on an interim measure that was applicable to the United States.[4]

Finally in 2021 two decisions on interim measures were both issued by emergency arbitrators, including one case approved and another rejected.[5]

As we can see, the system of Emergency Arbitration has been gaining track in recent years in China and a revision of the Arbitration Law, the draft of which currently includes the recognition of emergency powers by the arbitration institutions (→ Ch. 4) will certainly speed up such process.

Emergency Arbitrator Procedures

Article 1
Application for the Emergency Arbitrator Procedures

1. A party requiring emergency relief may apply for the Emergency Arbitrator Procedures based upon the applicable law or the agreement of the parties.

2. The party applying for the Emergency Arbitrator Procedures (the "Applicant") shall submit its Application for the Emergency Arbitrator Procedures to the Arbitration Court or the arbitration court of the relevant sub-commission/arbitration center of CIETAC administering the case prior to the formation of the arbitral tribunal.

3. The Application for the Emergency Arbitrator Procedures shall include the following information:

(a) the names and other basic information of the parties involved in the Application;

---

[1] BAC/BIAC, Annual Yearbooks of BAC/BIAC 2019.

[2] Shanghai Arbitration Commission's First Arbitration Case Involving Emergency Arbitrator Procedures Enters Enforcement Proceedings in the High Court of Hong Kong.

[3] BAC/BIAC, Annual Yearbook of BAC/BIAC 2020.

[4] BAC/BIAC, Annual Yearbook of BAC/BIAC 2020.

[5] BAC/BIAC, Annual Yearbooks of BAC/BIAC 2021.

(b) a description of the underlying dispute giving rise to the Application and the reasons why emergency relief is required;
(c) a statement of the emergency measures sought and the reasons why the applicant is entitled to such emergency relief;
(d) other necessary information required to apply for the emergency relief; and
(e) comments on the applicable law and the language of the Emergency Arbitrator Procedures.

When submitting its Application, the Applicant shall attach the relevant documentary and other evidence on which the Application is based, including but not limited to the arbitration agreement and any other agreements giving rise to the underlying dispute.

The Application, evidence and other documents shall be submitted in triplicate. Where there are multiple parties, additional copies shall be provided accordingly.

4. The Applicant shall advance the costs for the Emergency Arbitrator Procedures.

5. Where the parties have agreed on the language of arbitration, such language shall be the language of the Emergency Arbitrator Procedures. In the absence of such agreement, the language of the Procedures shall be determined by the Arbitration Court.

Article 2
Acceptance of Application and Appointment of the Emergency Arbitrator

1. After a preliminary review on the basis of the Application, the arbitration agreement and relevant evidence submitted by the Applicant, the Arbitration Court shall decide whether the Emergency Arbitrator Procedures shall apply. If the Arbitration Court decides to apply the Emergency Arbitrator Procedures, the President of the Arbitration Court shall appoint an emergency arbitrator within one (1) day from his/her receipt of both the Application and the advance payment of the costs for the Emergency Arbitrator Procedures.

2. Once the emergency arbitrator has been appointed by the President of the Arbitration Court, the Arbitration Court shall promptly transmit the Notice of Acceptance and the Applicant's application file to the appointed emergency arbitrator and the party against whom the emergency measures are sought, meanwhile copying the Notice of Acceptance to each of the other parties to the arbitration and the Chairman of CIETAC.

Article 3
Disclosure and Challenge of the Emergency Arbitrator

1. An emergency arbitrator shall not represent either party, and shall be and remain independent of the parties and treat them equally.

2. Upon acceptance of the appointment, an emergency arbitrator shall sign a Declaration and disclose to the Arbitration Court any facts or circumstances likely to give rise to justifiable doubts as to his/her impartiality or independence. If circumstances that need to be disclosed arise during the Emergency Arbitrator Procedures, the emergency arbitrator shall promptly disclose such circumstances in writing.

3. The Declaration and/or the disclosure of the emergency arbitrator shall be communicated to the parties by the Arbitration Court.

4. Upon receipt of the Declaration and/or the written disclosure of an emergency arbitrator, a party wishing to challenge the arbitrator on the grounds of the facts or circumstances disclosed by the emergency arbitrator shall forward the challenge in writing within two (2) days from the date of such receipt. If a party fails to file a challenge within the above time period, it may not subsequently challenge the emergency arbitrator on the basis of the matters disclosed by the emergency arbitrator. Where a party becomes aware of a reason for a challenge thereafter, the party may challenge the emergency arbitrator in writing within two (2) days after such reason has become known, but no later than the formation of the arbitral tribunal.

5. A party which has justifiable doubts as to the impartiality or independence of the appointed emergency arbitrator may challenge that emergency arbitrator in writing and shall state the facts and reasons on which the challenge is based with supporting evidence.

6. The President of the Arbitration Court shall make a final decision on the challenge of the emergency arbitrator. If the challenge is accepted, the President of the Arbitration Court shall reappoint an emergency arbitrator within one (1) day from the date of the decision confirming the challenge, and copy the decision to the Chairman of CIETAC. The emergency arbitrator who has been challenged shall continue to perform his/her functions until a final decision on the challenge has been made.

The disclosure and challenge proceedings shall apply equally to the reappointed emergency arbitrator.

7. Unless otherwise agreed by the parties, the emergency arbitrator shall not accept nomination or appointment to act as a member of the arbitral tribunal in any arbitration relating to the underlying dispute.

Article 4
Place of the Emergency Arbitrator Proceedings

Unless otherwise agreed by the parties, the place of the emergency arbitrator proceedings shall be the place of arbitration, which is determined in accordance with Article 7 of the Arbitration Rules.

Article 5
The Emergency Arbitrator Proceedings

1. The emergency arbitrator shall establish a procedural timetable for the emergency arbitrator proceedings within a time as short as possible, best within two (2) days from his/her acceptance of the appointment. The emergency arbitrator shall conduct the proceedings in the manner the emergency arbitrator considers to be appropriate, taking into account the nature and the urgency of the emergency relief, and shall ensure that each party has a reasonable opportunity to present its case.

2. The emergency arbitrator may order the provision of appropriate security by the party seeking the emergency relief as the precondition of taking emergency measures.

3. The power of the emergency arbitrator and the emergency arbitrator proceedings shall cease on the date of the formation of the arbitral tribunal.

4. The emergency arbitrator proceedings shall not affect the right of the parties to seek interim measures from a competent court pursuant to the applicable law.

Article 6
Decision of the Emergency Arbitrator

1. The emergency arbitrator has the power to make a decision to order or award necessary emergency relief, and shall make every reasonable effort to ensure that the decision is valid.

2. The decision of the emergency arbitrator shall be made within fifteen (15) days from the date of that arbitrator's acceptance of the appointment. The President of the Arbitration Court may extend the time period upon the request of the emergency arbitrator only if the President of the Arbitration Court considers it reasonable.

3. The decision of the emergency arbitrator shall state the reasons for taking the emergency measures, be signed by the emergency arbitrator and stamped with the seal of the Arbitration Court or the arbitration court of its relevant sub-commission/arbitration center.

4. The decision of the emergency arbitrator shall be binding upon both parties. A party may seek enforcement of the decision from a competent court pursuant to the relevant law provisions of the

enforcing state or region. Upon a reasoned request of a party, the emergency arbitrator or the arbitral tribunal to be formed may modify, suspend or terminate the decision.

5. The emergency arbitrator may decide to dismiss the application of the Applicant and terminate the emergency arbitrator proceedings, if that arbitrator considers that circumstances exist where emergency measures are unnecessary or unable to be taken for various reasons.

6. The decision of the emergency arbitrator shall cease to be binding:

(a) if the emergency arbitrator or the arbitral tribunal terminates the decision of the emergency arbitrator;
(b) if the President of the Arbitration Court decides to accept a challenge against the emergency arbitrator;
(c) upon the rendering of a final award by the arbitral tribunal, unless the arbitral tribunal decides that the decision of the emergency arbitrator shall continue to be effective;
(d) upon the Applicant's withdrawal of all claims before the rendering of a final award;
(e) if the arbitral tribunal is not formed within ninety (90) days from the date of the decision of the emergency arbitrator. This period of time may be extended by agreement of the parties or by the Arbitration Court under circumstances it considers appropriate; or
(f) if the arbitration proceedings have been suspended for sixty (60) consecutive days after the formation of the arbitral tribunal.

Article 7
Costs of the Emergency Arbitrator Proceedings

1. The Applicant shall advance an amount of RMB 30,000 as the costs of the emergency arbitrator proceedings, consisting of the remuneration of the emergency arbitrator and the administrative fee of CIETAC. The Arbitration Court may require the Applicant to advance any other additional and reasonable actual costs.

A party applying to the CIETAC Hong Kong Arbitration Center for emergency relief shall advance the costs of the emergency arbitrator proceedings in accordance with the CIETAC Arbitration Fee Schedule III (Appendix II).

2. The emergency arbitrator shall determine in its decision in what proportion the costs of the emergency arbitrator proceedings shall be borne by the parties, subject to the power of the arbitral tribunal to finally determine the allocation of such costs at the request of a party.

3. The Arbitration Court may fix the amount of the costs of the emergency arbitrator proceedings refundable to the Applicant if such proceedings terminate before the emergency arbitrator has made a decision.

Article 8
Miscellaneous

These rules for the Emergency Arbitrator Procedures shall be interpreted by CIETAC.

Annex 1
Changes to CIETAC Arbitration Rules 2015 (English)*

China International Economic and Trade Arbitration Commission (CIETAC) Arbitration Rules

CIETAC 2015	CIETAC 2024
Revised and Adopted by the China Council for the Promotion of International Trade/China Chamber of International Commerce on November 4, 2014. *Effective as of January 1, 2015.*	Discussed and Adopted by the Conference of Chairmen of CIETAC on August 22, 2023 and approved by the China Council for the Promotion of International Trade on September 2, 2023. **Effective as of January 1, 2024.**

Chapter I
General Provisions

Article 2
Structure and Duties

CIETAC 2015	CIETAC 2024
(6) The parties may agree to submit their disputes to CIETAC or a sub-commission/arbitration center of CIETAC for arbitration. Where the parties have agreed to arbitration by CIETAC, the Arbitration Court shall accept the arbitration application and administer the case. Where the parties have agreed to arbitration by a sub-commission/arbitration center, the arbitration court of the sub-commission/arbitration center *agreed upon by the parties* shall accept the arbitration application and administer the case. Where the sub-commission/arbitration center agreed upon by the parties does not exist or its authorization has been terminated, or where the agreement is ambiguous, the Arbitration Court shall accept the arbitration application and administer the case. In the event of any dispute, a decision shall be made by CIETAC.	(6) The parties may agree to submit their disputes to CIETAC or a sub-commission/arbitration center of CIETAC for arbitration. Where the parties have agreed to arbitration by CIETAC, the Arbitration Court shall accept the arbitration application and administer the case. Where the parties have agreed to arbitration by a CIETAC sub-commission/arbitration center, **or have agreed to arbitrate or conduct the oral hearing in the province, autonomous region, or centrally-administered municipality where a CIETAC sub-commission/arbitration center is located,** the arbitration court of **that** sub-commission/arbitration center shall accept the arbitration application and administer the case **unless otherwise agreed by the parties. The Arbitration Court may authorize and designate a sub-commission/arbitration center to administer relevant cases having regard to the circumstances of such cases.** Where the sub-commission/arbitration center agreed upon by the parties does not exist or its authorization has been terminated, or where the agreement is ambiguous, the Arbitration Court shall accept the arbitration application and administer the case. In the event of any dispute, a decision shall be made by CIETAC.

* The following table only features the provisions changed via the CIETAC 2024.

	(7) Upon the agreement or request of the parties, CIETAC may provide administration and supporting services for ad hoc arbitration, including but not limited to offering guidance and consultation on the application of the arbitration rules, appointing arbitrators and deciding on the challenge of arbitrators, providing oral hearing services, scrutinizing draft awards, managing arbitrators' remuneration, etc., unless such agreement is inoperative or in conflict with a mandatory provision of the law applicable to the arbitral proceedings.

Article 6
Objection to Arbitration Agreement and/or Jurisdiction

(1) CIETAC has the power to determine the existence and validity of an arbitration agreement and its jurisdiction over an arbitration case. CIETAC *may, where necessary, delegate* such power to the arbitral tribunal.	(1) CIETAC has the power to determine the existence and validity of an arbitration agreement and its jurisdiction over an arbitration case. Such power **is delegated to** the arbitral tribunal **once it is formed**.
(2) Where CIETAC is satisfied by prima facie evidence that a valid arbitration agreement exists, it *may make a decision based on such evidence* that it has jurisdiction over the arbitration case, and the arbitration shall proceed. Such a decision shall not prevent CIETAC from making a new decision on jurisdiction *based on* facts and/or evidence found by the arbitral tribunal during the arbitral proceedings that are inconsistent with the prima facie evidence.	(2) Where CIETAC is satisfied by prima facie evidence that a valid arbitration agreement exists **and decides** that it has jurisdiction over the arbitration case, the arbitration shall proceed. Such a decision shall not prevent the arbitral tribunal from making a new decision on jurisdiction based on facts and/or evidence it found during the arbitral proceedings that are inconsistent with the prima facie evidence.
(3) *Where CIETAC has delegated the power to determine jurisdiction to the arbitral tribunal,* the arbitral tribunal may either make a separate decision on jurisdiction during the arbitral proceedings or incorporate the decision in the final arbitral award.	(3) When deciding on jurisdiction, the arbitral tribunal may either make a separate decision on jurisdiction during the arbitral proceedings or incorporate the decision in the final arbitral award.
(4) Any objection to an arbitration agreement and/or the jurisdiction over an arbitration case shall be raised in writing before the first oral hearing held by the arbitral tribunal. Where a case is to be decided on the basis of documents only, such an objection shall be raised before the submission of the first substantive defense.	(4) Any objection to an arbitration agreement and/or the jurisdiction over an arbitration case shall be raised in writing before the first oral hearing held by the arbitral tribunal. Where a case is to be decided on the basis of documents only, such an objection shall be raised before the submission of the first substantive defense. **Where the law applicable to the arbitral proceedings provides otherwise, such provision shall prevail.**
(5)	**(5)**
(6)	**(6)**
(7) CIETAC or *its authorized* arbitral tribunal shall decide to dismiss the case upon finding that CIETAC has no jurisdiction over an arbitration case. Where a case is to be dismissed before the formation of the arbitral tribunal, the decision shall be made by the President of the Arbitration Court. Where the	(7) CIETAC or the arbitral tribunal shall decide to dismiss the case upon finding of lack of jurisdiction. Where a case is to be dismissed before the formation of the arbitral tribunal, the decision shall be made by the President of the Arbitration Court. Where the case is to be dismissed after the formation of the arbitral

case is to be dismissed after the formation of the arbitral tribunal, the decision shall be made by the arbitral tribunal.

tribunal, the decision shall be made by the arbitral tribunal.

Article 8
Service of Documents and Periods of Time

(1) All documents, notices and written materials in relation to the arbitration may be delivered in person or sent by registered mail or express mail, fax, or by any other means considered proper by the Arbitration Court or the arbitral tribunal.

(2) The arbitration documents *referred to in the preceding Paragraph 1* shall be sent to the address provided by the party itself or by its representative(s), or to an address agreed by the parties. Where a party or its representative(s) has not provided an address or the parties have not agreed on an address, the arbitration documents shall be sent to such party's address as provided by the other party or its representative(s).

(3) Any arbitration correspondence to a party or its representative(s) shall be deemed to have been properly served on the party if delivered to the addressee or sent to the addressee's place of business, place of registration, domicile, habitual residence or mailing address, or where, after reasonable inquiries by the other party, none of the aforesaid addresses can be found, the arbitration correspondence is sent by the Arbitration Court to the addressee's last known place of business, place of registration, domicile, habitual residence or mailing address by registered or express mail, or by any other means that can provide a record of the attempt at delivery, including but not limited to service by public notary, entrustment or retention.

(4) The periods of time specified in these Rules shall begin on the day following the day when the party receives or should have received ***the arbitration correspondence, notices or written materials*** sent by the Arbitration Court.

(1) All documents, notices and materials in relation to the arbitration (**"arbitration documents"**) may be delivered in person or by registered or express mail, by fax, **by electronic means or any other means of communication with a delivery record**, or by any other means considered proper by the Arbitration Court or thc arbitral tribunal. **Electronic means of delivery includes service of arbitration documents by electronic means to the email addresses or other electronic addresses agreed/designated by the parties, or via the digitalized information exchange system of CIETAC or other information system easily accessible to all parties, etc.**

(2) Arbitration documents may be served by electronic means as a preferred way of delivery.

(3) Arbitration documents shall be sent to the address provided by a party itself or by its representative(s), or to an address agreed by the parties. Where a party or its representative(s) has not provided an address or the parties have not agreed on an address, the arbitration documents shall be sent to such party's address as provided by the other party or its representative(s).

(4) Any arbitration documents sent to a party or its representative(s) shall be deemed to have been properly served on the party if delivered to the addressee or sent to the addressee's place of business, place of registration, domicile, habitual residence or address of communication, or where, after reasonable inquiries by the other party, none of the aforesaid addresses can be found, the arbitration documents are sent by the Arbitration Court to the addressee's last known place of business, place of registration, domicile, habitual residence or mailing address by registered or express mail, or by any other means that can provide a record of the attempt at delivery, including but not limited to service by public notary, entrustment or retention.

(5) The periods of time specified in these Rules shall begin on the day following the day when the party receives or should have received **the arbitration documents** sent by the Arbitration Court.

Article 10
Waiver of Right to Object

A party shall be deemed to have waived its right to object where it knows or should have known that any provision of, or requirement under, these Rules has not been complied with and yet participates in or proceeds with the arbitral proceedings without promptly and explicitly submitting its objection in writing to such non-compliance.

A party shall be deemed to have waived its right to object where it knows or should have known that any provision of, or requirement under, these Rules has not been complied with and does not promptly and explicitly submit its objection in writing to such non-compliance, yet participates in or proceeds with the arbitral proceedings **or fails to participate in the hearing without a justifiable reason after being duly notified.**

Chapter II
Arbitral Proceedings

Section 1
Request for Arbitration, Defense and Counterclaim

Article 11
Commencement of Arbitration

The arbitral proceedings shall commence on the day on which the Arbitration Court receives a Request for Arbitration.

The arbitral proceedings shall commence on the day on which the Arbitration Court receives a Request for Arbitration. **Where the Claimant submits a Request for Arbitration in writing and/or via CIETAC's online case filing system, the arbitral proceedings shall commence on the day when such Request is first received.**

Article 12
Application for Arbitration

A party applying for arbitration under these Rules shall:

(1) Submit a Request for Arbitration in writing signed and/or sealed by the Claimant or its authorized representative(s), which shall, inter alia, include:

1. the names and addresses of the Claimant and the Respondent, including the zip code, telephone, fax, email, or any other means of electronic telecommunications;

2. a reference to the arbitration agreement that is invoked;

3. a statement of the facts of the case and the main issues in dispute;

4. the claim of the Claimant; [and]

5. the facts and grounds on which the claim is based.

(1) A party applying for arbitration under these Rules shall:

1. Submit a Request for Arbitration in writing signed and/or sealed by the Claimant or its authorized representative(s), which shall, inter alia, include:

a. the names and addresses of the Claimant and the Respondent, including the zip code, telephone, fax, email, or any other means of electronic telecommunications;

b. a reference to the arbitration agreement that is invoked;

c. a statement of the facts of the case and the main issues in dispute;

d. the claim of the Claimant; [and]

e. the facts and grounds on which the claim is based.

(2) Attach to the Request for Arbitration the relevant documentary and other evidence on which the Claimant's claim is based.

(3) Pay the arbitration fee in advance to CIETAC in accordance with its Arbitration Fee Schedule.

2. Attach to the Request for Arbitration the relevant documentary and other evidence on which the Claimant's claim is based.

3. Pay the arbitration fee in advance to CIETAC in accordance with its Arbitration Fee Schedule.

(2) Where it is agreed in the arbitration agreement that negotiation or mediation shall be conducted before arbitration, the Claimant may apply for arbitration after conducting negotiation or mediation. However, failure to negotiate or mediate shall neither prevent the Claimant from applying for arbitration nor prevent the Arbitration Court from accepting the case, unless the law applicable to the arbitral proceedings or the arbitration agreement expressly provides otherwise.

Article 14
Multiple Contracts

The Claimant may initiate a single arbitration concerning disputes arising out of or in connection with multiple contracts, provided that:

1. such contracts consist of a principal contract and its ancillary contract(s), or such contracts involve the same parties as well as legal relationships of the same nature;

2. the disputes arise out of the same transaction or the same series of transactions; [and]

3. the arbitration agreements in such contracts are identical or compatible.

Article 14
Multiple Contracts and Adding Contract(s) in Arbitration

(1) The Claimant may initiate a single arbitration concerning disputes arising out of or in connection with multiple contracts, provided that:

1. such contracts consist of a principal contract and its ancillary contract(s), or such contracts involve the same parties as well as legal relationships of the same nature, or such contracts involve related subject matters;

2. the disputes **in such contracts** arise out of the same transaction or the same series of transactions; [and]

3. the arbitration agreements in such contracts are identical or compatible.

(2) If all of the circumstances set forth in the preceding Paragraph 1 Nr.1, 2, 3 are met, the Claimant may apply to add contract(s) during the arbitral proceedings. However, such application may be denied if it is too late and may delay the arbitral proceedings.

(3) The procedural matters in the preceding Paragraph 1 and 2 shall be decided by the Arbitration Court. Where the application for adding contract(s) is made after the formation of the arbitral tribunal, such decision shall be made by the arbitral tribunal.

Article 18
Joinder of Additional Parties

(3) Where any party objects to the arbitration agreement and/or jurisdiction over the arbitration with respect to the joinder proceed-

(3) Where any party objects to the arbitration agreement and/or jurisdiction over the arbitration with respect to the joinder proceed-

ings, *CIETAC has the power to decide on its jurisdiction based on the arbitration agreement and relevant evidence.*

ings, **the decision on jurisdiction shall be made in accordance with Article 6 of these Rules.**

Article 19
Consolidation of Arbitrations

(1) At the request of a party, CIETAC may consolidate two or more arbitrations pending under these Rules into a single arbitration if:

1. all of the claims in the arbitrations are made under the same arbitration agreement;

2. the claims in the arbitrations are made under *multiple arbitration agreements* that are identical or compatible *and the arbitrations* involve the same parties as well as legal relationships of the same nature;

3. the claims in the arbitrations are made under *multiple arbitration agreements* that are identical or compatible *and* the multiple contracts *involved* consist of a principle contract and its ancillary contract(s); [or]

4. all the parties to the arbitrations have agreed to consolidation.

(1) At the request of a party, CIETAC may consolidate two or more arbitrations pending under these Rules into a single arbitration if:

1. all of the claims in the arbitrations are made under the same arbitration agreement;

2. the claims in the arbitrations are made under **the arbitration agreements in multiple contracts** that consist of a principle contract and its ancillary contract(s), **or** involve the same parties as well as legal relationships of the same nature, or **involve related subject matters, and the arbitration agreements in such contracts** are identical or compatible; [or]

3. all the parties to the arbitrations have agreed to the consolidation.

Article 21
Copies of Arbitration Documents

When submitting the Request for Arbitration, the Statement of Defense, the Statement of Counterclaim, evidence, and other arbitration documents, the parties shall make their submissions in quintuplicate. Where there are multiple parties, additional copies shall be provided accordingly. Where the party applies for preservation of property or protection of evidence, it shall also provide additional copies accordingly. Where the arbitral tribunal is composed of a sole arbitrator, the number of copies submitted may be reduced by two.

Article 21
Means of Submission and Copies of Arbitration Documents

(1) When submitting the Request for Arbitration, the Statement of Defense, the Statement of Counterclaim, evidence, and other arbitration documents, the parties **may use electronic communication as a preferred means.**

(2) Where parties submit arbitration documents by electronic means, identical hard copies may be required if the Arbitration Court or the arbitral tribunal deems it necessary. Where the electronic version is not identical with the hard copies, the electronic version shall prevail; unless otherwise agreed by the parties.

(3) Where parties make their submissions in hard copies, such submissions shall be in quintuplicate. Where there are multiple parties, additional copies shall be provided accordingly.

Where the party applies for conservatory measures, additional copies shall be provided accordingly. Where the arbitral tribunal is composed of a sole arbitrator, the number of copies submitted may be reduced by two.

Article 22
Representation

A party may be represented by its authorized Chinese and/or foreign representative(s) in handling matters relating to the arbitration. In such a case, a Power of Attorney shall be forwarded to the Arbitration Court by the party or its authorized representative(s).

(1) A party may be represented by its authorized Chinese and/or foreign representative(s) in handling matters relating to the arbitration. In such a case, a Power of Attorney shall be submitted to the Arbitration Court by the party or its authorized representative(s), **and the Arbitration Court shall forward such Power of Attorney to the other parties and the arbitral tribunal.**

(2) If a party changes or adds representative (s) after the arbitral tribunal is formed, the President of the Arbitration Court may take necessary measures to prevent the occurrence of conflicts of interest on the arbitrator(s) as a result of the change including exclusion of the new representative(s) from participating in the arbitral proceedings, having regard to factors such as the parties' opinions made within a reasonable time on the challenge of arbitrator (s) and the progress of the arbitral tribunal's hearing of the case.

Article 23
Conservatory and Interim Measures

(1) Where a party applies for conservatory measures *pursuant to the laws of the People's Republic of China*, CIETAC shall forward the party's application to the competent court designated by that party in accordance with the law.

Article 23
Conservatory Measures and Interim Measures

(1) Where a party applies for conservatory measures, CIETAC shall forward the party's application to the competent court designated by that party.

Upon the request of a party, CIETAC may forward its application for conservatory measures to such court in advance of issuing the Notice of Arbitration.

Section 2
Arbitrators and the Arbitral Tribunal

Article 24
Duties of Arbitrator

An arbitrator shall not represent either party, and shall be and remain independent of the parties and treat them equally.

(1) An arbitrator shall not represent either party, and shall be and remain **impartial and** independent of the parties and treat them equally.

(2) Upon acceptance of appointment/nomination, the arbitrator shall perform his/her duties in accordance with these Rules and carry out the arbitral proceedings diligently and efficiently.

Article 26
Nomination or Appointment of Arbitrator

(3) The arbitral tribunal shall be formed in accordance with these Rules, unless otherwise agreed by the parties.

(4) If the procedure of forming the arbitral tribunal agreed by the parties is manifestly unfair or unjust, or if a party abuses its rights in a way that results in undue delay of the arbitral proceedings, the Chairman of CIETAC may determine the procedure of formation of the arbitral tribunal or appoint any member of the arbitral tribunal.

Article 27
Three-Arbitrator Tribunal

(3) The parties may each recommend one to five arbitrators as candidates for the presiding arbitrator and shall each submit a list of recommended candidates within the time period specified in the preceding Paragraph 2. Where there is only one common candidate on the lists, such candidate shall be the presiding arbitrator jointly nominated by the parties. Where there is more than one common candidate on the lists, the Chairman of CIETAC shall choose the presiding arbitrator from among the common candidates having regard to the circumstances of the case, and he/she shall act as the presiding arbitrator jointly nominated by the parties. Where there is no common candidate on the lists, the presiding arbitrator shall be appointed by the Chairman of CIETAC.

(3) The Claimant and the Respondent may agree that the arbitrators they each nominate shall jointly nominate the presiding arbitrator, and the two arbitrators so nominated shall jointly nominate, or entrust the Chairman of CIETAC to appoint the presiding arbitrator within seven (7) days from the date of their acceptance of the nomination. Failing such joint nomination or entrustment within the above time limit, the presiding arbitrator shall be appointed by the Chairman of CIETAC.

(4) The parties may each recommend one to five arbitrators as candidates for the presiding arbitrator and shall each submit a list of recommended candidates within the time period specified in the preceding Paragraph 2. Where there is only one common candidate on the lists, such candidate shall be the presiding arbitrator jointly nominated by the parties. Where there is more than one common candidate on the lists, the Chairman of CIETAC shall choose the presiding arbitrator from among the common candidates having regard to the circumstances of the case, and he/she shall act as the presiding arbitrator jointly nominated by the parties. Where there is no common candidate on the lists, the presiding arbitrator shall be appointed by the Chairman of CIETAC from **outside the lists.**

(5) In accordance with the parties' agreement or upon the parties' joint requests, the Chair-

(4) Where the parties have failed to jointly nominate the presiding arbitrator according to the above provisions, the presiding arbitrator shall be appointed by the Chairman of CIETAC.

man of CIETAC may provide a list of three candidates for the parties to nominate the presiding arbitrator within seven (7) days upon receipt of such list.

In such case, unless otherwise agreed by the parties, the presiding arbitrator shall be appointed/nominated in the following manner:

1. Each party may exclude one or more candidates to whom it objects and submit the list of remaining candidates to the Arbitration Court.

2. Where there is only one common candidate on the lists of remaining candidates submitted by the parties, such candidate shall be the presiding arbitrator jointly nominated by the parties. Where there is more than one common candidate on the lists, the Chairman of CIETAC shall choose the presiding arbitrator from among the common candidates having regard to the circumstances of the case, and he/she shall act as the presiding arbitrator jointly nominated by the parties. Where there is no common candidate on the lists, the presiding arbitrator shall be appointed by the Chairman of CIETAC from outside the lists.

(6) Where the parties have failed to jointly nominate the presiding arbitrator according to the above provisions, the presiding arbitrator shall be appointed by the Chairman of CIETAC.[1]

Article 28
Sole-Arbitrator Tribunal

Where the arbitral tribunal is composed of one arbitrator, the sole arbitrator shall be nominated pursuant to the procedures stipulated in Paragraphs 2, *3* and 4 of Article 27 of these Rules.

Where the arbitral tribunal is composed of one arbitrator, the sole arbitrator shall be nominated pursuant to the procedures stipulated in Paragraphs 2, 4, **5 and 6** of Article 27 of these Rules.

Article 29
Multiple-Party Tribunal

(2) The presiding arbitrator or the sole arbitrator shall be nominated in accordance with the procedures stipulated in Paragraphs 2, *3* and 4 of Article 27 of these Rules. When making such nomination pursuant to *Paragraph 3 of* Article 27 of these Rules, the Claimant side

(2) The presiding arbitrator or the sole arbitrator shall be nominated in accordance with the procedures stipulated in Paragraphs 2, 4, **5 and 6** of Article 27 of these Rules. When making such nomination pursuant to Article 27 of these Rules, the Claimant side and/or the Re-

[1] Article 27(6) appears in the version published by CCPIT on September 5, 2023, but not in the version published by CIETAC on its website. CCPIT is the Chinese organisation in charge of CIETAC, the authors assume therefore that the CCPIT version should be the governing version.

and/or the Respondent side, following discussion, shall each submit a list of their jointly agreed candidates.

spondent side, following discussion, shall each submit a list of their jointly agreed candidates.

Article 30
Considerations in Appointing Arbitrators

When appointing arbitrators pursuant to these Rules, the Chairman of CIETAC shall take into consideration the law applicable to the dispute, the place of arbitration, the language of arbitration, the nationalities of the parties, and any other factor(s) the Chairman considers relevant.

When appointing arbitrators pursuant to these Rules, the Chairman of CIETAC shall take into consideration the law applicable to the dispute, the place of arbitration, the language of arbitration, the nationalities of the parties, **the type of dispute,** and any other factor(s) the Chairman considers relevant.

Article 31
Disclosure

(2) If circumstances that need to be disclosed arise during the arbitral proceedings, the arbitrator shall promptly disclose such circumstances in writing.

(3) The Declaration and/or the disclosure of the arbitrator shall be submitted to the Arbitration Court to be forwarded to the parties.

(2) If **facts or** circumstances that need to be disclosed arise during the arbitral proceedings, the arbitrator shall promptly disclose such facts or circumstances in writing.

(3) The Declaration and/or the disclosure of the arbitrator shall be submitted to the Arbitration Court to be forwarded to the parties **and other members of the arbitral tribunal.**

Articlc 32
Challenge to Arbitrator

(7) An arbitrator *who has been challenged* shall continue to serve on the arbitral tribunal until a final decision on the challenge has been made by the Chairman of CIETAC.

(7) An arbitrator **whose challenge has been applied** shall continue to serve on the arbitral tribunal until a final decision on the challenge has been made by the Chairman of CIETAC.

Article 33
Replacement of Arbitrator

(3) In the event that an arbitrator is unable to fulfill his/her functions due to challenge or replacement, a substitute arbitrator shall be nominated or appointed within the time period specified by the Arbitration Court according to the same procedure that applied to the nomination or appointment of the arbitrator being challenged or replaced. If a party fails to nominate or appoint a substitute arbitrator accordingly, the substitute arbitrator shall be appointed by the Chairman of CIETAC.

(3) In the event that an arbitrator is unable to fulfill his/her functions due to challenge or replacement, a substitute arbitrator shall be nominated or appointed within the **reasonable** time period specified by the Arbitration Court according to the same procedure that applied to the nomination or appointment of the arbitrator being challenged or replaced. If a party fails to nominate or appoint a substitute arbitrator accordingly, the substitute arbitrator shall be appointed by the Chairman of CIETAC.

Section 3
Hearing

Article 36
Place of Oral Hearing

(1) Where the parties have agreed on the place of an oral hearing, the case shall be heard at that agreed place except in the circumstances stipulated in *Paragraph 3 of Article 82* of these Rules.

(1) Where the parties have agreed on the place of an oral hearing, the case shall be heard at that agreed place except in the circumstances stipulated in **Paragraph 3 of Article 85** of these Rules.

Article 37
Notice of Oral Hearing

Article 37
Oral Hearing

(4) Where a case is to be examined by way of an oral hearing, the parties and their authorized representative(s) shall have the right to participate in the oral hearing. The arbitral tribunal shall decide whether other relevant participants to the arbitration may participate in the oral hearing. Unless otherwise agreed by the parties and the arbitral tribunal, persons other than the participants to the arbitration may not participate in the oral hearing.

(5) After consultation with the parties and taking into consideration of the circumstances of the case, the arbitral tribunal may, at its own discretion, decide to conduct the oral hearing in person, by remote virtual conference, or by other appropriate means of electronic communication.

(6) The Arbitration Court provides oral hearing facilities as well as administrative and logistical support for remote virtual hearings.

Article 39
Default *[of parties]*[2]

Article 39
Default [in Hearing][3]

Article 40
Record of Oral Hearing

(2) Where the parties and other relevant participants to the arbitration believe there is an omission or error in the written record of their statements, they may apply for correction. Such application shall be kept in the record if denied by the arbitral tribunal.

[2] Added by the editor. The text of Art. 39 was not changed in CIETAC 2024.
[3] Added by the editor. The text of Art. 39 was not changed in CIETAC 2024.

(2) The written record, the minutes and the audio-visual record of an oral hearing shall be available for use and reference by the arbitral tribunal.

(3) At the request of a party, the Arbitration Court may, having regard to the specific circumstances of the arbitration, decide to engage a stenographer to make a stenographic record of an oral hearing, the cost of which shall be advanced by the parties.

(3) The written record, the minutes and the audio-visual record of an oral hearing shall be available for use and reference by the arbitral tribunal.

(4) At the request of a party, the Arbitration Court may, having regard to the specific circumstances of the arbitration, decide to engage a stenographer to make a stenographic record of an oral hearing, the cost of which shall be advanced by the parties.

Article 41
Evidence

(4) Unless otherwise agreed by the parties, the arbitral tribunal may decide to apply in whole or in part the CIETAC Guidelines on Evidence ("Guidelines on Evidence") to hear the case. However, the Guidelines on Evidence do not constitute an integral part of these Rules.

Article 42
Examination of Evidence

(1) Where a case is examined by way of an oral hearing, the evidence shall be produced at the oral hearing and may be examined by the parties.

(1) **Unless otherwise agreed by the parties,** where a case is examined by way of an oral hearing, the evidence shall be produced at the oral hearing and may be examined by the parties.

Article 44
Expert's Report and Appraiser's Report

(3) Copies of the expert's report and the appraiser's report shall be forwarded to the parties for their comments. *At the request of either party and with the approval of the arbitral tribunal,* the expert or appraiser shall participate in an oral hearing and give explanations on the report when the arbitral tribunal considers it necessary.

(3) Copies of the expert's report and the appraiser's report shall be forwarded to the parties for their comments. **Upon the application of either party or the request of the arbitral tribunal,** the expert or appraiser shall participate in an oral hearing and explain the report when the arbitral tribunal considers it necessary.

Article 46
Withdrawal *[of the claim]*[4] and Dismissal *[of the cases]*[5]

(2) A party may be deemed to have withdrawn its claim or counterclaim if the arbitral proceedings cannot proceed for reasons attributable to that party.

Article 46
Withdrawal and Dismissal

(2) A party may be deemed to have withdrawn its claim or counterclaim if the arbitral proceedings cannot proceed for reasons attributable to that party **or due to relevant provisions of law.**

[4] Added by the editor.
[5] Added by the editor.

Article 48
Third Party Funding

(1) Once a third party funding agreement is concluded, the funded party shall communicate to the Arbitration Court, without any delay, the existence of the third party funding arrangement, the financial interest therein, the name and address of the third party funder and other relevant information. The Arbitration Court shall forward such information to the other parties and the arbitral tribunal. The arbitral tribunal may order the funded party to disclose other relevant information of the funding if it deems necessary.

(2) When deciding the costs of arbitration and other fees in the award, the arbitral tribunal may take into account of the existence of the third party funding arrangement and the fact whether the requirements set forth in the preceding Paragraph 1 are complied with by the funded party.

Article 49
Interim Award

(1) Where the arbitral tribunal deems necessary, or where a party requests and the arbitral tribunal approves, the arbitral tribunal may render an interim award on any issue in the case before rendering the final award.

(2) Failure of either party to perform an interim award shall neither affect the arbitral proceedings nor prevent the arbitral tribunal from making the final award.

Article 50
Early Dismissal

(1) A party may request for the early dismissal of a claim or counterclaim in whole or in part on the ground that the claim or counterclaim is manifestly without legal merit, or is manifestly outside the jurisdiction of the arbitral tribunal ("Request for Early Dismissal").

(2) A Request for Early Dismissal shall be in writing and shall state the facts and legal basis supporting the application. In order to prevent the abuse of the request to delay the arbitral proceedings, the arbitral tribunal may require the requesting party to provide justifiable grounds for the request and to demonstrate that the early dismissal process will expedite the overall proceedings. A Request for Early Dismis-

sal by the parties shall not prevent the arbitral tribunal from proceeding with the arbitration.

(3) Unless otherwise decided by the arbitral tribunal, a Request for Early Dismissal shall be made as early as possible and no later than the submission of the Statement of Defense or the Reply to the Counterclaim.

(4) The arbitral tribunal shall have the power to decide on whether to accept and consider a Request for Early Dismissal after inviting the parties to express their views.

(5) The arbitral tribunal shall render a decision or an award on the request for early dismissal with reasons stated within sixty (60) days from the date on which such request is made. At the request of the arbitral tribunal, the President of the Arbitration Court may extend the time period if he/she considers such extension justified and necessary.

(6) Where the arbitral tribunal renders an award granting the Request for Early Dismissal, in whole or in part, such award shall not prevent the arbitral tribunal from continuing the hearing of other claims or counterclaims.

Chapter III
Arbitral Award

Article 48
Time Period for Rendering Award

Article 49
Making of Award

(2) Where the parties have agreed on the law applicable to the merits of their dispute, the parties' agreement shall prevail. In the absence of such an agreement or where such agreement is in conflict with a mandatory provision of the law, the arbitral tribunal shall determine *the law applicable to the merits of the dispute.*

(7) Unless the arbitral award is made in accordance with the opinion of the presiding arbitrator or the sole arbitrator and signed by the same, the arbitral award shall be signed by a majority of the arbitrators. An arbitrator who has a dissenting opinion may or may not sign his/her name on the award.

(9) The arbitral award is final and binding upon both parties. *Neither party may bring a lawsuit before a court or make a request to any other organization for revision of the award.*

Article 51
Time Period for Rendering Award

Article 52
Making of Award

(2) Where the parties have agreed on the law applicable to the merits of their dispute, the parties' agreement shall prevail. In the absence of such agreement or where such agreement is in conflict with a mandatory provision of the law, the arbitral tribunal shall determine **the applicable substantive law or principles of law.**

(7) Unless the arbitral award is made in accordance with the opinion of the presiding arbitrator or the sole arbitrator and signed by the same, the arbitral award shall be signed by a majority of the arbitrators. An arbitrator who has a dissenting opinion may or may not sign his/her name on the award. **An electronic signature of an arbitrator bears the same effect of his/her handwritten signature.**

(9) The arbitral award is final and binding upon both parties.

(10) The arbitral award shall be delivered to the parties in hard copies. Where the parties agree, or where CIETAC deems it necessary, the arbitral award may be delivered to the parties in an electronic form.

Article 50 Partial Award

Article 51 Scrutiny of Draft Award

Article 52 Allocation of Fees

Article 53 Correction of Award

(1) Within a reasonable time after the award is made, the arbitral tribunal may, on its own initiative, make corrections in writing of any clerical, typographical or calculation errors, or any errors of a similar nature contained in the award.

(2) Within thirty (30) days from its receipt of the arbitral award, either party may request the arbitral tribunal in writing for a correction of any clerical, typographical or calculation errors, or any errors of a similar nature contained in the award. If such an error does exist in the award, the arbitral tribunal shall make the correction in writing within thirty (30) days of its receipt of the written request for the correction.

(3) The above written correction shall form a part of the arbitral award and shall be subject to the provisions in *Paragraphs 4 to 9 of Article 49* of these Rules.

Article 54 Additional Award

(1) Where any *matter* which should have been decided by the arbitral tribunal was omitted from the arbitral award, the arbitral tribunal may, on its own initiative, make an additional award within a reasonable time after the award is made.

(3) Such additional award shall form a part of the arbitral award and shall be subject to the provisions in *Paragraphs 4 to 9 of Article 49* of these Rules.

Article 53 Partial Award

Article 54 Scrutiny of Draft Award

Article 55 Allocation of Fees

Article 56 Correction of Award

(1) Within a reasonable time after the award is made, the arbitral tribunal may, on its own initiative, make corrections in writing of any clerical, typographical or calculation errors, or any errors of a similar nature, **or omissions** contained in the award.

(2) Within thirty (30) days from its receipt of the arbitral award, either party may request the arbitral tribunal in writing for a correction of any clerical, typographical or calculation errors, or any errors of a similar nature, **or omissions** contained in the award. If such an error does exist in the award, the arbitral tribunal shall make the correction in writing within thirty (30) days of its receipt of the written request for the correction.

(3) The above written correction shall form a part of the arbitral award and shall be subject to the provisions in **Paragraphs 4 to 10 of Article 52** of these Rules.

Article 57 Additional Award

(1) Where any **claim or counterclaim** which should have been decided by the arbitral tribunal was omitted from the arbitral award, the arbitral tribunal may, on its own initiative, make an additional award within a reasonable time after the award is made.

(3) Such additional award shall form a part of the arbitral award and shall be subject to the provisions in **Paragraphs 4 to 10 of Article 52** of these Rules.

Article 55
Performance of Award

Article 58
Performance of Award

Chapter IV
Summary Procedure

Article 56
Application

Article 57
Notice of Arbitration

Where after examination the Claimant's arbitration application *is accepted* for arbitration under the Summary Procedure, the Arbitration Court shall send a Notice of Arbitration to both parties.

Article 59
Application

Article 60
Acceptance of a Case

Where the Arbitration Court, after examination of the Claimant's **Request for Arbitration and its attachments upon receipt, finds that the Request meets the requirements specified in Article 12 of these Rules** and that the Summary Procedure shall apply, it shall send a Notice of Arbitration to both parties.

Article 58
Formation of the Arbitral Tribunal

Article 59
Defense and Counterclaim

(2) The Claimant shall file its Statement of Defense to the Respondent's counterclaim within twenty (20) days of its receipt of *the counterclaim and its attachments.*

Article 61
Formation of the Arbitral Tribunal

Article 62
Defense and Counterclaim

(2) The Claimant shall file its Statement of Defense to the Respondent's counterclaim within twenty (20) days of its receipt of **the Notice of Acceptance of the Counterclaim.**

Article 60
Conduct of Hearing

Article 61
***Notice of* Oral Hearing**

Article 62
Time Period for Rendering Award

Article 63
Change of Procedure

Article 64
Context Reference

Article 63
Conduct of Hearing

Article 64
[Trial of] Oral Hearing

Article 65
Time Period for Rendering Award

Article 66
Change of Procedure

Article 67
Context Reference

Chapter V
Special Provisions for Domestic Arbitration

Article 65
Application

(2) The provisions of the Summary Procedure in Chapter IV shall apply if a domestic arbitration case falls within the scope of *Article 56* of these Rules.

Article 66
Acceptance of a Case

(1) Upon receipt of a Request for Arbitration, where the Arbitration Court finds the Request to meet the requirements specified in Article 12 of these Rules, the Arbitration Court shall notify the parties accordingly *within five (5) days* from its receipt of the Request. *Where a Request for Arbitration is found not to be in conformity with the requirements, the Arbitration Court shall notify the party in writing of its refusal of acceptance with reasons stated.*

(2) Upon receipt of a Request for Arbitration, where after examination, the Arbitration Court finds the Request not to be in conformity with the formality requirements specified in Article 12 of these Rules, it may request the Claimant to comply with the requirements within a specified time period.

Article 67
Formation of the Arbitral Tribunal

Article 68
Defense and Counterclaim

(2) The Claimant shall file its Statement of Defense to the Respondent's counterclaim within twenty (20) days from the date of its receipt of *the counterclaim and its attachments.*

Article 68
Application

(2) The provisions of the Summary Procedure in Chapter IV shall apply if a domestic arbitration case falls within the scope of **Article 59** of these Rules.

Article 69
Acceptance of a Case

Where the Arbitration Court, after **examination** of the **Claimant's** Request for Arbitration and its attachments **upon receipt**, finds that the Request meets the requirements specified in Article 12 of these Rules **and that the Special Provisions for Domestic Arbitration shall apply**, it shall **send a Notice of Arbitration to both parties.**

Article 70
Formation of the Arbitral Tribunal

Article 71
Defense and Counterclaim

(2) The Claimant shall file its Statement of Defense to the Respondent's counterclaim within twenty (20) days from the date of its receipt of **the Notice of Acceptance of the Counterclaim**.

Article 69 *Notice of* Oral Hearing	Article 72 [Trial of] Oral Hearing
Article 70 Record of Oral Hearing	Article 73 Record of Oral Hearing
Article 71 Time Period for Rendering Award	Article 74 Time Period for Rendering Award
Article 72 Context Reference	Article 75 Context Reference

Chapter VI
Special Provisions for Hong Kong Arbitration

Article 73 Application	Article 76 Application
Article 74 Place of Arbitration and Law Applicable to the Arbitral Proceedings	Article 77 Place of Arbitration and Law Applicable to the Arbitral Proceedings
Article 75 Decision on Jurisdiction	Article 78 Decision on Jurisdiction
Article 76 Nomination or Appointment of Arbitrator	Article 79 Nomination or Appointment of Arbitrator
Article 77 Interim Measures and Emergency Relief	Article 80 Interim Measures and Emergency Relief
Article 78 Seal on Award	Article 81 Seal on Award
Article 79 Arbitration Fees	Article 82 Arbitration Fees
Article 80 Context Reference	Article 83 Context Reference

Chapter VII
Supplementary Provisions

Article 81
Language

(1) Where the parties have agreed on the language of arbitration, their agreement shall prevail. In the absence of such agreement, the language of arbitration to be used in the proceedings shall be Chinese. CIETAC may also designate *another language* as the language of arbitration having *regard to the circumstances of the case.*

(2) If a party or its representative(s) or witness(es) requires interpretation at an oral hearing, an interpreter may be provided either by the Arbitration Court or by the party.

(3) The arbitral tribunal or the Arbitration Court may, if it considers it necessary, require the parties to submit a corresponding translation of their documents and evidence into Chinese or other languages.

Article 82
Arbitration Fees and Costs

(1) Apart from the arbitration fees charged in accordance with its Arbitration Fee Schedule, CIETAC may charge the parties for any other additional and reasonable actual costs, including but not limited to arbitrators' special remuneration, their travel and accommodation expenses incurred in dealing with the case, engagement fees of stenographers, as well as the costs and expenses of experts, appraisers or interpreters appointed by the arbitral tribunal. *The Arbitration Court shall, after hearing from the arbitrator and the party concerned,* determine the arbitrator's special remuneration with reference to the standards of arbitrators' fees and expenses set forth in the CIETAC Arbitration Fee Schedule III (Appendix II).

Article 84
Language

(1) Where the parties have agreed on the language of arbitration, their agreement shall prevail.

(2) In the absence of such agreement, the language of arbitration shall be Chinese. CIETAC may also designate **one or more language(s) as the language(s) of arbitration after taking into proper consideration of all the circumstances of the case including the language(s) of the contract. The arbitral tribunal, after it is formed,** may **redesignate the language(s) to be used in the proceedings having regard to the circumstances** of the case.

(3) If a party or its representative(s) or witness(es) requires interpretation at an oral hearing, an interpreter may be provided either by the Arbitration Court or by the party.

(4) The arbitral tribunal or the Arbitration Court may, if it considers it necessary, require the parties to submit a corresponding translation of their documents and evidence into Chinese or other languages.

Article 85
Arbitration Fees and Costs

(1) Apart from the arbitration fees charged in accordance with its Arbitration Fee Schedule, CIETAC may charge the parties for any other additional and reasonable actual costs, including but not limited to arbitrators' special remuneration, their travel and accommodation expenses incurred in dealing with the case, engagement fees of stenographers, as well as the costs and expenses of experts, appraisers or interpreters appointed by the arbitral tribunal. The special remuneration of an arbitrator **may be based on an hourly rate, if agreed by the parties or proposed by the arbitrator with the consent of the Arbitration Court after consulting the parties concerned , and** may be determined with reference to the standards set forth **in Article III, Paragraph B** Arbitrator's

Article 83
Interpretation

Article 84
Coming into Force

These Rules shall be effective as of *January 1, 2015*. For cases administered by CIETAC or its sub-commissions/arbitration centers before these Rules come into force, the Arbitration Rules effective at the time of acceptance shall apply, or where both parties agree, these Rules shall apply.

Fees and Expenses **(Based on an Hourly Rate)** of the CIETAC Arbitration Fee Schedule III (Appendix II).

(5) When providing ad hoc arbitration service to the parties in accordance with Paragraph 7 of Article 2 of these Rules, CIETAC may, taking into account of the request of the parties and the circumstances of the case, and after consulting with the parties, decide to charge the parties relevant arbitration fees and notify the parties to pay within a specified time period. Where the parties fail to pay or pay in full, CIETAC may suspend its ad hoc arbitration service in whole or in part, and the relevant service request of the parties may be deemed to have been withdrawn.

Article 86
Limitation of Liability

CIETAC, its staff members, the arbitrators, the emergency arbitrators and relevant persons engaged by the arbitral tribunal, shall not bear any civil liability to any person for any act, including any negligence, action or omission, in connection with any arbitration under these Rules, and shall not bear any obligation to testify, unless otherwise provided in the law applicable to the arbitration.

Article 87
Interpretation

Article 88
Coming into Force

These Rules shall be effective as of **January 1, 2024**. For cases administered by CIETAC or its sub-commissions/arbitration centers before these Rules come into force, the Arbitration Rules effective at the time of acceptance shall apply, or where both parties agree, these Rules shall apply.

Annex 2
Changes to CIETAC Arbitration Rules 2015 (full Chinese versions)

中国国际经济贸易仲裁委员会仲裁规则

(2014 年 11 月 4 日中国国际贸易促进委员会/中国国际商会修订并通过，自 2015 年 1 月 1 日起施行)	**(2023 年 8 月 22 日贸仲主任会议审议通过，经中国贸促会 2023 年 9 月 2 日核准，自 2024 年 1 月 1 日起施行)**
第一章 总 则	第一章 总 则
第一条 仲裁委员会	第一条 仲裁委员会
(一)中国国际经济贸易仲裁委员会(以下简称“仲裁委员会”)，原名中国国际贸易促进委员会对外贸易仲裁委员会、中国国际贸易促进委员会对外经济贸易仲裁委员会，同时使用“中国国际商会仲裁院”名称。	(一)中国国际经济贸易仲裁委员会(以下简称“仲裁委员会”)，原名中国国际贸易促进委员会对外贸易仲裁委员会、中国国际贸易促进委员会对外经济贸易仲裁委员会，同时使用“中国国际商会仲裁院”名称。
(二)当事人在仲裁协议中订明由中国国际贸易促进委员会/中国国际商会仲裁，或由中国国际贸易促进委员会/中国国际商会的仲裁委员会或仲裁院仲裁的,或使用仲裁委员会原名称为仲裁机构的，均视为同意由中国国际经济贸易仲裁委员会仲裁。	(二)当事人在仲裁协议中订明由中国国际贸易促进委员会/中国国际商会仲裁，或由中国国际贸易促进委员会/中国国际商会的仲裁委员会或仲裁院仲裁的,或使用仲裁委员会原名称为仲裁机构的，均视为同意由中国国际经济贸易仲裁委员会仲裁。
第二条 机构及职责	第二条 机构及职责
(一)仲裁委员会主任履行本规则赋予的职责。副主任根据主任的授权可以履行主任的职责。	(一)仲裁委员会主任履行本规则赋予的职责。副主任根据主任的授权可以履行主任的职责。
(二)仲裁委员会设有仲裁院,在授权的副主任和仲裁院院长的领导下履行本规则规定的职责。	(二)仲裁委员会设有仲裁院,在授权的副主任和仲裁院院长的领导下履行本规则规定的职责。
(三)仲裁委员会设在北京。仲裁委员会设有分会或仲裁中心(本规则附件一)。仲裁委员会的分会/仲裁中心是仲裁委员会的派出机构,根据仲裁委员会的授权,接受仲裁申请,管理仲裁案件。	(三)仲裁委员会设在北京。仲裁委员会设有分会或仲裁中心(本规则附件一)。仲裁委员会的分会/仲裁中心是仲裁委员会的派出机构,根据仲裁委员会的授权,接受仲裁申请,管理仲裁案件。
(四)分会/仲裁中心设仲裁院,在分会/仲裁中心仲裁院院长的领导下履行本规则规定由仲裁委员会仲裁院履行的职责。	(四)分会/仲裁中心设仲裁院,在分会/仲裁中心仲裁院院长的领导下履行本规则规定由仲裁委员会仲裁院履行的职责。
(五)案件由分会/仲裁中心管理的，本规则规定由仲裁委员会仲裁院院长履行的职责，由仲裁委员会仲裁院院长授权的分会/仲裁中心仲裁院院长履行。	(五)案件由分会/仲裁中心管理的，本规则规定由仲裁委员会仲裁院院长履行的职责，由仲裁委员会仲裁院院长授权的分会/仲裁中心仲裁院院长履行。
(六)当事人可以约定将争议提交仲裁委员会或仲裁委员会分会/仲裁中心进行仲裁;约定由仲裁委员会进行仲裁的，由仲裁委员会仲裁院接受仲裁申请并管理案件;约定由分会/仲裁中心仲裁的，由所约定的分会/仲裁中心仲裁院接受仲裁申请并管理案件。约定的分会/仲裁中心不存在、被终止授权或约定不明的，由仲裁委员会仲裁院接受仲裁申请	(六)当事人可以约定将争议提交仲裁委员会或仲裁委员会分会/仲裁中心进行仲裁约定由仲裁委员会进行仲裁的，由仲裁委员会仲裁院接受仲裁申请并管理案件约定由分会/仲裁中心仲裁**或约定开庭地、仲裁地在分会/仲裁中心所在省、自治区、直辖市辖域内的**，由**该**分会/仲裁中心仲裁院接受仲裁申请并管理案件，**当事人另有约定的除外**。

并管理案件。如有争议，由仲裁委员会作出决定。

第三条 受案范围

(一)仲裁委员会根据当事人的约定受理契约性或非契约性的经济贸易等争议案件。

(二)前款所述案件包括:

1、国际或涉外争议案件;

2、涉及香港特别行政区、澳门特别行政区及台湾地区的争议案件;

3、国内争议案件。

第四条 规则的适用

(一)本规则统一适用于仲裁委员会及其分会/仲裁中心。

(二)当事人约定将争议提交仲裁委员会仲裁的,视为同意按照本规则进行仲裁。

(三)当事人约定将争议提交仲裁委员会仲裁但对本规则有关内容进行变更或约定适用其他仲裁规则的，从其约定，但其约定无法实施或与仲裁程序适用法强制性规定相抵触者除外。当事人约定适用其他仲裁规则的，由仲裁委员会履行相应的管理职责。

(四)当事人约定按照本规则进行仲裁但未约定仲裁机构的，视为同意将争议提交仲裁委员会仲裁。

(五)当事人约定适用仲裁委员会专业仲裁规则的，从其约定，但其争议不属于该专业仲裁规则适用范围的，适用本规则。

第五条 仲裁协议

(一)仲裁协议指当事人在合同中订明的仲裁条款或以其他方式达成的提交仲裁的书面协议。

(二)仲裁协议应当采取书面形式。书面形式包括合同书、信件、电报、电传、传真、电子数据交换和电子邮件等可以有形地表现所载内容的形式。在仲裁申请书和仲裁答辩书的交换中，一方当事人声称有仲裁协议而另一方当事人不做否认表示的，视为存在书面仲裁协议。

(三)仲裁协议的适用法对仲裁协议的形式及效力另有规定的，从其规定。

(四)合同中的仲裁条款应视为与合同其他条款分离的、独立存在的条款，附属于合同的

仲裁委员会仲裁院可根据案件具体情形授权并指定分会/仲裁中心管理相关案件。

约定的分会/仲裁中心不存在、被终止授权或约定不明的，由仲裁委员会仲裁院接受仲裁申请并管理案件。如有争议，由仲裁委员会作出决定。

(七)仲裁委员会可以根据当事人约定和请求为临时仲裁提供管理和辅助服务，包括并不限于适用仲裁规则咨询指引性服务、仲裁员指定/回避、提供秘书和庭审服务、核阅裁决草稿、代为管理仲裁员报酬等仲裁服务。但当事人约定无法实施或与仲裁程序适用法强制性规定相抵触者除外。

第三条 受案范围

(一)仲裁委员会根据当事人的约定受理契约性或非契约性的经济贸易等争议案件。

(二)前款所述案件包括:

1、国际或涉外争议案件;

2、涉及香港特别行政区、澳门特别行政区及台湾地区的争议案件;

3、国内争议案件。

第四条 规则的适用

(一)本规则统一适用于仲裁委员会及其分会/仲裁中心。

(二)当事人约定将争议提交仲裁委员会仲裁的,视为同意按照本规则进行仲裁。

(三)当事人约定将争议提交仲裁委员会仲裁但对本规则有关内容进行变更或约定适用其他仲裁规则的，从其约定，但其约定无法实施或与仲裁程序适用法强制性规定相抵触者除外。当事人约定适用其他仲裁规则的，由仲裁委员会履行相应的管理职责。

(四)当事人约定按照本规则进行仲裁但未约定仲裁机构的，视为同意将争议提交仲裁委员会仲裁。

(五)当事人约定适用仲裁委员会专业仲裁规则的，从其约定，但其争议不属于该专业仲裁规则适用范围的，适用本规则。

第五条 仲裁协议

(一)仲裁协议指当事人在合同中订明的仲裁条款或以其他方式达成的提交仲裁的书面协议。

(二)仲裁协议应当采取书面形式。书面形式包括合同书、信件、电报、电传、传真、电子数据交换和电子邮件等可以有形地表现所载内容的形式。在仲裁申请书和仲裁答辩书的交换中，一方当事人声称有仲裁协议而另一方当事人不作否认表示的，视为存在书面仲裁协议。

(三)仲裁协议的适用法对仲裁协议的形式及效力另有规定的，从其规定。

(四)合同中的仲裁条款应视为与合同其他条款分离的、独立存在的条款，附属于合同的

仲裁协议也应视为与合同其他条款分离的、独立存在的一个部分;合同的变更、解除、终止、转让、失效、无效、未生效、被撤销以及成立与否，均不影响仲裁条款或仲裁协议的效力。

第六条 对仲裁协议及/或管辖权的异议

(一)仲裁委员会有权对仲裁协议的存在、效力以及仲裁案件的管辖权作出决定。如有必要，仲裁委员会也可以授权仲裁庭作出管辖权决定。

(二)仲裁委员会依表面证据认为存在有效仲裁协议的，可根据表面证据作出仲裁委员会有管辖权的决定，仲裁程序继续进行。仲裁委员会依表面证据作出的管辖权决定并不妨碍其根据仲裁庭在审理过程中发现的与表面证据不一致的事实及/或证据重新作出管辖权决定。

(三)仲裁庭依据仲裁委员会的授权作出管辖权决定时，可以在仲裁程序进行中单独作出，也可以在裁决书中一并作出。

(四)当事人对仲裁协议及/或仲裁案件管辖权的异议，应当在仲裁庭首次开庭前书面提出;书面审理的案件，应当在第一次实体答辩前提出。

(五)对仲裁协议及/或仲裁案件管辖权提出异议不影响仲裁程序的继续进行。

(六)上述管辖权异议及/或决定包括仲裁案件主体资格异议及/或决定。

(七)仲裁委员会或经仲裁委员会授权的仲裁庭作出无管辖权决定的，应当作出撤销案件的决定。撤案决定在仲裁庭组成前由仲裁委员会仲裁院院长作出，在仲裁庭组成后，由仲裁庭作出。

第七条 仲裁地

(一)当事人对仲裁地有约定的，从其约定。

(二)当事人对仲裁地未作约定或约定不明的，以管理案件的仲裁委员会或其分会/仲裁中心所在地为仲裁地;仲裁委员会也可视案件的具体情形确定其他地点为仲裁地。

(三)仲裁裁决视为在仲裁地作出。

第八条 送达及期限

(一)有关仲裁的一切文书、通知、材料等均可采用当面递交、挂号信、特快专递、传真或仲裁委员会仲裁院或仲裁庭认为适当的其他方式发送。

仲裁协议也应视为与合同其他条款分离的、独立存在的一个部分;合同的变更、解除、终止、转让、失效、无效、未生效、被撤销以及成立与否，均不影响仲裁条款或仲裁协议的效力。

第六条 对仲裁协议及/或管辖权的异议

(一)仲裁委员会有权对仲裁协议的存在、效力以及仲裁案件的管辖权作出决定。**仲裁庭组成后**，仲裁委员会**授权**仲裁庭作出管辖权决定。

(二)仲裁委员会依表面证据认为存在有效仲裁协议**并作出**仲裁委员会有管辖权决定的，仲裁程序继续进行。仲裁委员会依表面证据作出的管辖权决定并不妨碍仲裁庭在审理过程中发现的与表面证据不 致的事实及/或证据重新作出管辖权决定。

(三)仲裁庭作出管辖权决定时，可以在仲裁程序进行中单独作出，也可以在裁决书中一并作出。

(四)当事人对仲裁协议及/或仲裁案件管辖权的异议，应当在仲裁庭首次开庭前书面提出书面审理的案件，应当在第一次实体答辩前提出。**仲裁程序适用法另有规定的，从其规定。**

(五)对仲裁协议及/或仲裁案件管辖权提出异议不影响仲裁程序的继续进行。

(六)上述管辖权异议及/或决定包括仲裁案件主体资格异议及/或决定。

(七)仲裁委员会或仲裁庭作出无管辖权决定的，应当作出撤销案件的决定。撤案决定在仲裁庭组成前由仲裁委员会仲裁院院长作出，在仲裁庭组成后，由仲裁庭作出。

第七条 仲裁地

(一)当事人对仲裁地有约定的，从其约定。

(二)当事人对仲裁地未作约定或约定不明的，以管理案件的仲裁委员会或其分会/仲裁中心所在地为仲裁地;仲裁委员会也可视案件的具体情形确定其他地点为仲裁地。

(三)仲裁裁决视为在仲裁地作出。

第八条 送达及期限

(一)有关仲裁的一切文书、通知、材料**(以下简称"仲裁文件")**等均可采用当面递交、挂号信、特快专递、传真、**电子送达方式及其他任何能提供投递记录的通讯手段**，或仲裁委员会仲裁院或仲裁庭认为适当的其他方式发送。**电子送达方式包括向当事人约定/指定的电子邮箱、其他电子通讯地址，以及经由仲裁委员会信息化存储系统、各方可无障碍存取的信息系统等以电子形式送达仲裁文件。**

(二)仲裁文件可优先采用电子送达。

(二)上述第(一)款所述仲裁文件应发送当事人或其仲裁代理人自行提供的或当事人约定的地址;当事人或其仲裁代理人没有提供地址或当事人对地址没有约定的，按照对方当事人或其仲裁代理人提供的地址发送。	
(三)向一方当事人或其仲裁代理人发送的仲裁文件，如经当面递交收件人或发送至收件人的营业地、注册地、住所地、惯常居住地或通讯地址，或经对方当事人合理查询不能找到上述任一地点，仲裁委员会仲裁院以挂号信或特快专递或能提供投递记录的包括公证送达、委托送达和留置送达在内的其他任何手段投递给收件人最后一个为人所知的营业地、注册地、住所地、惯常居住地或通讯地址，即视为有效送达。	(三)仲裁文件应发送当事人或其仲裁代理人自行提供的或当事人约定的地址，当事人或其仲裁代理人没有提供地址或当事人对地址没有约定的，按照对方当事人或其仲裁代理人提供的地址发送。
(四)本规则所规定的期限，应自当事人收到或应当收到仲裁委员会仲裁院向其发送的文书、通知、材料等之日的次日起计算。	(四)向一方当事人或其仲裁代理人发送的仲裁文件，如经当面递交收件人或发送至收件人的营业地、注册地、住所地、惯常居住地或通讯地址，或经对方当事人合理查询不能找到上述任一地点，仲裁委员会仲裁院以挂号信或特快专递或能提供投递记录的包括公证送达、委托送达和留置送达在内的其他任何手段投递给收件人最后一个为人所知的营业地、注册地、住所地、惯常居住地或通讯地址，即视为有效送达。
	(五)本规则所规定的期限，应自当事人收到或应当收到仲裁委员会仲裁院向其发送的**仲裁文件**之日的次日起计算。
第九条 诚实信用	第九条 诚实信用
仲裁参与人应遵循诚实信用原则，进行仲裁程序。	仲裁参与人应遵循诚实信用原则，进行仲裁程序。
第十条 放弃异议	第十条 放弃异议
一方当事人知道或理应知道本规则或仲裁协议中规定的任何条款或情事未被遵守，仍参加仲裁程序或继续进行仲裁程序而且不对此不遵守情况及时地、明示地提出书面异议的，视为放弃其提出异议的权利。	一方当事人知道或理应知道本规则或仲裁协议中规定的任何条款或情事未被遵守，仍参加仲裁程序或继续进行仲裁程序**或经有效通知无正当理由缺席审理**而且不对此不遵守情况及时地、明示地提出书面异议的，视为放弃其提出异议的权利。

第二章 仲裁程序

第一节 仲裁申请、答辩、反请求

第十一条 仲裁程序的开始	第十一条 仲裁程序的开始
仲裁程序自仲裁委员会仲裁院收到仲裁申请书之日起开始。	仲裁程序自仲裁委员会仲裁院收到仲裁申请书之日起开始。**申请人向仲裁委员会书面提交仲裁申请及/或通过仲裁委员会网上立案系统申请仲裁的，仲裁程序开始于最先收到的日期。**
第十二条 申请仲裁	第十二条 申请仲裁
当事人依据本规则申请仲裁时应:	(一)当事人依据本规则申请仲裁时应
(一)提交由申请人或申请人授权的代理人签名及/或盖章的仲裁申请书。仲裁申请书应写明:	1. 提交由申请人或申请人授权的代理人签名及/或盖章的仲裁申请书。仲裁申请书应写明

1、申请人和被申请人的名称和住所，包括邮政编码、电话、传真、电子邮箱或其他电子通讯方式;	(1) 申请人和被申请人的名称和住所，包括邮政编码、电话、传真、电子邮箱或其他电子通讯方式
2、申请仲裁所依据的仲裁协议;	(2) 申请仲裁所依据的仲裁协议
3、案情和争议要点;	(3) 案情和争议要点
4、申请人的仲裁请求;	(4) 申请人的仲裁请求
5、仲裁请求所依据的事实和理由。	(5) 仲裁请求所依据的事实和理由。
(二)在提交仲裁申请书时，附具申请人请求所依据的证据材料以及其他证明文件。	2. 在提交仲裁申请书时，附具申请人请求所依据的证据材料以及其他证明文件。
(三)按照仲裁委员会制定的仲裁费用表的规定预缴仲裁费。	3. 按照仲裁委员会制定的仲裁费用表的规定预缴仲裁费。
	(二)仲裁协议约定仲裁前应进行协商、调解程序的，可协商、调解后提交仲裁申请，但未协商、未调解，不影响申请人提起仲裁申请及仲裁委员会仲裁院受理仲裁案件，除非所适用的法律或仲裁协议对此明确作出了相反规定。
第十三条 案件的受理	第十三条 案件的受理
(一)仲裁委员会根据当事人在争议发生之前或在争议发生之后达成的将争议提交仲裁委员会仲裁的仲裁协议和一方当事人的书面申请，受理案件。	(一)仲裁委员会根据当事人在争议发生之前或在争议发生之后达成的将争议提交仲裁委员会仲裁的仲裁协议和一方当事人的书面申请，受理案件。
(二)仲裁委员会仲裁院收到申请人的仲裁申请书及其附件后，经审查，认为申请仲裁的手续完备的,应将仲裁通知、仲裁委员会仲裁规则和仲裁员名册各一份发送给双方当事人;申请人的仲裁申请书及其附件也应同时发送给被申请人。	(二)仲裁委员会仲裁院收到申请人的仲裁申请书及其附件后，经审查，认为申请仲裁的手续完备的,应将仲裁通知、仲裁委员会仲裁规则和仲裁员名册各一份发送给双方当事人;申请人的仲裁申请书及其附件也应同时发送给被申请人。
(三)仲裁委员会仲裁院经审查认为申请仲裁的手续不完备的，可以要求申请人在一定的期限内予以完备。申请人未能在规定期限内完备申请仲裁手续的，视同申请人未提出仲裁申请;申请人的仲裁申请书及其附件，仲裁委员会仲裁院不予留存。	(三)仲裁委员会仲裁院经审查认为申请仲裁的手续不完备的，可以要求申请人在一定的期限内予以完备。申请人未能在规定期限内完备申请仲裁手续的，视同申请人未提出仲裁申请;申请人的仲裁申请书及其附件，仲裁委员会仲裁院不予留存。
(四)仲裁委员会受理案件后，仲裁委员会仲裁院应指定一名案件秘书协助仲裁案件的程序管理。	(四)仲裁委员会受理案件后，仲裁委员会仲裁院应指定一名案件秘书协助仲裁案件的程序管理。
第十四条 多份合同的仲裁	**第十四条 多合同仲裁及仲裁中追加合同**
申请人就多份合同项下的争议可在同一仲裁案件中合并提出仲裁申请，但应同时符合下列条件:	(一)申请人就多个合同项下的争议可在单个仲裁案件中合并提出仲裁申请，但应同时符合下列条件
1、多份合同系主从合同关系;或多份合同所涉当事人相同且法律关系性质相同;	1. 多个合同系主从合同关系，或多个合同所涉当事人相同且法律关系性质相同，**或多个合同所涉标的具有牵连关系**
2、争议源于同一交易或同一系列交易;	2. **多个合同所涉**争议源于同一交易或同一系列交易
3、多份合同中的仲裁协议内容相同或相容。	3. 多个合同中的仲裁协议内容相同或相容。

Annex 2

第十五条 答辩

(一)被申请人应自收到仲裁通知后 45 天内提交答辩书。被申请人确有正当理由请求延长提交答辩期限的，由仲裁庭决定是否延长答辩期限;仲裁庭尚未组成的，由仲裁委员会仲裁院作出决定。

(二)答辩书由被申请人或被申请人授权的代理人签名及/或盖章，并应包括下列内容及附件:

1、被申请人的名称和住所，包括邮政编码、电话、传真、电子邮箱或其他电子通讯方式;

2、对仲裁申请书的答辩及所依据的事实和理由;

3、答辩所依据的证据材料以及其他证明文件。

(三)仲裁庭有权决定是否接受逾期提交的答辩书。

(四)被申请人未提交答辩书，不影响仲裁程序的进行。

第十六条 反请求

(一)被申请人如有反请求，应自收到仲裁通知后 45 天内以书面形式提交。被申请人确有正当理由请求延长提交反请求期限的，由仲裁庭决定是否延长反请求期限;仲裁庭尚未组成的，由仲裁委员会仲裁院作出决定。

(二)被申请人提出反请求时，应在其反请求申请书中写明具体的反请求事项及其所依据的事实和理由，并附具有关的证据材料以及其他证明文件。

(三)被申请人提出反请求，应按照仲裁委员会制定的仲裁费用表在规定的时间内预缴仲裁费。被申请人未按期缴纳反请求仲裁费的，视同未提出反请求申请。

(四)仲裁委员会仲裁院认为被申请人提出反请求的手续已完备的，应向双方当事人发出反请求受理通知。申请人应在收到反请求受理通知后 30 天内针对被申请人的反请求提交答辩。申请人确有正当理由请求延长提交答辩期限的，由仲裁庭决定是否延长答辩期限;仲裁庭尚未组成的，由仲裁委员会仲裁院作出决定。

(五)仲裁庭有权决定是否接受逾期提交的反请求和反请求答辩书。

(六)申请人对被申请人的反请求未提出书面答辩的，不影响仲裁程序的进行。

(二)同时符合上述第(一)款 1、2、3 项规定情形的，申请人可在仲裁程序中申请追加合同，但上述申请过迟影响仲裁程序正常进行的，可决定不予追加合同。

(三)上述第(一)(二)款程序事项，由仲裁委员会仲裁院决定。在仲裁庭组成后提出追加合同申请的，由仲裁庭决定。

第十五条 答辩

(一)被申请人应自收到仲裁通知后 45 天内提交答辩书。被申请人确有正当理由请求延长提交答辩期限的，由仲裁庭决定是否延长答辩期限;仲裁庭尚未组成的，由仲裁委员会仲裁院作出决定。

(二)答辩书由被申请人或被申请人授权的代理人签名及/或盖章，并应包括下列内容及附件:

1、被申请人的名称和住所，包括邮政编码、电话、传真、电子邮箱或其他电子通讯方式;

2、对仲裁申请书的答辩及所依据的事实和理由;

3、答辩所依据的证据材料以及其他证明文件。

(三)仲裁庭有权决定是否接受逾期提交的答辩书。

(四)被申请人未提交答辩书，不影响仲裁程序的进行。

第十六条 反请求

(一)被申请人如有反请求，应自收到仲裁通知后 45 天内以书面形式提交。被申请人确有正当理由请求延长提交反请求期限的，由仲裁庭决定是否延长反请求期限;仲裁庭尚未组成的，由仲裁委员会仲裁院作出决定。

(二)被申请人提出反请求时，应在其反请求申请书中写明具体的反请求事项及其所依据的事实和理由，并附具有关的证据材料以及其他证明文件。

(三)被申请人提出反请求，应按照仲裁委员会制定的仲裁费用表在规定的时间内预缴仲裁费。被申请人未按期缴纳反请求仲裁费的，视同未提出反请求申请。

(四)仲裁委员会仲裁院认为被申请人提出反请求的手续已完备的，应向双方当事人发出反请求受理通知。申请人应在收到反请求受理通知后 30 天内针对被申请人的反请求提交答辩。申请人确有正当理由请求延长提交答辩期限的，由仲裁庭决定是否延长答辩期限;仲裁庭尚未组成的，由仲裁委员会仲裁院作出决定。

(五)仲裁庭有权决定是否接受逾期提交的反请求和反请求答辩书。

(六)申请人对被申请人的反请求未提出书面答辩的，不影响仲裁程序的进行。

第十七条 变更仲裁请求或反请求

申请人可以申请对其仲裁请求进行变更，被申请人也可以申请对其反请求进行变更;但是仲裁庭认为其提出变更的时间过迟而影响仲裁程序正常进行的，可以拒绝其变更请求。

第十八条 追加当事人

(一)在仲裁程序中，一方当事人依据表面上约束被追加当事人的案涉仲裁协议可以向仲裁委员会申请追加当事人。在仲裁庭组成后申请追加当事人的，如果仲裁庭认为确有必要，应在征求包括被追加当事人在内的各方当事人的意见后，由仲裁委员会作出决定。

仲裁委员会仲裁院收到追加当事人申请之日视为针对该被追加当事人的仲裁开始之日。

(二)追加当事人申请书应包含现有仲裁案件的案号，涉及被追加当事人在内的所有当事人的名称、住所及通讯方式，追加当事人所依据的仲裁协议、事实和理由，以及仲裁请求。

当事人在提交追加当事人申请书时，应附具其申请所依据的证据材料以及其他证明文件。

(三)任何一方当事人就追加当事人程序提出仲裁协议及/或仲裁案件管辖权异议的，仲裁委员会有权基于仲裁协议及相关证据作出是否具有管辖权的决定。

(四)追加当事人程序开始后，在仲裁庭组成之前，由仲裁委员会仲裁院就仲裁程序的进行作出决定;在仲裁庭组成之后，由仲裁庭就仲裁程序的进行作出决定。

(五)在仲裁庭组成之前追加当事人的，本规则有关当事人选定或委托仲裁委员会主任指定仲裁员的规定适用于被追加当事人。仲裁庭的组成应按照本规则第二十九条的规定进行。

在仲裁庭组成后决定追加当事人的，仲裁庭应就已经进行的包括仲裁庭组成在内的仲裁程序征求被追加当事人的意见。被追加当事人要求选定或委托仲裁委员会主任指定仲裁员的，双方当事人应重新选定或委托仲裁委员会主任指定仲裁员。仲裁庭的组成应按照本规则第二十九条的规定进行。

(六)本规则有关当事人提交答辩及反请求的规定适用于被追加当事人。被追加当事人提交答辩及反请求的期限自收到追加当事人仲裁通知后起算。

(七)案涉仲裁协议表面上不能约束被追加当事人或存在其他任何不宜追加当事人的情形的，仲裁委员会有权决定不予追加。

第十九条 合并仲裁

(一)符合下列条件之一的，经一方当事人请求，仲裁委员会可以决定将根据本规则进行

第十七条 变更仲裁请求或反请求

申请人可以申请对仲裁请求进行变更，被申请人也可以申请对反请求进行变更但是仲裁庭认为提出变更的时间过迟而影响仲裁程序正常进行的，可以拒绝受理变更请求申请。

第十八条 追加当事人

(一)在仲裁程序中，一方当事人依据表面上约束被追加当事人的案涉仲裁协议可以向仲裁委员会申请追加当事人。在仲裁庭组成后申请追加当事人的，如果仲裁庭认为确有必要，应在征求包括被追加当事人在内的各方当事人的意见后，由仲裁委员会作出决定。

仲裁委员会仲裁院收到追加当事人申请之日视为针对该被追加当事人的仲裁开始之日。

(二)追加当事人申请书应包含现有仲裁案件的案号，涉及被追加当事人在内的所有当事人的名称、住所及通讯方式，追加当事人所依据的仲裁协议、事实和理由，以及仲裁请求。

当事人在提交追加当事人申请书时，应附具其申请所依据的证据材料以及其他证明文件。

(三)任何一方当事人就追加当事人程序提出仲裁协议及/或仲裁案件管辖权异议的，适用本规则第六条规定作出管辖权决定。

(四)追加当事人程序开始后，在仲裁庭组成之前，由仲裁委员会仲裁院就仲裁程序的进行作出决定在仲裁庭组成之后，由仲裁庭就仲裁程序的进行作出决定。

(五)在仲裁庭组成之前追加当事人的，本规则有关当事人选定或委托仲裁委员会主任指定仲裁员的规定适用于被追加当事人。仲裁庭的组成应按照本规则第二十九条的规定进行。

在仲裁庭组成后决定追加当事人的，仲裁庭应就已经进行的包括仲裁庭组成在内的仲裁程序征求被追加当事人的意见。被追加当事人要求选定或委托仲裁委员会主任指定仲裁员的，双方当事人应重新选定或委托仲裁委员会主任指定仲裁员。仲裁庭的组成应按照本规则第二十九条的规定进行。

(六)本规则有关当事人提交答辩及反请求的规定适用于被追加当事人。被追加当事人提交答辩及反请求的期限自收到追加当事人仲裁通知后起算。

(七)案涉仲裁协议表面上不能约束被追加当事人或存在其他任何不宜追加当事人的情形的，仲裁委员会有权决定不予追加。

十九条 合并仲裁

(一)符合下列条件之一的，经一方当事人请求，仲裁委员会可以决定将根据本规则进行

的两个或两个以上的仲裁案件合并为一个仲裁案件，进行审理。

1、各案仲裁请求依据同一个仲裁协议提出;

2、各案仲裁请求依据多份仲裁协议提出，该多份仲裁协议内容相同或相容，且各案当事人相同、各争议所涉及的法律关系性质相同;

3、各案仲裁请求依据多份仲裁协议提出，该多份仲裁协议内容相同或相容，且涉及的多份合同为主从合同关系;

4、所有案件的当事人均同意合并仲裁。

(二)根据上述第(一)款决定合并仲裁时，仲裁委员会应考虑各方当事人的意见及相关仲裁案件之间的关联性等因素，包括不同案件的仲裁员的选定或指定情况。

(三)除非各方当事人另有约定，合并的仲裁案件应合并至最先开始仲裁程序的仲裁案件。

(四)仲裁案件合并后，在仲裁庭组成之前，由仲裁委员会仲裁院就程序的进行作出决定;仲裁庭组成后，由仲裁庭就程序的进行作出决定。

第二十条 仲裁文件的提交与交换

(一)当事人的仲裁文件应提交至仲裁委员会仲裁院。

(二)仲裁程序中需发送或转交的仲裁文件，由仲裁委员会仲裁院发送或转交仲裁庭及当事人，当事人另有约定并经仲裁庭同意或仲裁庭另有决定者除外。

第二十一条 仲裁文件的份数

当事人提交的仲裁申请书、答辩书、反请求书和证据材料以及其他仲裁文件，应一式五份;多方当事人的案件，应增加相应份数;当事人提出财产保全申请或证据保全申请的，应增加相应份数;仲裁庭组成人数为一人的，应相应减少两份。

第二十二条 仲裁代理人

当事人可以授权中国及/或外国的仲裁代理人办理有关仲裁事项。当事人或其仲裁代理人应向仲裁委员会仲裁院提交授权委托书。

的两个或两个以上的仲裁案件合并为一个仲裁案件进行审理。

1. 各案仲裁请求依据同一个仲裁协议提出

2. 各案仲裁请求依据**多个合同仲裁协议**提出，**该多个合同**系主从合同关系、**或多个合同所涉**当事人相同及法律关系性质相同、**或多个合同所涉标的具有牵连关系，且多个合同仲裁协议**内容相同或相容

3. 所有案件的当事人均同意合并仲裁。

(二)根据上述第(一)款决定合并仲裁时，仲裁委员会应考虑各方当事人的意见及相关仲裁案件之间的关联性等因素，包括不同案件的仲裁员的选定或指定情况。

(三)除非各方当事人另有约定，合并的仲裁案件应合并至最先开始仲裁程序的仲裁案件。

(四)仲裁案件合并后，在仲裁庭组成之前，由仲裁委员会仲裁院就程序的进行作出决定仲裁庭组成后，由仲裁庭就程序的进行作出决定。

第二十条 仲裁文件的提交与交换

(一)当事人的仲裁文件应提交至仲裁委员会仲裁院。

(二)仲裁程序中需发送或转交的仲裁文件，由仲裁委员会仲裁院发送或转交仲裁庭及当事人，当事人另有约定并经仲裁庭同意或仲裁庭另有决定者除外。

第二十一条 仲裁文件的份数

(一)当事人提交的仲裁申请书、答辩书、反请求书和证据材料以及其他仲裁文件**可优先采用电子方式。**

(二)当事人以电子方式提交的，如仲裁委员会仲裁院或仲裁庭认为有必要，可要求其提交相同的纸质文本。电子文本与纸质文本不一致的，以电子文本为准，除非当事人另有约定。

(三)当事人以纸质方式提交的，应一式五份多方当事人的案件，应增加相应份数当事人提出保全措施申请的，应增加相应份数仲裁庭组成人数为一人的，应相应减少两份。

第二十二条 仲裁代理人

(一)当事人可以授权中国及/或外国的仲裁代理人办理有关仲裁事项。当事人或其仲裁代理人应向仲裁委员会仲裁院提交授权委托书，**仲裁委员会仲裁院应将授权委托书转交相关当事人和仲裁庭。**

(二)仲裁庭组成后当事人变更或新增仲裁代理人的，仲裁委员会仲裁院院长可考虑当事人在合理期限内对仲裁员回避事项发表意见的情况、仲裁庭审理案件的进展等因素，采取必要措施防止仲裁员因当事人代理人的变化而产生的利益冲突，包括排除新的仲裁代理人参与仲裁程序。

第二十三条 保全及临时措施

(一)当事人依据中国法律申请保全的，仲裁委员会应当依法将当事人的保全申请转交当事人指明的有管辖权的法院。

(二)根据所适用的法律或当事人的约定，当事人可以依据《中国国际经济贸易仲裁委员会紧急仲裁员程序》(本规则附件三)向仲裁委员会仲裁院申请紧急性临时救济。紧急仲裁员可以决定采取必要或适当的紧急性临时救济措施。紧急仲裁员的决定对双方当事人具有约束力。

(三)经一方当事人请求，仲裁庭依据所适用的法律或当事人的约定可以决定采取其认为必要或适当的临时措施，并有权决定由请求临时措施的一方当事人提供适当的担保。

第二十三条 保全措施及临时措施

(一)当事人申请保全措施的，仲裁委员会应当将当事人的保全措施申请转交当事人指明的有管辖权的法院。

仲裁委员会可依据当事人的请求，将其提交的保全措施申请在仲裁通知发出前先行转交上述法院。

(二)根据所适用的法律或当事人的约定，当事人可以依据《中国国际经济贸易仲裁委员会紧急仲裁员程序》(本规则附件三)向仲裁委员会仲裁院申请紧急性临时救济。紧急仲裁员可以决定采取必要或适当的紧急性临时救济措施。紧急仲裁员决定对双方当事人具有约束力。

(三)经一方当事人请求，仲裁庭依据所适用的法律或当事人的约定可以决定采取其认为必要或适当的临时措施，并有权决定由请求临时措施的一方当事人提供适当的担保。

第二节 仲裁员及仲裁庭

第二十四条 仲裁员的义务

仲裁员不代表任何一方当事人，应独立于各方当事人，平等地对待各方当事人。

第二十四条 仲裁员的义务

(一)仲裁员不代表任何一方当事人，应保持中立并独立于各方当事人，平等地对待各方当事人。

(二)仲裁员接受指定/选定的，应按本规则履行职责，勤勉高效推进仲裁程序。

第二十五条 仲裁庭的人数

(一)仲裁庭由一名或三名仲裁员组成。

(二)除非当事人另有约定或本规则另有规定，仲裁庭由三名仲裁员组成。

第二十五条 仲裁庭的人数

(一)仲裁庭由一名或三名仲裁员组成。

(二)除非当事人另有约定或本规则另有规定，仲裁庭由三名仲裁员组成。

第二十六条 仲裁员的选定或指定

(一)仲裁委员会制定统一适用于仲裁委员会及其分会/仲裁中心的仲裁员名册;当事人从仲裁委员会制定的仲裁员名册中选定仲裁员。

(二)当事人约定在仲裁委员会仲裁员名册之外选定仲裁员的，当事人选定的或根据当事人约定指定的人士经仲裁委员会主任确认后可以担任仲裁员。

第二十六条 仲裁员的选定或指定

(一)仲裁委员会制定统一适用于仲裁委员会及其分会/仲裁中心的仲裁员名册当事人从仲裁委员会制定的仲裁员名册中选定仲裁员。

(二)当事人约定在仲裁委员会仲裁员名册之外选定仲裁员的，当事人选定的或根据当事人约定指定的人士经仲裁委员会主任确认后可以担任仲裁员。

(三)仲裁庭根据本规则规定组成，但当事人另有约定者除外。

(四)如果当事人约定的组庭方式存在显著的不公平或不公正，或当事人滥用权利导致仲裁程序不必要的拖延，仲裁委员会主任可依据公平原则确定组庭方式或指定仲裁庭的任一组成人员。

Annex 2

第二十七条 三人仲裁庭的组成	第二十七条 三人仲裁庭的组成
(一)申请人和被申请人应各自在收到仲裁通知后 15 天内选定或委托仲裁委员会主任指定一名仲裁员。当事人未在上述期限内选定或委托仲裁委员会主任指定的，由仲裁委员会主任指定。	(一)申请人和被申请人应各自在收到仲裁通知后 15 天内选定或委托仲裁委员会主任指定一名仲裁员。当事人未在上述期限内选定或委托仲裁委员会主任指定的，由仲裁委员会主任指定。
(二)第三名仲裁员由双方当事人在被申请人收到仲裁通知后 15 天内共同选定或共同委托仲裁委员会主任指定。第三名仲裁员为仲裁庭的首席仲裁员。	(二)第三名仲裁员由双方当事人在被申请人收到仲裁通知后 15 天内共同选定或共同委托仲裁委员会主任指定。第三名仲裁员为仲裁庭的首席仲裁员。
	(三)双方当事人可以约定由其各自选定的两名仲裁员共同选定首席仲裁员，在该两名仲裁员分别接受选定后 7 天内共同选定或共同委托仲裁委员会主任指定首席仲裁员。逾期未选定的，由仲裁委员会主任指定首席仲裁员。
(三)双方当事人可以各自推荐一至五名候选人作为首席仲裁员人选，并按照上述第(二)款规定的期限提交推荐名单。双方当事人的推荐名单中有一名人选相同的，该人选为双方当事人共同选定的首席仲裁员;有一名以上人选相同的，由仲裁委员会主任根据案件的具体情况在相同人选中确定一名首席仲裁员，该名首席仲裁员仍为双方共同选定的首席仲裁员;推荐名单中没有相同人选时，由仲裁委员会主任指定首席仲裁员。	(四)双方当事人可以各自推荐一至五名候选人作为首席仲裁员人选，并按照上述第(二)款规定的期限提交推荐名单。双方当事人的推荐名单中有一名人选相同的，该人选为双方当事人共同选定的首席仲裁员有一名以上人选相同的，由仲裁委员会主任根据案件的具体情况在相同人选中确定一名首席仲裁员，该名首席仲裁员仍为双方共同选定的首席仲裁员推荐名单中没有相同人选时，由仲裁委员会主任**在推荐名单外**指定首席仲裁员。
	(五)经双方当事人约定或共同请求，仲裁委员会主任可以提名 3 名首席仲裁员人选供其在收到提名名单后 7 日内选定首席仲裁员。 除非当事人另有约定，本款应使用下述名单方法指定/选定首席仲裁员 1. 每一方当事人可排除其反对的一个或数人并将提名名单上保留的人选名单提交仲裁委员会仲裁院。 2. 如双方当事人保留名单有一名相同人选的，则该人选为双方当事人共同选定的首席仲裁员如双方当事人保留名单有两名或以上相同人选的，则由仲裁委员会主任根据案件的具体情况确定其中一名人选为首席仲裁员，该名首席仲裁员仍为双方共同选定的首席仲裁员双方当事人未选定相同人选时，由仲裁委员会主任在提名名单外指定首席仲裁员。
(四)双方当事人未能按照上述规定共同选定首席仲裁员的，由仲裁委员会主任指定首席仲裁员。	(六)双方当事人未能按照上述规定共同选定首席仲裁员的，由仲裁委员会主任指定首席仲裁员。[1]
第二十八条 独任仲裁庭的组成	第二十八条 独任仲裁庭的组成
仲裁庭由一名仲裁员组成的，按照本规则第二十七条第(二)、(三)、(四)款规定的程序，选定或指定独任仲裁员。	仲裁庭由一名仲裁员组成的，按照本规则第二十七条第(二)(四)**(五)(六)**款规定的程序，选定或指定独任仲裁员。

[1] 第六款出现于中国贸促会 2023 年 9 月 5 日发布的版本。

第二十九条 多方当事人仲裁庭的组成

(一)仲裁案件有两个或两个以上申请人及/或被申请人时,申请人方及/或被申请人方应各自协商，各方共同选定或共同委托仲裁委员会主任指定一名仲裁员。

(二)首席仲裁员或独任仲裁员应按照本规则第二十七条第(二)、(三)、(四)款规定的程序选定或指定。申请人方及/或被申请人方按照本规则第二十七条第(三)款的规定选定首席仲裁员或独任仲裁员时，应各方共同协商，提交各方共同选定的候选人名单。

(三)如果申请人方及/或被申请人方未能在收到仲裁通知后 15 天内各方共同选定或各方共同委托仲裁委员会主任指定一名仲裁员，则由仲裁委员会主任指定仲裁庭三名仲裁员，并从中确定一人担任首席仲裁员。

第三十条 指定仲裁员的考虑因素

仲裁委员会主任根据本规则的规定指定仲裁员时，应考虑争议的适用法律、仲裁地、仲裁语言、当事人国籍，以及仲裁委员会主任认为应考虑的其他因素。

第三十一条 披露

(一)被选定或被指定的仲裁员应签署声明书，披露可能引起对其公正性和独立性产生合理怀疑的任何事实或情况。

(二)在仲裁程序中出现应披露情形的，仲裁员应立即书面披露。

(三)仲裁员的声明书及/或披露的信息应提交仲裁委员会仲裁院并转交各方当事人。

第三十二条 仲裁员的回避

(一)当事人收到仲裁员的声明书及/或书面披露后，如果以披露的事实或情况为理由要求该仲裁员回避，则应于收到仲裁员的书面披露后 10 天内书面提出。逾期没有申请回避的，不得以仲裁员曾经披露的事项为由申请该仲裁员回避。

(二)当事人对被选定或被指定的仲裁员的公正性和独立性产生具有正当理由的怀疑时，可以书面提出要求该仲裁员回避的请求，但应说明提出回避请求所依据的具体事实和理由，并举证。

(三)对仲裁员的回避请求应在收到组庭通知后 15 天内以书面形式提出;在此之后得知要求回避事由的，可以在得知回避事由后 15 天内提出，但应不晚于最后一次开庭终结。

(四)当事人的回避请求应当立即转交另一方当事人、被请求回避的仲裁员及仲裁庭其他成员。

(五)如果一方当事人请求仲裁员回避，另一方当事人同意回避请求，或被请求回避的仲裁员主动提出不再担任该仲裁案件的仲裁员，则该仲裁员不再担任仲裁员审理本案。

第二十九条 多方当事人仲裁庭的组成

(一)仲裁案件有两个或两个以上申请人及/或被申请人时,申请人方及/或被申请人方应各自协商，各方共同选定或共同委托仲裁委员会主任指定一名仲裁员。

(二)首席仲裁员或独任仲裁员应按照本规则第二十七条第(二)(四)**(五)(六)**款规定的程序选定或指定。申请人方及/或被申请人方按照本规则第二十七条的规定选定首席仲裁员或独任仲裁员时，应各方共同协商，提交各方共同选定的候选人名单。

(三)如果申请人方及/或被申请人方未能在收到仲裁通知后 15 天内各方共同选定或各方共同委托仲裁委员会主任指定一名仲裁员，则由仲裁委员会主任指定仲裁庭三名仲裁员，并从中确定一人担任首席仲裁员。

第三十条 指定仲裁员的考虑因素

仲裁委员会主任根据本规则的规定指定仲裁员时，应考虑争议的适用法律、仲裁地、仲裁语言、当事人国籍、**争议类型**，以及仲裁委员会主任认为应考虑的其他因素。

第三十一条 披露

(一)被选定或被指定的仲裁员应签署声明书，披露可能引起对其公正性和独立性产生合理怀疑的任何事实或**情形**。

(二)在仲裁程序中出现应披露的**事实或**情形的，仲裁员应立即书面披露。

(三)仲裁员的声明书及/或披露的信息应提交仲裁委员会仲裁院并转交各方当事人**及其他仲裁庭组成人员**。

第三十二条 仲裁员的回避

(一)当事人收到仲裁员的声明书及/或书面披露后，如果以披露的事实或情况为理由要求该仲裁员回避，则应于收到仲裁员的书面披露后 10 天内书面提出。逾期没有申请回避的，不得以仲裁员曾经披露的事项为由申请该仲裁员回避。

(二)当事人对被选定或被指定的仲裁员的公正性和独立性产生具有正当理由的怀疑时，可以书面提出要求该仲裁员回避的请求，但应说明提出回避请求所依据的具体事实和理由，并举证。

(三)对仲裁员的回避请求应在收到组庭通知后 15 天内以书面形式提出在此之后得知要求回避事由的，可以在得知回避事由后 15 天内提出，但应不晚于最后一次开庭终结。

(四)当事人的回避请求应当立即转交另一方当事人、被请求回避的仲裁员及仲裁庭其他成员。

(五)如果一方当事人请求仲裁员回避，另一方当事人同意回避请求，或被请求回避的仲裁员主动提出不再担任该仲裁案件的仲裁员，则该仲裁员不再担任仲裁员审理本案。

上述情形并不表示当事人提出回避的理由成立。
(六)除上述第(五)款规定的情形外，仲裁员是否回避，由仲裁委员会主任作出终局决定并可以不说明理由。
(七)在仲裁委员会主任就仲裁员是否回避作出决定前，被请求回避的仲裁员应继续履行职责。

第三十三条 仲裁员的更换

(一)仲裁员在法律上或事实上不能履行职责，或没有按照本规则的要求或在本规则规定的期限内履行应尽职责时，仲裁委员会主任有权决定将其更换;该仲裁员也可以主动申请不再担任仲裁员。

(二)是否更换仲裁员，由仲裁委员会主任作出终局决定并可以不说明理由。

(三)在仲裁员因回避或更换不能履行职责时，应按照原选定或指定仲裁员的方式在仲裁委员会仲裁院规定的期限内选定或指定替代的仲裁员。当事人未选定或指定替代仲裁员的，由仲裁委员会主任指定替代的仲裁员。

(四)重新选定或指定仲裁员后，由仲裁庭决定是否重新审理及重新审理的范围。

第三十四条 多数仲裁员继续仲裁程序

最后一次开庭终结后，如果三人仲裁庭中的一名仲裁员因死亡或被除名等情形而不能参加合议及/或作出裁决，另外两名仲裁员可以请求仲裁委员会主任按照第三十三条的规定更换该仲裁员;在征求双方当事人意见并经仲裁委员会主任同意后，该两名仲裁员也可以继续进行仲裁程序，作出决定或裁决。仲裁委员会仲裁院应将上述情况通知双方当事人。

上述情形并不表示当事人提出回避的理由成立。
(六)除上述第(五)款规定的情形外，仲裁员是否回避，由仲裁委员会主任作出终局决定并可以不说明理由。
(七)在仲裁委员会主任就仲裁员是否回避作出决定前，**被申请回避**的仲裁员应继续履行职责。

第三十三条 仲裁员的更换

(一)仲裁员在法律上或事实上不能履行职责，或没有按照本规则的要求或在本规则规定的期限内履行应尽职责时，仲裁委员会主任有权决定将其更换该仲裁员也可以主动申请不再担任仲裁员。

(二)是否更换仲裁员，由仲裁委员会主任作出终局决定并可以不说明理由。

(三)在仲裁员因回避或更换不能履行职责时，应按照原选定或指定仲裁员的方式在仲裁委员会仲裁院规定的**合理**期限内选定或指定替代的仲裁员。当事人未选定或指定替代仲裁员的，由仲裁委员会主任指定替代的仲裁员。

(四)重新选定或指定仲裁员后，由仲裁庭决定是否重新审理及重新审理的范围。

第三十四条 多数仲裁员继续仲裁程序

最后一次开庭终结后，如果三人仲裁庭中的一名仲裁员因死亡或被除名等情形而不能参加合议及/或作出裁决，另外两名仲裁员可以请求仲裁委员会主任按照第三十三条的规定更换该仲裁员;在征求双方当事人意见并经仲裁委员会主任同意后，该两名仲裁员也可以继续进行仲裁程序，作出决定或裁决。仲裁委员会仲裁院应将上述情况通知双方当事人。

第三节 审 理

第三十五条 审理方式

(一)除非当事人另有约定，仲裁庭可以按照其认为适当的方式审理案件。在任何情形下，仲裁庭均应公平和公正地行事，给予双方当事人陈述与辩论的合理机会。

(二)仲裁庭应开庭审理案件，但双方当事人约定并经仲裁庭同意或仲裁庭认为不必开庭审理并征得双方当事人同意的，可以只依据书面文件进行审理。

(三)除非当事人另有约定，仲裁庭可以根据案件的具体情况采用询问式或辩论式的庭审方式审理案件。

(四)仲裁庭可以在其认为适当的地点以其认为适当的方式进行合议。

(五)除非当事人另有约定，仲裁庭认为必要时可以就所审理的案件发布程序令、发出问题单、制作审理范围书、举行庭前会议等。经仲裁庭其他成员授权，首席仲裁员可以单独就仲裁案件的程序安排作出决定。

第三十五条 审理方式

(一)除非当事人另有约定，仲裁庭可以按照其认为适当的方式审理案件。在任何情形下，仲裁庭均应公平和公正地行事，给予双方当事人陈述与辩论的合理机会。

(二)仲裁庭应开庭审理案件，但双方当事人约定并经仲裁庭同意或仲裁庭认为不必开庭审理并征得双方当事人同意的，可以只依据书面文件进行审理。

(三)除非当事人另有约定，仲裁庭可以根据案件的具体情况采用询问式或辩论式的庭审方式审理案件。

(四)仲裁庭可以在其认为适当的地点以其认为适当的方式进行合议。

(五)除非当事人另有约定，仲裁庭认为必要时可以就所审理的案件发布程序令、发出问题单、制作审理范围书、举行庭前会议等。经仲裁庭其他成员授权，首席仲裁员可以单独就仲裁案件的程序安排作出决定。

第三十六条 开庭地

(一)当事人约定了开庭地点的,仲裁案件的开庭审理应当在约定的地点进行，但出现本规则第八十二条第(三)款规定的情形的除外。

(二)除非当事人另有约定,由仲裁委员会仲裁院或其分会/仲裁中心仲裁院管理的案件应分别在北京或分会/仲裁中心所在地开庭审理;如仲裁庭认为必要，经仲裁委员会仲裁院院长同意，也可以在其他地点开庭审理。

第三十七条 开庭通知

(一)开庭审理的案件，仲裁庭确定第一次开庭日期后，应不晚于开庭前 20 天将开庭日期通知双方当事人。当事人有正当理由的，可以请求延期开庭，但应于收到开庭通知后 5 天内提出书面延期申请;是否延期，由仲裁庭决定。

(二)当事人有正当理由未能按上述第(一)款规定提出延期开庭申请的，是否接受其延期申请，由仲裁庭决定。

(三)再次开庭审理的日期及延期后开庭审理日期的通知及其延期申请，不受上述第(一)款期限的限制。

第三十八条 保密

(一)仲裁庭审理案件不公开进行。双方当事人要求公开审理的，由仲裁庭决定是否公开审理。

(二)不公开审理的案件，双方当事人及其仲裁代理人、仲裁员、证人、翻译、仲裁庭咨询的专家和指定的鉴定人，以及其他有关人员，均不得对外界透露案件实体和程序的有关情况。

第三十九条 当事人缺席

(一)申请人无正当理由开庭时不到庭的，或在开庭审理时未经仲裁庭许可中途退庭的，可以视为撤回仲裁申请;被申请人提出反请求的，不影响仲裁庭就反请求进行审理，并作出裁决。

(二)被申请人无正当理由开庭时不到庭的，或在开庭审理时未经仲裁庭许可中途退庭的，仲裁庭可以进行缺席审理并作出裁决;被申请人提出反请求的，可以视为撤回反请求。

第三十六条 开庭地

(一)当事人约定开庭地点的,仲裁案件的开庭审理应当在约定的地点进行，但出现本规则**第八十五条第(三)款**规定的情形的除外。

(二)除非当事人另有约定,由仲裁委员会仲裁院或其分会/仲裁中心仲裁院管理的案件应分别在北京或分会/仲裁中心所在地开庭审理如仲裁庭认为必要，经仲裁委员会仲裁院院长同意，也可以在其他地点开庭审理。

第三十七条 开庭审理

(一)开庭审理的案件，仲裁庭确定第一次开庭日期后，应不晚于开庭前 20 天将开庭日期通知双方当事人。当事人有正当理由的，可以请求延期开庭，但应于收到开庭通知后 5 天内提出书面延期申请是否延期，由仲裁庭决定。

(二)当事人有正当理由未能按上述第(一)款规定提出延期开庭申请的，是否接受其延期申请，由仲裁庭决定。

(三)再次开庭审理的日期及延期后开庭审理日期的通知及其延期申请，不受上述第(一)款期限的限制。

(四)开庭审理的案件，当事人及其仲裁代理人有权参加开庭。其他仲裁参与人参加开庭由仲裁庭决定。除非经仲裁庭和当事人同意，仲裁参与人之外的人员不得出席。

(五)仲裁庭可在商各方当事人意见后，根据仲裁案件的具体情况，自行决定以现场出席、远程视频及其他适当的电子通讯方式开庭。

(六)仲裁委员会仲裁院提供开庭设施及远程视频开庭的行政后勤支持。

第三十八条 保密

(一)仲裁庭审理案件不公开进行。双方当事人要求公开审理的，由仲裁庭决定是否公开审理。

(二)不公开审理的案件，双方当事人及其仲裁代理人、仲裁员、证人、翻译、仲裁庭咨询的专家和指定的鉴定人，以及其他有关人员，均不得对外界透露案件实体和程序的有关情况。

第三十九条 缺席审理

(一)申请人无正当理由开庭时不到庭的，或在开庭审理时未经仲裁庭许可中途退庭的，可以视为撤回仲裁申请;被申请人提出反请求的，不影响仲裁庭就反请求进行审理，并作出裁决。

(二)被申请人无正当理由开庭时不到庭的，或在开庭审理时未经仲裁庭许可中途退庭的，仲裁庭可以进行缺席审理并作出裁决;被申请人提出反请求的，可以视为撤回反请求。

Annex 2

第四十条 庭审笔录	**第四十条 庭审笔录**
(一)开庭审理时，仲裁庭可以制作庭审笔录及/或影音记录。仲裁庭认为必要时，可以制作庭审要点，并要求当事人及/或其代理人、证人及/或其他有关人员在庭审笔录或庭审要点上签字或盖章。	(一)开庭审理时，仲裁庭可以制作庭审笔录及/或影音记录。仲裁庭认为必要时，可以制作庭审要点，并要求当事人及/或其代理人、证人及/或其他有关人员在庭审笔录或庭审要点上签字或盖章。
	(二)当事人和其他仲裁参与人认为对自己陈述的记录有遗漏或有差错的，可以申请补正仲裁庭不同意其补正的，应将该申请记录在案。
(二)庭审笔录、庭审要点和影音记录供仲裁庭查用。	(三)庭审笔录、庭审要点和影音记录供仲裁庭查用。
(三)应一方当事人申请，仲裁委员会仲裁院视案件具体情况可以决定聘请速录人员速录庭审笔录，当事人应当预交由此产生的费用。	(四)应一方当事人申请，仲裁委员会仲裁院视案件具体情况可以决定聘请速录人员记录庭审笔录，当事人应当预交由此产生的费用。
第四十一条 举证	**第四十一条 举证**
(一)当事人应对其申请、答辩和反请求所依据的事实提供证据加以证明，对其主张、辩论及抗辩要点提供依据。	(一)当事人应对其申请、答辩和反请求所依据的事实提供证据加以证明，对其主张、辩论及抗辩要点提供依据。
(二)仲裁庭可以规定当事人提交证据的期限。当事人应在规定的期限内提交证据。逾期提交的，仲裁庭可以不予接受。当事人在举证期限内提交证据材料确有困难的，可以在期限届满前申请延长举证期限。是否延长，由仲裁庭决定。	(二)仲裁庭可以规定当事人提交证据的期限。当事人应在规定的期限内提交证据。逾期提交的，仲裁庭可以不予接受。当事人在举证期限内提交证据材料确有困难的，可以在期限届满前申请延长举证期限。是否延长，由仲裁庭决定。
(三)当事人未能在规定的期限内提交证据，或虽提交证据但不足以证明其主张的，负有举证责任的当事人承担因此产生的后果。	(三)当事人未能在规定的期限内提交证据，或虽提交证据但不足以证明其主张的，负有举证责任的当事人承担因此产生的后果。
	(四)除非当事人另有约定，仲裁庭可以决定适用或部分适用《中国国际经济贸易仲裁委员会证据指引》(以下简称《证据指引》)审理案件，但该《证据指引》不构成本规则的组成部分。
第四十二条 质证	**第四十二条 质证**
(一)开庭审理的案件，证据应在开庭时出示，当事人可以质证。	(一)**除非当事人另有约定或协商一致**，开庭审理的案件，证据应在开庭时出示，当事人可以质证。
(二)对于书面审理的案件的证据材料，或对于开庭后提交的证据材料且当事人同意书面质证的，可以进行书面质证。书面质证时，当事人应在仲裁庭规定的期限内提交书面质证意见。	(二)对于书面审理的案件的证据材料，或对于开庭后提交的证据材料且当事人同意书面质证的，可以进行书面质证。书面质证时，当事人应在仲裁庭规定的期限内提交书面质证意见。
第四十三条 仲裁庭调查取证	**第四十三条 仲裁庭调查取证**
(一)仲裁庭认为必要时,可以调查事实，收集证据。	(一)仲裁庭认为必要时,可以调查事实，收集证据。
(二)仲裁庭调查事实、收集证据时，可以通知当事人到场。经通知，一方或双方当事人不到场的，不影响仲裁庭调查事实和收集证据。	(二)仲裁庭调查事实、收集证据时，可以通知当事人到场。经通知，一方或双方当事人不到场的，不影响仲裁庭调查事实和收集证据。
(三)仲裁庭调查收集的证据，应转交当事人，给予当事人提出意见的机会。	(三)仲裁庭调查收集的证据，应转交当事人，给予当事人提出意见的机会。

第四十四条 专家报告及鉴定报告	**第四十四条 专家报告及鉴定报告**
(一)仲裁庭可以就案件中的专门问题向专家咨询或指定鉴定人进行鉴定。专家和鉴定人可以是中国或外国的机构或自然人。	(一)仲裁庭可以就案件中的专门问题向专家咨询或指定鉴定人进行鉴定。专家和鉴定人可以是中国或外国的机构或自然人。
(二)仲裁庭有权要求当事人、当事人也有义务向专家或鉴定人提供或出示任何有关资料、文件或财产、实物，以供专家或鉴定人审阅、检验或鉴定。	(二)仲裁庭有权要求当事人、当事人也有义务向专家或鉴定人提供或出示任何有关资料、文件或财产、实物，以供专家或鉴定人审阅、检验或鉴定。
(三)专家报告和鉴定报告的副本应转交当事人，给予当事人提出意见的机会。一方当事人要求专家或鉴定人参加开庭的，经仲裁庭同意，专家或鉴定人应参加开庭,并在仲裁庭认为必要时就所作出的报告进行解释。	(三)专家报告和鉴定报告的副本应转交当事人，给予当事人提出意见的机会。**一方当事人申请或仲裁庭要求**专家或鉴定人参加开庭的，专家或鉴定人应参加开庭,并在仲裁庭认为必要时就所作出的报告进行解释。
第四十五条 程序中止	**第四十五条 程序中止**
(一)双方当事人共同或分别请求中止仲裁程序，或出现其他需要中止仲裁程序的情形的，仲裁程序可以中止。	(一)双方当事人共同或分别请求中止仲裁程序，或出现其他需要中止仲裁程序的情形的，仲裁程序可以中止。
(二)中止程序的原因消失或中止程序期满后，仲裁程序恢复进行。	(二)中止程序的原因消失或中止程序期满后，仲裁程序恢复进行。
(三)仲裁程序的中止及恢复，由仲裁庭决定;仲裁庭尚未组成的，由仲裁委员会仲裁院院长决定。	(三)仲裁程序的中止及恢复，由仲裁庭决定;仲裁庭尚未组成的，由仲裁委员会仲裁院院长决定。
第四十六条 撤回申请和撤销案件	**第四十六条 撤回申请和撤销案件**
(一)当事人可以撤回全部仲裁请求或全部仲裁反请求。申请人撤回全部仲裁请求的，不影响仲裁庭就被申请人的仲裁反请求进行审理和裁决。被申请人撤回全部仲裁反请求的，不影响仲裁庭就申请人的仲裁请求进行审理和裁决。	(一)当事人可以撤回全部仲裁请求或全部仲裁反请求。申请人撤回全部仲裁请求的，不影响仲裁庭就被申请人的仲裁反请求进行审理和裁决。被申请人撤回全部仲裁反请求的，不影响仲裁庭就申请人的仲裁请求进行审理和裁决。
(二)因当事人自身原因致使仲裁程序不能进行的，可以视为其撤回仲裁请求。	(二)因当事人自身原因**或相关法律规定**致使仲裁程序不能进行的，可以视为其撤回仲裁请求。
(三)仲裁请求和反请求全部撤回的，案件可以撤销。在仲裁庭组成前撤销案件的，由仲裁委员会仲裁院院长作出撤案决定;仲裁庭组成后撤销案件的，由仲裁庭作出撤案决定。	(三)仲裁请求和反请求全部撤回的，案件可以撤销。在仲裁庭组成前撤销案件的，由仲裁委员会仲裁院院长作出撤案决定仲裁庭组成后撤销案件的，由仲裁庭作出撤案决定。
(四)上述第(三)款及本规则第六条第(七)款所述撤案决定应加盖“中国国际经济贸易仲裁委员会”印章。	(四)上述第(三)款及本规则第六条第(七)款所述撤案决定应加盖“中国国际经济贸易仲裁委员会”印章。
第四十七条 仲裁与调解相结合	**第四十七条 仲裁与调解相结合**
(一)双方当事人有调解愿望的，或一方当事人有调解愿望并经仲裁庭征得另一方当事人同意的，仲裁庭可以在仲裁程序中对案件进行调解。双方当事人也可以自行和解。	(一)双方当事人有调解愿望的，或一方当事人有调解愿望并经仲裁庭征得另一方当事人同意的，仲裁庭可以在仲裁程序中对案件进行调解。双方当事人也可以自行和解。
(二)仲裁庭在征得双方当事人同意后可以按照其认为适当的方式进行调解。	(二)仲裁庭在征得双方当事人同意后可以按照其认为适当的方式进行调解。
(三)调解过程中，任何一方当事人提出终止调解或仲裁庭认为已无调解成功的可能时，仲裁庭应终止调解。	(三)调解过程中，任何一方当事人提出终止调解或仲裁庭认为已无调解成功的可能时，仲裁庭应终止调解。
(四)双方当事人经仲裁庭调解达成和解或自行和解的，应签订和解协议。	(四)双方当事人经仲裁庭调解达成和解或自行和解的，应签订和解协议。

(五)当事人经调解达成或自行达成和解协议的，可以撤回仲裁请求或反请求，也可以请求仲裁庭根据当事人和解协议的内容作出裁决书或制作调解书。

(六)当事人请求制作调解书的,调解书应当写明仲裁请求和当事人书面和解协议的内容，由仲裁员署名，并加盖“中国国际经济贸易仲裁委员会”印章，送达双方当事人。

(七)调解不成功的，仲裁庭应当继续进行仲裁程序并作出裁决。

(八)当事人有调解愿望但不愿在仲裁庭主持下进行调解的，经双方当事人同意，仲裁委员会可以协助当事人以适当的方式和程序进行调解。

(九)如果调解不成功，任何一方当事人均不得在其后的仲裁程序、司法程序和其他任何程序中援引对方当事人或仲裁庭在调解过程中曾发表的意见、提出的观点、作出的陈述、表示认同或否定的建议或主张作为其请求、答辩或反请求的依据。

(十)当事人在仲裁程序开始之前自行达成或经调解达成和解协议的，可以依据由仲裁委员会仲裁的仲裁协议及其和解协议，请求仲裁委员会组成仲裁庭，按照和解协议的内容作出仲裁裁决。除非当事人另有约定，仲裁委员会主任指定一名独任仲裁员成立仲裁庭，由仲裁庭按照其认为适当的程序进行审理并作出裁决。具体程序和期限，不受本规则其他条款关于程序和期限的限制。

(五)当事人经调解达成或自行达成和解协议的，可以撤回仲裁请求或反请求，也可以请求仲裁庭根据当事人和解协议的内容作出裁决书或制作调解书。

(六)当事人请求制作调解书的,调解书应当写明仲裁请求和当事人书面和解协议的内容，由仲裁员署名，并加盖“中国国际经济贸易仲裁委员会”印章，送达双方当事人。

(七)调解不成功的，仲裁庭应当继续进行仲裁程序并作出裁决。

(八)当事人有调解愿望但不愿在仲裁庭主持下进行调解的，经双方当事人同意，仲裁委员会可以协助当事人以适当的方式和程序进行调解。

(九)如果调解不成功，任何一方当事人均不得在其后的仲裁程序、司法程序和其他任何程序中援引对方当事人或仲裁庭在调解过程中曾发表的意见、提出的观点、作出的陈述、表示认同或否定的建议或主张作为其请求、答辩或反请求的依据。

(十)当事人在仲裁程序开始之前自行达成或经调解达成和解协议的，可以依据由仲裁委员会仲裁的仲裁协议及其和解协议，请求仲裁委员会组成仲裁庭，按照和解协议的内容作出仲裁裁决。除非当事人另有约定，仲裁委员会主任指定一名独任仲裁员成立仲裁庭，由仲裁庭按照其认为适当的程序进行审理并作出裁决。具体程序和期限，不受本规则其他条款关于程序和期限的限制。

第四十八条 第三方资助

(一)获得第三方资助的当事应在签署资助协议后，毫不迟延地将第三方资助安排的事实、经济利益、第三方的名称与住址等情况提交仲裁委员会仲裁院。仲裁委员会仲裁院应转交相关当事人和仲裁庭。仲裁庭认为必要的，可要求获得第三方资助的当事人披露相关情况。

(二)在就仲裁费用和其他相关费用作出裁决时，仲裁庭可以考虑是否存在第三方资助的情形，以及当事是否遵守第(一)款的规定。

第四十九条 中间裁决

(一)仲裁庭认为必要或当事人提出请求并经仲裁庭同意的，仲裁庭可以在作出最终裁决之前，就案件的任何问题作出中间裁决。

(二)任何一方当事人不履行中间裁决，不影响仲裁程序的继续进行，也不影响仲裁庭作出最终裁决。

第五十条 早期驳回程序

(一)当事人可以以仲裁请求或反请求明显缺乏法律依据或明显超出仲裁庭的管辖范围为由申请早期驳回全部或部分仲裁请求或反请求(以下简称“早期驳回程序申请”)。

(二)当事人应以书面形式提出早期驳回程序申请，并应说明其事实和法律依据。仲裁庭可要求提出请求的一方当事人提供正当理由，并可要求其证明实施早期驳回程序将加快整个仲裁程序，以防止当事人滥用早期驳回程序申请拖延仲裁程序。当事人提起早期驳回申请不影响仲裁庭继续进行仲裁程序。

(三)当事人应尽可能及早提交早期驳回程序申请，除非仲裁庭另有决定，早期驳回程序申请最迟应不晚于提交答辩书或反请求答辩书时提出。

(四)在征询双方当事人意见后，仲裁庭可以对早期驳回程序申请作出是否受理决定。

(五)仲裁庭应在早期驳回程序申请提出之日起 60 天内对该请求作出裁决，并附具理由。经仲裁庭请求，仲裁委员会仲裁院院长认为确有正当理由和必要的，可以适当延长该期限。

(六)仲裁庭裁决支持或部分支持早期驳回程序申请的，可以根据审理情况作出裁决，该裁决不影响仲裁庭对其他仲裁请求和反请求的继续审理。

第三章 裁 决

第四十八条 作出裁决的期限

(一)仲裁庭应在组庭后 6 个月内作出裁决书。

(二)经仲裁庭请求，仲裁委员会仲裁院院长认为确有正当理由和必要的，可以延长该期限。

(三)程序中止的期间不计入上述第(一)款规定的裁决期限。

第四十九条 裁决的作出

(一)仲裁庭应当根据事实和合同约定，依照法律规定，参考国际惯例，公平合理、独立公正地作出裁决。

(二)当事人对于案件实体适用法有约定的，从其约定。当事人没有约定或其约定与法律强制性规定相抵触的，由仲裁庭决定案件实体的法律适用。

(三)仲裁庭在裁决书中应写明仲裁请求、争议事实、裁决理由、裁决结果、仲裁费用的承担、裁决的日期和地点。当事人协议不写明争议事实和裁决理由的，以及按照双方当事人和解协议的内容作出裁决书的，可以不写明争议事实和裁决理由。仲裁庭有权在裁决书中确定当事人履行裁决的具体期限及逾期履行所应承担的责任。

(四)裁决书应加盖“中国国际经济贸易仲裁委员会”印章。

(五)由三名仲裁员组成的仲裁庭审理的案件，裁决依全体仲裁员或多数仲裁员的意见作出。少数仲裁员的书面意见应附卷，并可以附在裁决书后，该书面意见不构成裁决书的组成部分。

第五十一条 作出裁决的期限

(一)仲裁庭应在组庭后 6 个月内作出裁决书。

(二)经仲裁庭请求，仲裁委员会仲裁院院长认为确有正当理由和必要的，可以延长该期限。

(三)程序中止的期间不计入上述第(一)款规定的裁决期限。

第五十二条 裁决的作出

(一)仲裁庭应当根据事实和合同约定，依照法律规定，参考国际惯例，公平合理、独立公正地作出裁决。

(二)当事人对于案件实体适用法有约定的，从其约定。当事人没有约定或其约定与法律强制性规定相抵触的，由仲裁庭决定案件实体**应适用的法律或法律规则**。

(三)仲裁庭在裁决书中应写明仲裁请求、争议事实、裁决理由、裁决结果、仲裁费用的承担、裁决的日期和地点。当事人协议不写明争议事实和裁决理由的，以及按照双方当事人和解协议的内容作出裁决书的，可以不写明争议事实和裁决理由。仲裁庭有权在裁决书中确定当事人履行裁决的具体期限及逾期履行所应承担的责任。

(四)裁决书应加盖“中国国际经济贸易仲裁委员会”印章。

(五)由三名仲裁员组成的仲裁庭审理的案件，裁决依全体仲裁员或多数仲裁员的意见作出。少数仲裁员的书面意见应附卷，并可以附在裁决书后，该书面意见不构成裁决书的组成部分。

(六)仲裁庭不能形成多数意见的，裁决依首席仲裁员的意见作出。其他仲裁员的书面意见应附卷，并可以附在裁决书后，该书面意见不构成裁决书的组成部分。

(七)除非裁决依首席仲裁员意见或独任仲裁员意见作出并由其署名，裁决书应由多数仲裁员署名。持有不同意见的仲裁员可以在裁决书上署名，也可以不署名。

(八)作出裁决书的日期，即为裁决发生法律效力的日期。

(九)裁决是终局的，对双方当事人均有约束力。任何一方当事人均不得向法院起诉，也不得向其他任何机构提出变更仲裁裁决的请求。

第五十条 部分裁决

(一)仲裁庭认为必要或当事人提出请求并经仲裁庭同意的，仲裁庭可以在作出最终裁决之前，就当事人的某些请求事项先行作出部分裁决。部分裁决是终局的，对双方当事人均有约束力。

(二)一方当事人不履行部分裁决，不影响仲裁程序的继续进行，也不影响仲裁庭作出最终裁决。

第五十一条 裁决书草案的核阅

仲裁庭应在签署裁决书之前将裁决书草案提交仲裁委员会核阅。在不影响仲裁庭独立裁决的情况下，仲裁委员会可以就裁决书的有关问题提请仲裁庭注意。

第五十二条 费用承担

(一)仲裁庭有权在裁决书中裁定当事人最终应向仲裁委员会支付的仲裁费和其他费用。

(二)仲裁庭有权根据案件的具体情况在裁决书中裁定败诉方应补偿胜诉方因办理案件而支出的合理费用。仲裁庭裁定败诉方补偿胜诉方因办理案件而支出的费用是否合理时，应具体考虑案件的裁决结果、复杂程度、胜诉方当事人及/或代理人的实际工作量以及案件的争议金额等因素。

第五十三条 裁决书的更正

(一)仲裁庭可以在发出裁决书后的合理时间内自行以书面形式对裁决书中的书写、打印、计算上的错误或其他类似性质的错误作出更正。

(二)任何一方当事人均可以在收到裁决书后30天内就裁决书中的书写、打印、计算上的错误或其他类似性质的错误，书面申请仲裁庭作出更正;如确有错误，仲裁庭应在收到书面申请后30天内作出书面更正。

(六)仲裁庭不能形成多数意见的，裁决依首席仲裁员的意见作出。其他仲裁员的书面意见应附卷，并可以附在裁决书后，该书面意见不构成裁决书的组成部分。

(七)除非裁决依首席仲裁员意见或独任仲裁员意见作出并由其署名，裁决书应由多数仲裁员署名。持有不同意见的仲裁员可以在裁决书上署名，也可以不署名。**仲裁员电子签名与手写署名具有同等效力。**

(八)作出裁决书的日期，即为裁决发生法律效力的日期。

(九)裁决是终局的，对双方当事人均有约束力。

(十)向双方当事人送达的裁决书应为纸质文本。如双方当事人约定，或仲裁委员会认为有必要的，裁决书可以电子文本送达。

第五十三条 部分裁决

(一)仲裁庭认为必要或当事人提出请求并经仲裁庭同意的，仲裁庭可以在作出最终裁决之前，就当事人的某些请求事项先行作出部分裁决。部分裁决是终局的，对双方当事人均有约束力。

(二)一方当事人不履行部分裁决，不影响仲裁程序的继续进行，也不影响仲裁庭作出最终裁决。

第五十四条 裁决书草案的核阅

仲裁庭应在签署裁决书之前将裁决书草案提交仲裁委员会核阅。在不影响仲裁庭独立裁决的情况下，仲裁委员会可以就裁决书的有关问题提请仲裁庭注意。

第五十五条 费用承担

(一)仲裁庭有权在裁决书中裁定当事人最终应向仲裁委员会支付的仲裁费和其他费用。

(二)仲裁庭有权根据案件的具体情况在裁决书中裁定败诉方应补偿胜诉方因办理案件而支出的合理费用。仲裁庭裁定败诉方补偿胜诉方因办理案件而支出的费用是否合理时，应具体考虑案件的裁决结果、复杂程度、胜诉方当事人及/或代理人的实际工作量以及案件的争议金额等因素。

第五十六条 裁决书的更正

(一)仲裁庭可以在发出裁决书后的合理时间内自行以书面形式对裁决书中的书写、打印、计算上的错误或其他类似性质的错误**或遗漏事项**作出更正。

(二)任何一方当事人均可以在收到裁决书后30天内就裁决书中的书写、打印、计算上的错误或其他类似性质的错误**或遗漏事项**，书面申请仲裁庭作出更正如确有错误，仲裁庭应在收到书面申请后30天内作出书面更正。

(三)上述书面更正构成裁决书的组成部分，应适用本规则第四十九条第(四)至(九)款的规定。	(三)上述书面更正构成裁决书的组成部分，应适用本规则第五十二条第(四)至(十)款的规定。
第五十四条 补充裁决	**第五十七条 补充裁决**
(一)如果裁决书中有遗漏事项，仲裁庭可以在发出裁决书后的合理时间内自行作出补充裁决。	(一)如果裁决书中对仲裁请求/反请求有漏裁事项，仲裁庭可以在发出裁决书后的合理时间内自行作出补充裁决。
(二)任何一方当事人可以在收到裁决书后30天内以书面形式请求仲裁庭就裁决书中遗漏的事项作出补充裁决;如确有漏裁事项，仲裁庭应在收到上述书面申请后30天内作出补充裁决。	(二)任何一方当事人可以在收到裁决书后30天内以书面形式请求仲裁庭就裁决书中漏裁的事项作出补充裁决如确有漏裁事项，仲裁庭应在收到上述书面申请后30天内作出补充裁决。
(三)该补充裁决构成裁决书的一部分，应适用本规则第四十九条第(四)至(九)款的规定。	(三)该补充裁决构成裁决书的一部分，应适用本规则第五十二条第(四)至(十)款的规定。
第五十五条 裁决的履行	**第五十八条 裁决的履行**
(一)当事人应依照裁决书写明的期限履行仲裁裁决;裁决书未写明履行期限的，应立即履行。	(一)当事人应依照裁决书写明的期限履行仲裁裁决;裁决书未写明履行期限的，应立即履行。
(二)一方当事人不履行裁决的，另一方当事人可以依法向有管辖权的法院申请执行。	(二)一方当事人不履行裁决的，另一方当事人可以依法向有管辖权的法院申请执行。

第四章 简易程序

第五十六条 简易程序的适用	**第五十九条 简易程序的适用**
(一)除非当事人另有约定，凡争议金额不超过人民币500万元，或争议金额超过人民币500万元但经一方当事人书面申请并征得另一方当事人书面同意的，或双方当事人约定适用简易程序的，适用简易程序。	(一)除非当事人另有约定，凡争议金额不超过人民币500万元，或争议金额超过人民币500万元但经一方当事人书面申请并征得另一方当事人书面同意的，或双方当事人约定适用简易程序的，适用简易程序。
(二)没有争议金额或争议金额不明确的，由仲裁委员会根据案件的复杂程度、涉及利益的大小以及其他有关因素综合考虑决定是否适用简易程序。	(二)没有争议金额或争议金额不明确的，由仲裁委员会根据案件的复杂程度、涉及利益的大小以及其他有关因素综合考虑决定是否适用简易程序。
第五十七条 仲裁通知	**第六十条 案件的受理**
申请人提出仲裁申请，经审查可以受理并适用简易程序的，仲裁委员会仲裁院应向双方当事人发出仲裁通知。	仲裁委员会仲裁院收到申请人的仲裁申请书及其附件后，经审查，认为符合本规则第十二条规定的受理条件并适用简易程序的，应向双方当事人发出仲裁通知。
第五十八条 仲裁庭的组成	**第六十一条 仲裁庭的组成**
除非当事人另有约定，适用简易程序的案件，依照本规则第二十八条的规定成立独任仲裁庭审理案件。	除非当事人另有约定，适用简易程序的案件，依照本规则第二十八条的规定成立独任仲裁庭审理案件。
第五十九条 答辩和反请求	**第六十二条 答辩和反请求**
(一)被申请人应在收到仲裁通知后20天内提交答辩书及证据材料以及其他证明文件;如有反请求，也应在此期限内提交反请求书及证据材料以及其他证明文件。	(一)被申请人应在收到仲裁通知后20天内提交答辩书及证据材料以及其他证明文件如有反请求，也应在此期限内提交反请求书及证据材料以及其他证明文件。
(二)申请人应在收到反请求书及其附件后20天内针对被申请人的反请求提交答辩。	(二)申请人应在收到反请求受理通知后20天内针对被申请人的反请求提交答辩。
(三)当事人确有正当理由请求延长上述期限的，由仲裁庭决定是否延长;仲裁庭尚未组成的，由仲裁委员会仲裁院作出决定。	(三)当事人确有正当理由请求延长上述期限的，由仲裁庭决定是否延长仲裁庭尚未组成的，由仲裁委员会仲裁院作出决定。

Annex 2

第六十条 审理方式

仲裁庭可以按照其认为适当的方式审理案件，可以在征求当事人意见后决定只依据当事人提交的书面材料和证据进行书面审理，也可以决定开庭审理。

第六十一条 开庭通知

(一)对于开庭审理的案件，仲裁庭确定第一次开庭日期后，应不晚于开庭前 15 天将开庭日期通知双方当事人。当事人有正当理由的，可以请求延期开庭，但应于收到开庭通知后 3 天内提出书面延期申请;是否延期，由仲裁庭决定。

(二)当事人有正当理由未能按上述第(一)款规定提出延期开庭申请的，是否接受其延期申请，由仲裁庭决定。

(三)再次开庭审理的日期及延期后开庭审理日期的通知及其延期申请，不受上述第(一)款期限的限制。

第六十二条 作出裁决的期限

(一)仲裁庭应在组庭后 3 个月内作出裁决书。

(二)经仲裁庭请求，仲裁委员会仲裁院院长认为确有正当理由和必要的，可以延长该期限。

(三)程序中止的期间不计入上述第(一)款规定的裁决期限。

第六十三条 程序变更

仲裁请求的变更或反请求的提出，不影响简易程序的继续进行。经变更的仲裁请求或反请求所涉争议金额分别超过人民币 500 万元的案件，除非当事人约定或仲裁庭认为有必要变更为普通程序，继续适用简易程序。

第六十四条 本规则其他条款的适用

本章未规定的事项，适用本规则其他各章的有关规定。

第六十三条 审理方式

仲裁庭可以按照其认为适当的方式审理案件，可以在征求当事人意见后决定只依据当事人提交的书面材料和证据进行书面审理，也可以决定开庭审理。

第六十四条 开庭审理

(一)对于开庭审理的案件，仲裁庭确定第一次开庭日期后，应不晚于开庭前 15 天将开庭日期通知双方当事人。当事人有正当理由的，可以请求延期开庭，但应于收到开庭通知后 3 天内提出书面延期申请;是否延期，由仲裁庭决定。

(二)当事人有正当理由未能按上述第(一)款规定提出延期开庭申请的，是否接受其延期申请，由仲裁庭决定。

(三)再次开庭审理的日期及延期后开庭审理日期的通知及其延期申请，不受上述第(一)款期限的限制。

第六十五条 作出裁决的期限

(一)仲裁庭应在组庭后 3 个月内作出裁决书。

(二)经仲裁庭请求，仲裁委员会仲裁院院长认为确有正当理由和必要的，可以延长该期限。

(三)程序中止的期间不计入上述第(一)款规定的裁决期限。

第六十六条 程序变更

仲裁请求的变更或反请求的提出，不影响简易程序的继续进行。经变更的仲裁请求或反请求所涉争议金额分别超过人民币 500 万元的案件，除非当事人约定或仲裁庭认为有必要变更为普通程序，继续适用简易程序。

第六十七条 本规则其他条款的适用

本章未规定的事项，适用本规则其他各章的有关规定

第五章 国内仲裁的特别规定

第六十五条 本章的适用

(一)国内仲裁案件，适用本章规定。

(二)符合本规则第五十六条规定的国内仲裁案件，适用第四章简易程序的规定。

第六十六条 案件的受理

(一)收到仲裁申请书后，仲裁委员会仲裁院认为仲裁申请符合本规则第十二条规定的受理条件的，应当在 5 天内通知当事人~~;认为不符合受理条件的，应书面通知当事人不予受理，并说明理由~~。

(二)收到仲裁申请书后，仲裁委员会仲裁院经审查认为申请仲裁的手续不符合本规则第十二条规定的，可以要求当事人在规定的期限内予以完备。

第六十八条 本章的适用

(一)国内仲裁案件，适用本章规定。

(二)符合本规则第五十九条规定的国内仲裁案件，适用第四章简易程序的规定。

第六十九条 案件的受理

仲裁委员会仲裁院收到申请人的仲裁申请书及其附件后，经审查，认为符合本规则第十二条规定的受理条件并适用国内仲裁程序的，应向双方当事人发出仲裁通知。

第六十七条 仲裁庭的组成

仲裁庭应按照本规则第二十五条、第二十六条、第二十七条、第二十八条、第二十九条和第三十条的规定组成。

第六十八条 答辩和反请求

(一)被申请人应在收到仲裁通知后 20 天内提交答辩书及所依据的证据材料以及其他证明文件;如有反请求，也应在此期限内提交反请求书及所依据的证据材料以及其他证明文件。

(二)申请人应在收到反请求书及其附件后 20 天内针对被申请人的反请求提交答辩。

(三)当事人确有正当理由请求延长上述期限的，由仲裁庭决定是否延长;仲裁庭尚未组成的，由仲裁委员会仲裁院作出决定。

第六十九条 开庭通知

(一)对于开庭审理的案件，仲裁庭确定第一次开庭日期后，应不晚于开庭前 15 天将开庭日期通知双方当事人。当事人有正当理由的，可以请求延期开庭，但应于收到开庭通知后 3 天内提出书面延期申请;是否延期，由仲裁庭决定。

(二)当事人有正当理由未能按上述第(一)款规定提出延期开庭申请的，是否接受其延期申请，由仲裁庭决定。

(三)再次开庭审理的日期及延期后开庭审理日期的通知及其延期申请，不受上述第(一)款期限的限制。

第七十条 庭审笔录

(一)仲裁庭应将开庭情况记入笔录。当事人和其他仲裁参与人认为对自己陈述的记录有遗漏或有差错的，可以申请补正;仲裁庭不同意其补正的，应将该申请记录在案。

(二)庭审笔录由仲裁员、记录人员、当事人和其他仲裁参与人签名或盖章。

第七十一条 作出裁决的期限

(一)仲裁庭应在组庭后 4 个月内作出裁决书。

(二)经仲裁庭请求，仲裁委员会仲裁院院长认为确有正当理由和必要的，可以延长该期限。

(三)程序中止的期间不计入上述第(一)款规定的裁决期限。

第七十二条 本规则其他条款的适用

本章未规定的事项，适用本规则其他各章的有关规定。本规则第六章的规定除外。

第七十条 仲裁庭的组成

仲裁庭应按照本规则第二十五条、第二十六条、第二十七条、第二十八条、第二十九条和第三十条的规定组成。

第七十一条 答辩和反请求

(一)被申请人应在收到仲裁通知后 20 天内提交答辩书及所依据的证据材料以及其他证明文件如有反请求，也应在此期限内提交反请求书及所依据的证据材料以及其他证明文件。

(二)申请人应在收到反请求受理通知后 20 天内针对被申请人的反请求提交答辩。

(三)当事人确有正当理由请求延长上述期限的，由仲裁庭决定是否延长;仲裁庭尚未组成的，由仲裁委员会仲裁院作出决定。

第七十二条 开庭审理

(一)对于开庭审理的案件，仲裁庭确定第一次开庭日期后，应不晚于开庭前 15 天将开庭日期通知双方当事人。当事人有正当理由的，可以请求延期开庭，但应于收到开庭通知后 3 天内提出书面延期申请;是否延期，由仲裁庭决定。

(二)当事人有正当理由未能按上述第(一)款规定提出延期开庭申请的，是否接受其延期申请，由仲裁庭决定。

(三)再次开庭审理的日期及延期后开庭审理日期的通知及其延期申请，不受上述第(一)款期限的限制。

第七十三条 庭审笔录

(一)仲裁庭应将开庭情况记入笔录。当事人和其他仲裁参与人认为对自己陈述的记录有遗漏或有差错的，可以申请补正;仲裁庭不同意其补正的，应将该申请记录在案。

(二)庭审笔录由仲裁员、记录人员、当事人和其他仲裁参与人签名或盖章。

第七十四条 作出裁决的期限

(一)仲裁庭应在组庭后 4 个月内作出裁决书。

(二)经仲裁庭请求，仲裁委员会仲裁院院长认为确有正当理由和必要的，可以延长该期限。

(三)程序中止的期间不计入上述第(一)款规定的裁决期限。

第七十五条 本规则其他条款的适用

本章未规定的事项，适用本规则其他各章的有关规定。本规则第六章的规定除外。

第六章 香港仲裁的特别规定

第七十三条 本章的适用

(一)仲裁委员会在香港特别行政区设立仲裁委员会香港仲裁中心。本章适用于仲裁委员

第七十六条 本章的适用

(一)仲裁委员会在香港特别行政区设立仲裁委员会香港仲裁中心。本章适用于仲裁委员

会香港仲裁中心接受仲裁申请并管理的仲裁案件。

(二)当事人约定将争议提交仲裁委员会香港仲裁中心仲裁或约定将争议提交仲裁委员会在香港仲裁的，由仲裁委员会香港仲裁中心接受仲裁申请并管理案件。

第七十四条 仲裁地及程序适用法

除非当事人另有约定,仲裁委员会香港仲裁中心管理的案件的仲裁地为香港,仲裁程序适用法为香港仲裁法，仲裁裁决为香港裁决。

第七十五条 管辖权决定的作出

当事人对仲裁协议及/或仲裁案件管辖权的异议，应不晚于第一次实体答辩前提出。仲裁庭有权对仲裁协议的存在、效力以及仲裁案件的管辖权作出决定。

第七十六条 仲裁员的选定或指定

仲裁委员会现行仲裁员名册在仲裁委员会香港仲裁中心管理的案件中推荐使用，当事人可以在仲裁委员会仲裁员名册外选定仲裁员。被选定的仲裁员应经仲裁委员会主任确认。

第七十七条 临时措施和紧急救济

(一)除非当事人另有约定，应一方当事人申请，仲裁庭有权决定采取适当的临时措施。

(二)在仲裁庭组成之前，当事人可以按照《中国国际经济贸易仲裁委员会紧急仲裁员程序》(本规则附件三)申请紧急性临时救济。

第七十八条 裁决书的印章

裁决书应加盖“中国国际经济贸易仲裁委员会香港仲裁中心”印章。

第七十九条 仲裁收费

依本章接受申请并管理的案件适用《中国国际经济贸易仲裁委员会仲裁费用表(三)》(本规则附件二)。

第八十条 本规则其他条款的适用

本章未规定的事项，适用本规则其他各章的有关规定，本规则第五章的规定除外。

会香港仲裁中心接受仲裁申请并管理的仲裁案件。

(二)当事人约定将争议提交仲裁委员会香港仲裁中心仲裁或约定将争议提交仲裁委员会在香港仲裁的，由仲裁委员会香港仲裁中心接受仲裁申请并管理案件。

第七十七条 仲裁地及程序适用法

除非当事人另有约定,仲裁委员会香港仲裁中心管理的案件的仲裁地为香港,仲裁程序适用法为香港仲裁法，仲裁裁决为香港裁决。

第七十八条 管辖权决定的作出

当事人对仲裁协议及/或仲裁案件管辖权的异议，应不晚于第一次实体答辩前提出。仲裁庭有权对仲裁协议的存在、效力以及仲裁案件的管辖权作出决定。

第七十九条 仲裁员的选定或指定

仲裁委员会现行仲裁员名册在仲裁委员会香港仲裁中心管理的案件中推荐使用，当事人可以在仲裁委员会仲裁员名册外选定仲裁员。被选定的仲裁员应经仲裁委员会主任确认。

第八十条 临时措施和紧急救济

(一)除非当事人另有约定，应一方当事人申请，仲裁庭有权决定采取适当的临时措施。

(二)在仲裁庭组成之前，当事人可以按照《中国国际经济贸易仲裁委员会紧急仲裁员程序》(本规则附件三)申请紧急性临时救济。

第八十一条 裁决书的印章

裁决书应加盖“中国国际经济贸易仲裁委员会香港仲裁中心”印章。

第八十二条 仲裁收费

依本章接受申请并管理的案件适用《中国国际经济贸易仲裁委员会仲裁费用表(三)》(本规则附件二)。

第八十三条 本规则其他条款的适用

本章未规定的事项，适用本规则其他各章的有关规定，本规则第五章的规定除外。

第七章 附 则

第八十一条 仲裁语言

(一)当事人对仲裁语言有约定的，从其约定。当事人对仲裁语言没有约定的，以中文为仲裁语言。仲裁委员会也可以视案件的具体情形确定其他语言为仲裁语言。

第八十四条 仲裁语言

(一)当事人对仲裁语言有约定的，从其约定。

(二)当事人对仲裁语言没有约定的，以中文为仲裁语言。仲裁委员会也可以在适当考虑合同所用语言在内的所有情况后决定使用一种或数种语言进行仲裁。仲裁庭组成后，可根据案件具体情形重新确定仲裁程序使用的仲裁语言。

(二)仲裁庭开庭时，当事人或其代理人、证人需要语言翻译的，可由仲裁委员会仲裁院提供译员，也可由当事人自行提供译员。

(三)当事人提交的各种文书和证明材料，仲裁庭或仲裁委员会仲裁院认为必要时，可以要求当事人提供相应的中文译本或其他语言译本。

第八十二条 仲裁费用及实际费用

(一)仲裁委员会除按照制定的仲裁费用表向当事人收取仲裁费外,还可以向当事人收取其他额外的、合理的实际费用,包括仲裁员办理案件的特殊报酬、差旅费、食宿费、聘请速录员速录费，以及仲裁庭聘请专家、鉴定人和翻译等费用。仲裁员的特殊报酬由仲裁委员会仲裁院在征求相关仲裁员和当事人意见后，参照《中国国际经济贸易仲裁委员会仲裁费用表(三)》(本规则附件二)有关仲裁员报酬和费用标准确定。

(二)当事人未在仲裁委员会规定的期限内为其选定的仲裁员预缴特殊报酬、差旅费、食宿费等实际费用的，视为没有选定仲裁员。

(三)当事人约定在仲裁委员会或其分会/仲裁中心所在地之外开庭的，应预缴因此而发生的差旅费、食宿费等实际费用。当事人未在仲裁委员会规定的期限内预缴有关实际费用的，应在仲裁委员会或其分会/仲裁中心所在地开庭。

(四)当事人约定以两种或两种以上语言为仲裁语言的,或根据本规则第五十六条的规定适用简易程序的案件但当事人约定由三人仲裁庭审理的，仲裁委员会可以向当事人收取额外的、合理的费用。

第八十三条 规则的解释

(一)本规则条文标题不用于解释条文含义。

(二)本规则由仲裁委员会负责解释。

(三)仲裁庭开庭时，当事人或其代理人、证人需要语言翻译的，可由仲裁委员会仲裁院提供译员，也可由当事人自行提供译员。

(四)当事人提交的各种文书和证明材料，仲裁庭或仲裁委员会仲裁院认为必要时，可以要求当事人提供相应的中文译本或其他语言译本。

第八十五条 仲裁费用及实际费用

（一）仲裁委员会除按照制定的仲裁费用表向当事人收取仲裁费外,还可以向当事人收取其他额外的、合理的实际费用,包括仲裁员办理案件的特殊报酬、差旅费、食宿费、聘请速录员速录费，以及仲裁庭聘请专家、鉴定人和翻译等费用。仲裁员的特殊报酬由**双方当事人约定或仲裁员提出经由仲裁委员会仲裁院商相关当事人同意后可以小时费率为基础报价，并**参照《中国国际经济贸易仲裁委员会仲裁费用表(三)》(本规则附件二)有关三**(**二)仲裁员报酬和费用**(以小时费率为基础)**标准**及相关规**定确定。

(二)当事人未在仲裁委员会规定的期限内为其选定的仲裁员预缴特殊报酬、差旅费、食宿费等实际费用的，视为没有选定仲裁员。

(三)当事人约定在仲裁委员会或其分会/仲裁中心所在地之外开庭的，应预缴因此而发生的差旅费、食宿费等实际费用。当事人未在仲裁委员会规定的期限内预缴有关实际费用的，应在仲裁委员会或其分会/仲裁中心所在地开庭。

(四)当事人约定以两种或两种以上语言为仲裁语言的,或根据本规则第五十九条的规定适用简易程序的案件但当事人约定由三人仲裁庭审理的，仲裁委员会可以向当事人收取额外的、合理的费用。

(五)仲裁委员会为当事人提供本规则第二条第(七)款规定的临时仲裁服务的，视当事人请求及案件具体情况，经与双方当事人协商决定收取相关仲裁费用，并通知当事人在规定的期限内支付。当事人未缴纳或未足额缴纳的，仲裁委员会可全部或部分中止提供临时仲裁服务，并应当视为其撤回了相关请求。

第八十六条 责任限制

仲裁委员会及其工作人员、仲裁员、紧急仲裁员和仲裁程序中仲裁庭聘请的相关人员，不就其根据本规则进行的任何与仲裁有关的行为包括任何过失、作为和不作为，向任何人承担任何民事责任，且不负有作证义务，除非仲裁所适用的法律另有规定。

第八十七条 规则的解释

(一)本规则条文标题不用于解释条文含义。

(二)本规则由仲裁委员会负责解释。

Annex 2

第八十四条 规则的施行	第八十八条 规则的施行
本规则自2015年1月1日起施行。本规则施行前仲裁委员会及其分会/仲裁中心管理的案件，仍适用受理案件时适用的仲裁规则;双方当事人同意的，也可以适用本规则。	本规则自**2024**年**1**月**1**日起施行。本规则施行前仲裁委员会及其分会/仲裁中心管理的案件，仍适用受理案件时适用的仲裁规则;双方当事人同意的，也可以适用本规则。

Index

Figures in bold indicate Article numbers, Figures in light indicate margin numbers, Chapters are indicated by *Ch.*

Index